MASTER CLASS

MASTER CLASS

LESSONS FROM LEADING WRITERS

NANCY BUNGE

UNIVERSITY OF IOWA PRESS   IOWA CITY

University of Iowa Press, Iowa City 52242
http://www.uiowa.edu/uiowapress
Printed in the United States of America
Design by Richard Hendel

· The University of Iowa Press is a member of
Green Press Initiative and is committed to preserving
natural resources.

Printed on acid-free paper

Library of Congress
Cataloging-in-Publication Data
Bunge, Nancy L.
Master class: lessons from leading writers / by Nancy Bunge.
p.   cm.
Includes index.
ISBN 0-87745-965-7 (cloth), ISBN 0-87745-966-5 (paper)
1. Authorship.   2. Authorship—Study and teaching.   3. Authors—
Interviews.   I. Title.
·   PN147.B798 2005   2005047012
808'.02—dc22

05 06 07 08 09 C 5 4 3 2 1
05 06 07 08 09 P 5 4 3 2 1

Contents

PRACTICE

INTERVIEWS WITH AUTHORS ABOUT HOW THEY WORK

$\mathcal{A}$CKNOWLEDGMENTS

I owe an enormous debt to all the writers I interviewed; they were extremely generous with their time, energy, and insight. They not only answered all the questions, they also reviewed and approved the interviews as required by the Human Subjects rules at Michigan State University, where I teach. All of them left the substance of their remarks intact; those who made changes, smoothed edges so that their views would come through more clearly. Thanks also to the literary executors who gave me permission to use interviews. Dealing with so many talented and kind human beings has been the most rewarding part of this undertaking.

Mickey Pearlman, Sheila Friedling, and Anne Dubuisson Anderson offered terrific advice about this project, which I happily appropriated. As I traveled around interviewing, friends offered food, shelter, and support, including Catherine Cook, Janet Nussmann and Bob Cary, Margaret Sullivan, Mike Colleran and Julie Rosmond, and Sharon Furrow. I have three specific debts: The title *Master Class* is the short version of one suggested by Steve Ross; when I use a line from each talk as its title, I'm imitating Marvin Bell; and the University Press of Mississippi kindly allowed me to reprint Clarence Major's interview here even though the contract for *Conversations with Clarence Major* assigns them my copyright. Many thanks to all these people.

Finally, I'm very grateful to the University of Iowa Press. I especially thank Holly Carver for her patience as we sorted through the contract and the permissions, Sara Sauers and Deidre Woods for their help with publicity, Sarah Brown for her meticulous copyediting, and Charlotte Wright for keeping everything running smoothly. Thanks particularly to Prasenjit Gupta for suggestions that greatly improve the book, including its subtitle.

INTRODUCTION

When I selected writer-teachers to interview in the early eighties, I chose authors who excelled in a variety of ways. I talked with both the former Poet Laureate Richard Wilbur and the screenwriter and novelist Richard Price as well as the heads of several writing programs including John Leggett, then director of the Iowa Writers' Workshop; Wallace Stegner, who had recently retired from supervising the Stanford Writing Program; and Allen Ginsberg and Anne Waldman, the co-directors of the Jack Kerouac School of Disembodied Poetics. Despite the wide range of writers I interviewed, the *Washington Post* review of my collection *Finding the Words: Conversations with Writers Who Teach* appropriately noted that one piece of advice recurred with amazing consistency: to produce fresh, interesting work, aspiring writers must learn to trust themselves. As Wallace Stegner put it, "If you're not a person, if you're only a copy of a person, you aren't going to write very well."

This rule has an essential corollary: improving as a writer means constantly extending oneself with new knowledges and experiments — literary and otherwise. And, indeed, graduates of writing programs repeatedly report that they learned the most from watching their instructors model the blend of courage and integrity that facilitates a lifetime of self-education. Fortunately, the literary interview makes this instruction available to those who lack the time or money to attend an MFA program; for when writers talk about their work both in the classroom and at the desk, their honesty and vitality leap off the page. As a result, their comments offer readers both practical suggestions and an intuitive sense of the integrity and curiosity that allow one to put technique to good use.

In retrospect, I realized that by interviewing writer-teachers in the early eighties, I had unwittingly documented the teaching philosophies of a vanishing breed: writers who valued their social responsibilities as much as their own work and, as a result, taught as seriously as they wrote. Allen Ginsberg's willingness to teach at the Naropa Institute without remuneration makes explicit the generosity and idealism pervading the remarks of virtually every author-professor I encountered.

As a result, I talked with writer-teachers from the golden age of creative writing programs. During his twenty years at Stanford, Wallace Stegner mentored many of America's premier fiction and nonfiction writers, including Larry McMurtry, Tom McGuane, Scott Turow, Ernest Gaines, Robert Stone, N. Scott Momaday, and Wendell Berry. Allen Ginsberg and Anne Waldman attracted dozens of distinguished writers to their program, especially those of Beat lineage like William Burroughs and Gary Snyder. Meanwhile, a legion of distinguished poets and fiction writers moved through the classrooms of the Iowa Writers' Workshop as students, teachers, or both: Kurt Vonnegut, Philip Roth, Gail Godwin, Michael Harper, John Irving, Richard Yates, James Alan McPherson, John Casey, and Robert Bly, to name a very few. Other writers took more solitary residences in universities: Saul Bellow at the University of Chicago, William Stafford at Lewis and Clark College, and Elie Wiesel at Boston University.

When I later began to interview writers about the decisions and procedures that had led them through their careers, I eventually realized that these new talks validated and demonstrated the wisdom of those I'd interviewed in the eighties. Beneath the particulars of each writer's choices a pattern emerged: loyalty to a distinctive value scheme shaped both their subject matter and their working methods.

For instance, Scott Turow identifies the abuse of power as a compelling issue for him. He not only returns to it repeatedly in his books, he writes out of an openness that his manipulative characters could never achieve, letting ideas occur to him and then following them wherever they take him, even when things get so chaotic he suspects he's "nuts." Although he has produced one best-selling book after another, he does not write to the market; he notes that "the times pass me by" while he attends to whatever grips him at the moment. This accepting stance permeates the tone as well as the content of his interview; as he surveys his life as a successful lawyer and writer, he seems bemused, not self-satisfied.

On the other hand, Ivan Doig, who writes about his hard-working literal and spiritual relatives and who believes his success proves that doing things right pays, underlines that he is in control: "I want to keep emphasizing that all this writing career of mine has behind it is the best guessing eye of a person who set out to be a professional journalist from the spring of his senior year in high school." The times do not go by Ivan Doig: when he saw the Montana centennial approaching, he mapped out a trilogy based on Montana's history. While Turow records whatever occurs to him each day, Doig sits down at a desk surrounded by files, notebooks, and photographs that provide the information he will need to make the book he has in process as solid and accurate as possible.

But holding true to one's point of view does not mean stagnating in it. Successful writers also validate another lesson emphasized by an earlier generation of master teachers: writing better means constantly enlarging one's awareness and one's craft. Sue Miller sees learning as the heart of her writing process. She believes that even characters need exposure to situations that challenge their limits in order to lead interesting lives. When deciding what to write, Miller thinks not only about what would fascinate her and her audience but also about what technical problems she would enjoy engaging. When she writes well, she loses herself in her characters so completely that "there is an expansiveness to my imagination about someone." She also enjoys research because it gives her a way of "stepping into the world and finding out things." Miller's imaginative, emotional, and intellectual journey takes her out of herself while simultaneously giving her fresh perspective on both her craft and her life. As a result, she says about writing her most recent book: "I felt very far away from myself; on the other hand, I felt completely connected to myself."

Excellent writers across three generations agree that writing well requires that one rest in one's point of view while constantly broadening and deepening it with new material and perceptions. This collection of interviews with master writer-teachers from the eighties and with contemporary authors validates the enduring value of the writing advice I heard over twenty years ago, while displaying a variety of ways to follow it. The literary interview teaches these lessons not only by providing techniques for others to try but also with inspirational models whose energy and insight demonstrate the intellectual and emotional rewards for undertaking the endlessly difficult and fascinating task of learning to write better.

THEORY

INTERVIEWS WITH WRITER-TEACHERS

SOMETHING MY LIFE CAN TEACH OTHER PEOPLE

Sandra Gilbert reveals that even she had to struggle against the gender constraints she and Susan Gubar analyze in their groundbreaking books: The Madwoman in the Attic, No Man's Land, *and* Shakespeare's Sisters. *Gilbert structures her poetry writing classes in a way that coaxes her students to transcend their own limits by not only exposing them to different kinds of work but also by requiring them to try it all— even when it means attempting to translate a poem written in an unfamiliar foreign language. To make sure her students understand the eternal need for a poet to attempt and even fumble with new approaches, she does the assignments along with them, readily admitting when she trips.*

Gilbert currently teaches at the University of California at Davis; she has also taught at Princeton, Johns Hopkins, Williams, Stanford, and Indiana. Her publications include literary analyses, anthologies, a memoir, and poetry; her recent books are Invention of Farewell: A Book of Elegies *and* Kissing the Bread: New and Selected Poems.

■ *Did you publish poetry or criticism first?*

I published poetry first. When I was an undergraduate at Cornell I did quite well as a poet: not only did I regularly publish stuff in the *Writer*, the campus literary magazine, but I also had poems accepted by several "real" (professional) quarterlies. So I was sure I was going to become a famous poet when I grew up! (Laughter) But something strange happened. An editor at Knopf had written one of my professors and said, "Do you know of any good young poets?" and the professor wrote back, saying, "Oh yes, we have a person, Sandra Mortola." Then I became guest managing editor at *Mademoiselle* the summer after I graduated from college, which is an interesting bond I have with Sylvia Plath, who'd had the same position four years earlier. And I did actually receive a letter from the Knopf editor—and I also did have a manuscript of poems that I'd written for a senior creative writing workshop — so when I casually mentioned all this to Cyrilly Abels, the *Mademoiselle* editor with whom I worked, she took me out to a ritzy lunch with the Knopf editor. (Cyrilly, by the way, later became "Jay Cee" in *The Bell Jar*, a transformation that didn't make her happy!) Anyway, the Knopf editor, who happened to be quite an important one, turned to me as we were finishing our salad — which is, of course, *de rigueur*: no business until you're through with the chef's salad — and said, "Well, what about your manuscript? I hear you're very good and I'd love to see it." But to my own surprise — and quite bizarrely, I now think — I said, "Oh, I'm not ready to show that to anybody. I'm really not ready to publish a book of poems." And I could see that Cyrilly was absolutely dismayed. And rightly so, of course. She expected all of us guest editors to take ourselves seriously, and suddenly, despite my supposed ambitions, I *wasn't* serious.

Why? Well, I was about to get married and my fiancé had just been drafted! I couldn't think about much else right then. Besides, I was only twenty years old and even though I'd been successful in college I couldn't believe that anyone would *already* expect me to take myself seriously as a writer. So I said, "Oh, no, no, no." They looked at each other and he said to Cyrilly, "Well, I've never heard a young poet say anything like that." Later she let me know she was enraged. She gave me quite a lecture, but alas I never did anything more about the letter from the Knopf editor. And for me that was the beginning of four or five years of literary silence. Whatever happened to young women in the late fifties and early sixties had happened to me and I became very silent.

So then for a while I had nine-to-five jobs in New York, working for publishing houses and magazines, writing fashion copy and book-jacket copy. But my husband was an academic and I thought his life was far more interesting than mine and much simpler: he didn't have to get up really early if he didn't want to, he didn't have to punch any clocks, and he didn't seem as bored with his work as I was with mine. So I decided I would go to graduate school. I was just beginning to have children and it was relatively easy to go to graduate school and have children because I could study and write at home, and besides, I had a wonderful (and for those days very advanced) academic husband who could and did share child care.

But when I went to graduate school, I was still in some sense arrogant and perverse because although I started writing poetry again, I didn't think I needed to enroll in any workshops and consequently I didn't know many other poets. As a writer, I mostly stayed by myself in my lonely room, writing poems, not meeting other poets, and therefore not learning what was wrong with my work. So I made a lot of mistakes and I did *not* publish poems the way I had in college. For one thing, I didn't send them out much, and when I did, I usually sent them only to the *New Yorker!* Then, when they came back, I would cry and put them away in a drawer. Oh, and I sent a manuscript to the Yale Younger Poets Contest, and when it didn't win the first time, I thought, "Well, that's that." In fact, I had no sense of what you have to do to establish yourself as a poet because I had alienated myself from the *business* of poetry. So though I was always writing poetry and criticism at the same time, when I started my adult career my criticism was published earlier and more often than my poetry, which means that I got more established as a critic, even though I define myself as equally poet *and* critic.

One of the things I try to do for my students is tell them about this part of my life now and then. For instance, I tell them that when a submission comes back from an editor, if you're "comfortable" with the work (as we like to say in California), then you should immediately put it in another envelope and send it somewhere else. For a long time we had a journal called the *California Quarterly* at U.C. Davis—my husband was the editor—and a lot of our creative writing graduate students worked on it. It was marvelous for them because they learned, in the first place, that rejections shouldn't be taken personally in an emotional way; and in the second place, when they saw the huge mass of submissions they realized that sometimes a reader for a magazine is too exhausted to appreciate what a poem or story is doing; and perhaps most important, they learned, in the third place, that where a creative writing teacher needs only the slightest excuse to like a poem and try to help a student improve it, an editor wants only the slightest excuse to decide, no, this piece has problems, we can't use it. (Although of course if a problem was really tiny, we'd write and say, "Well, we love this poem except for that line" or "We're troubled by such and such," and encourage the author to revise and resubmit.) Anyway, once students understand these points, then when something comes back, they won't put it in a drawer and cry and never send it out again. (Laughter) So I hope there's something my anecdotes about my early career can do for my students, something my life can teach other people.

■ *Ruth Stone says she learned at the university that poets were men.*

Oh yes, I too was taught that poets were men. I don't think that as an undergraduate I ever studied a single work by a woman. Nor did I ever have a woman teacher in college. Nor did I have a woman teacher in graduate school. And if I had to read any works by women, they were perhaps a couple of novels by Jane Austen and Virginia Woolf. And indeed, even though I had to know those for my orals, I don't think I ever had any classes in which we actually *studied* them. I can't imagine what I was thinking when I contemplated a career as a poet and professor. It sometimes seems to me that all of us young women who had such ambitions must have been crazy.

And yet, even though I married young, had children early, and dropped out of academia and the literary world for some years, my aspirations were high: when I went to graduate school I expected to have a career like everyone else—meaning a career like the ones that all my male professors had. And most of my female contemporaries had the same expectations. To any objective observer we must all have seemed mad! But if we were, I'm glad about it because our generation ultimately brought about great changes in the MLA and the academic world, precisely because of our seemingly lunatic assumption that something completely outside our actual experience was possible. We crossed the threshold of the professional world, saw that things weren't happening the way we had supposed they would, and suddenly began screaming, "What's going on here?" True, we had great precursors among earlier feminists, but we were probably the first massive generation of women to go through college and graduate school, so we were a kind of a female population bulge. And therefore the looniness and dissonance of our experience made a significant difference in the whole conception (if I may risk a pun) of the "second wave" of feminism.

Even so, I still don't understand how we balanced our perception of literature as a male preserve and our aspirations and identifications as *literary* women. From the time I was thirteen, I consistently identified with women writers and yet I never studied them in school. When I was thirteen or fourteen, I started writing little pseudo–Emily Dickinson poems. And I wrote sonnets like Edna Millay's. As a high school student, I rarely imitated male writers. When I started writing fiction, I did go through a phase where I thought a bit about Joyce, but basically I wrote in the stream of consciousness style of Virginia Woolf. I remember writing one piece in which the protagonist's name was actually Virginia! And later I was continually aware of Sylvia Plath as a daunting older rival, but also as another potential self and as a model.

Lots of the breakthroughs in my poetry in fact came from Plath. I read her work in *Seventeen* even before I was in high school and from then on I followed her career with fascination. Years later, when I studied her manuscripts at Smith, I was tremendously moved by her craft and her aesthetic intelligence. But at the same time, before the *Ariel* poems came out I was both disappointed and competitive, thinking, "Oh, she's just such a dutiful poet, she writes poems they want to publish in the *New Yorker*—whereas mine come back and I cry."

Some people have also said that women's work gets reviewed differently than men's work.

Absolutely. *Absolutely.* Plath is almost always identified through the melodrama of her biography, in particular her suicide. Instead, we should discuss her poetry in terms of her canon and her process of composition. When you look at the manuscripts at Smith, you can see almost immediately that she isn't pouring out all the pathology of her soul in the way so many critics have accused her of doing. On the contrary, she's carefully revising and deliberately mythologizing and fictionalizing her life. She's an artist and a craftswoman. She gets accused of being a seductress who offers us a poisoned chalice to drink. Often the imagery that's used to moralize her career suggests that she's a sort of poetic femme fatale. But nobody talks that way about Berryman, for example, or Hart Crane, and yet there's the same kind of torment and passion and perhaps acrimony in the work of those two men and others like them, who were also suicides.

I assume that you teach both literature and creative writing.

Yes, I teach literature, women's studies, and creative writing. If I teach five courses a year, two are usually creative writing classes, and I love to teach them. They're wonderful for me as a teacher and as a poet. I assign exercises to the class and I very often do them myself because students are sometimes anxious about being asked to do exercises and I want to show that I think such exercises are good for everyone. If you ask students to write a specific kind of poem or do an imitation or something, they often fear it will bruise their imaginations. Graduate students are particularly sensitive on this point: "It might be OK for the freshman, but not for us, Sandra." So I explain that literary exercises can be considered comparable to the warm-up exercises a ballerina does at the barre or the drawings Picasso did over and over, that you have to perfect your craft, that you have to understand all the options available to you as a poet—and I add that if you think there'll be a time when you don't need to do that, you're very much mistaken and I'll prove my point by doing these exercises myself.

I've seen so much growth and change in people, it's amazing. I've reached the ripe old age where my students have begun to publish a lot of poems and at least half of the poems they publish when they start out have been assignment or exercise poems. They always say, "Well, this is just an exercise poem. I just did this because Sandra made us read *Life Studies*. She said, 'You should try to write a *Life Studies* kind of poem,' but I'm really interested in language poetry and I only read John Ashbery. I just did this because Sandra said we should do it." And then they'll write a wonderful poem and everybody in the class will say, "That's a marvelous poem. Why don't you send it to such and such?" and it'll get taken and they've learned that even if you only love to read John Ashbery, you can also write in another mode. So.

The other thing I do at the very beginning of the quarter is go around the table and find out what everybody has been reading lately and who their favorite poets are and how they identify themselves with poets. The gaps and blanks I find in students' backgrounds are sometimes astonishing. So I encourage them to broaden their literary horizons. But besides wanting them to read more, I want them to know they should try to write, say, sonnets and sestinas, no matter how they define themselves, because you can get a sense of form just from practicing strict forms. And I also want them to understand the range of visions and experiences a poet can explore. If they've heard that Lowell is somebody you just don't read anymore so they won't read Lowell, then they don't know that the kinds of things he examines in *Life Studies* might be useful to them. If they haven't read Neruda, they don't know the kinds of imaginative leaps a poet can make. Getting them to read lots of different poets and getting them to write in different modes is an important contribution I hope I can make as a teacher.

Once I've seen how students respond to new and different material,

I'm able to work with them individually on their strengths and weaknesses in a more significant way. If they're just writing the same stuff they've obsessively ground out all their lives—well, there's something to be said for obsession in poetry—but . . . there's a delicate balance. You don't want to tell somebody who is writing wonderful poems of a certain kind, "Stop doing that!" because these poems may be in a mode that person has to perfect, but there are ways you can help this writer perfect such a mode by showing what other poets do. So I try to do that.

One thing we've done that's been *tremendously* interesting is read poetry in other languages. I don't know whether because of some Bloomian anxiety of influence young poets are just daunted by the verbal brilliance of precursors in their own language, or whether it's just a matter of English being so familiar, but I find that it's often inspiring for students to read poetry in other languages, even languages they don't know, if they have literal translations on facing pages. Several times I've used Stanley Burnshaw's book, *The Poem Itself.* It's a wonderful book. It's got poems in German, French, Spanish, and Italian, and then it has prose translations so even when you don't know the language particularly well, you can follow the translation process, especially if you use a dictionary.

I ask students first to use the prose translation to make their own translation, to make a "working of the poem," and then to take some aspect of the poem which usually arises from its strangeness and its foreignness (since most Americans, even graduate students, aren't fluent in any other languages) and develop that into a variation of their own. That has worked marvelously. We've made some interesting discoveries—like how difficult Mallarmé is to translate. (Laughter) Nobody could do the "workings" of Mallarmé, not even me. Especially not me! We had a lot of trouble, but then we got wonderful variations and we learned *enormous* things about the way language works and about not just the problem of translation, but the problem of craft and of putting a poem together out of words that you find in another language and reconstitute in your own.

I make different decisions every quarter, usually very intuitively, based on whom I feel like reading. I tend to think, "Oh, it would be good to be reading Whitman and seeing what we could do with long lines and with self-dramatization and with that Whitmanesque mythologizing of the world." "It would be good to be reading early

Williams and see what we could do with the minimal notions of no ideas but in things." "It would be great to read *Life Studies* and see what we could do with family poems and snapshots of the past." "It would be fascinating to be reading Plath and thinking about the mythologizing of one's life and the kinds of strings of metaphors that she creates and the internal rhymes she uses." I tend to muse on what I want to do and start with one or two poets I'm interested in, then round out the curriculum with others who would balance those. It usually works quite well.

Some writers have complained that when academics teach or write about literature, they tend to look for the intellectual patterns rather than looking at the work itself.

That's true, but there you raise a problem that's difficult for me because as a person who is both an academic critic and a poet, I'm very conscious of the ways in which as an artist, as a poet or fiction writer, you want to be conscious of what you're doing in terms of craft and your own ideas, but it doesn't always help you to know what particular obsessions are driving you; or, if you know them, you don't always want to bring them to consciousness. But the critic and the scholar and the literary historian will need to find those patterns and will see in your work things that you can't or don't see when you're producing it. Maybe years later you'll understand that your poetry does something that you had no idea it was doing at the time you wrote it. When Susan Gubar and I were working on *The Madwoman in the Attic,* I went back to a lot of the poems that are in my first collection, *In the Fourth World,* and I discovered all kinds of things we studied in *The Madwoman* that I'd been doing in a lot of my own early poems, yet of course I'd had absolutely no consciousness when I was writing those poems that I was working in these particular modes that I was later to examine as a critic. Which is good, or so I believe. Poets have an experience that's essentially emotional and intuitive, an experience that usually involves a kind of epiphany, and that's where most poetic energy and vision come from; critics also have experiences like that, of suddenly understanding something and getting an idea intuitively rather than intellectually, but the critic then has to interpret and rationalize, systematize, analyze, and articulate her insight very carefully and logically. It's interesting for me, as a person who is both a critic and a poet, to experience that division even in myself.

■ *I thought I read somewhere that you don't*
see a division between forms.

I did say that. You're quite right. (Laughter) I don't feel that my work in criticism means it's impossible for me to write poetry. The more criticism I do, the more obsessed I become with certain kinds of critical thought, the more that inspires me as a poet. And the more poetry I write, the more I understand from my own experiences of the process of composition what other poets do, and this understanding helps my work as a critic. Each thing I do energizes the other; but that's not to say that as a poet I can allow myself the kind of intellectual consciousness that I have as a critic because in my opinion much of the energy of poetry has to come out of the right brain, or whatever it is that's the metaphor-making, gestalt-perceiving, intuitive part of the mind. And then later, as the poet part of me becomes aware of what she's trying to do, she's able to shape and refine her original flash of imagination. But the recognition of metaphor is a moment of revelation and it's a moment of revelation that I, for one, don't experience, for the *most* part, quite the way I experience the formulation of a critical hypothesis.

■ *In the introduction to your book on Lawrence, you say the*
assumption that critics know more than writers is false.

Maybe what I really meant, to try to achieve a compromise between that assertion and more recent assertions (by others) about critics indeed knowing more than writers, is that writers—poets and novelists—do "know" in deep ways if you look through their complete oeuvres. Everything that the writer says in some sense says the same thing, or is related to everything else that the writer says. There is a kind of world view that the writer has which is manifested everywhere, both in intellectual, discursive theoretical statements and in fiction and in poetry, and so the writer does know what he or she is doing and that knowing is manifested consciously and unconsciously. To bring this into line with what I claimed earlier: a critic studying a particular writer can achieve a distance from the writer that the writer can't achieve for himself or herself in order to perceive what it is that the writer is saying.

As an artist, you have to know what your intentions are, you have to know how you want to master the form of, say, a poem, and you have to know how to clarify its images and so on; but I don't think a poet can always consciously formulate the deep urge behind a specific poem, the emotional needs the poem may be satisfying, the sense of cosmic injustice it may be rectifying. I wouldn't disagree with a lot of Freud's points about the genesis of art. Art obviously comes out of unconscious needs and, like dreaming, it's obviously in some way a manifestation of unconscious forces.

December 29, 1982

ℐLLEN 𝒢INSBERG

Allen Ginsberg claims that learning to trust one's "ordinary mind" and resisting the temptation to defer to convention rests at the center of good writing. One learns this, he believes, from the example of people who function with integrity because those who "see beauty," inevitably "want to share it." He also thinks reading great literature helps students become "as intelligent as they secretly are."

Ginsberg co-founded the Jack Kerouac School of Disembodied Poetics at the Naropa Institute; he also taught at Brooklyn College. The author of numerous poetry collections, including Howl, Kaddish, Reality Sandwiches, *and* Planet News, *he won the National Book Award for* Fall of America, *the Poetry Society of America's Frost Medal, an award from the Before Columbus Foundation for lifetime achievement, and the medal of Chevalier de l'Ordre des Arts et Lettres.*

■ *I was confused by the tapes of your classes.*
Are they literature classes or writing classes?

I don't make a distinction. Although in writing classes people presumably write poems and bring them in and have them criticized and in literature classes people presumably study other people's texts and don't write, the best teachings I got from Kerouac and Burroughs was hearing them pointing out gems of language and rhythm and perception in world literature as well as in my own which turned me on to say, "I can do that" or "I did that" or "This is just like my brain." So what I'm doing is presenting texts which give the students permission to be as intelligent as they secretly are. It's a writing class and it's also a literature class, but I don't think the teaching of writing necessarily involves the full-time examination of the students' texts or the teacher's texts. I think it's a byplay of intelligence between the students and the teacher on anything, whether it's Shakespeare or a brick wall. It's indicating to the student how to use perception, not necessarily in written form, in terms of body English: how to sit in a chair, how to be aware of breath, how to walk across the street. Knowing how to walk across a street is the same thing as knowing how to write a haiku; learning how to walk across the street is the same thing as learning how to write *The Brothers Karamazov.*

■ *"If the mind is shapely, the art will be shapely."*

Yes. The thing is to get under the students' skin and arouse enough enthusiasm that they get under their own skin. This means allowing yourself to be yourself in class. My own best teachers were William Carlos Williams, William Burroughs, Gary Snyder, Gregory Corso, and Jack Kerouac. I learned by hanging around with them, from watching their reaction to cars going down the street or a story in the newspaper or TV or a movie image or a sunset or moon eclipse; when you see the intelligence of somebody reacting to the phenomenal world, you learn by imitation. You see beauty and you want to share it.

My best learning was just being myself with them and they giving me permission to be myself and then discovering myself with them— how funny I was. So you've got to encourage the student to discover himself and how funny he is and the only way you can do that is by letting yourself be yourself in class which means not teaching, but being there with the students and goofing off with them. The best teaching is done inadvertently.

The oriental theory is such, called *darshan.* People will go across India to visit Ghandi or Ramakrishna or Great Lama, to take *darshan,* which means just to look at them, see how they move their arms, how they carry themselves. It's not a mystical matter; it's seeing and examining someone whose intelligence is unobstructed, whose breath is unobstructed, whose body is unobstructed, whose psychophysical makeup is unobstructed or full of character. That isn't a rationalistic or mystical or mysterious matter—it's common sense.

You finally have to get down to cases and take a look at what the students put down on paper because you could talk beautifully and they could talk back intelligently and sympathetically and full of erotic clarity and you think they understood, but then when they write down something, it might turn out to be the most dreary, third-rate imitation of Rimbaud-Dylan . . . which happened to me the other day. I ran into a student who struck me as radiant and then I read what he wrote—he had only two vivid words out of a page and a half of romantic drivel. So you have to look at the work and see if students are on the level you think they are.

Williams taught me by going over my poetry, *Empty Mirror*. I sent him eighty pages of stuff and he separated forty pages that he thought were really good and he told me what he thought was "inactive" among those forty pages, said I ought to cut it out. I said, "But it's part of the writing, isn't it?" He said, "One active phrase is better than a whole page of inert writing because nobody will ever read or reread it, whereas the active phrase, even if it's not a complete sentence, is more interesting." He put two pages in front of me. One had an active phrase that didn't come to anything as a whole poem, but was fine as a fragment, like a Greek fragment, a piece of Sappho that's still brilliant even though it's only part of a clause versus a whole page of something that's not active. So he said, "Cut down to what's active."

There's another useful principle Mark Van Doren pointed out. He used to write book reviews for the *New York Herald Tribune* and almost every one of the reviews was intelligent and sympathetic; he was always talking about something absolutely marvelous. I said, "What do you do with a book you don't like?" and he said, "Why should I waste my time writing about something I'm not interested in?" So in looking at students' writing and teaching other poetry, it's a waste of time to try to tell them what they're doing wrong. It is not a waste of time to point out examples of active language to them and give them an arrow in the direction you think they should go. You might briefly give some explanation of what is wrong with a phrase like "a dim land of peace" or "I am suffering the terrible illusion of being born into the mystery of nature." You might try to analyze it, but it's like trying to explain what *isn't* there; so the best thing you can do is point to what *is* there. Use every situation to enlighten in the direction of what is practically apprehensible and useful. Point out that part of their nature that is already successful and apparent and concretized and palpable. Attacking what's impalpable is like attacking the ocean. Same thing in terms of poetry samples. Some teachers used to take great delight in mocking bad poetry; it might be more interesting to constantly up level the whole discourse by working with material that's active.

■ *As I understand it, you think that in order to write poetry well, one must let go of pretensions and accept whatever comes up.*
Yeah.

■ *That's hard to do.*
Then maybe you don't understand what it means because it seems to me easy. What's so hard about it?

■ *Well, you've said that Kerouac had to keep telling you to let go.*
Yes.

■ *And that it took you a long time to be able to do it.*
Yeah, because I thought I was supposed to do something different than what came naturally. It wasn't that I couldn't get to my nature. It was that I thought my nature was unacceptable for high class poetry. I thought that high class poetry meant something besides just ordinary mind; I thought it meant some other kind of mind than the one we've got.

Trying to fake another kind of mind or another kind of language or another kind of perception constantly leads poets into these paradoxical situations where they fake something that might be imitatively interesting, but, on the other hand, ultimately is *uninteresting to them*. They dry up at the age of forty or they have writing blocks because they're not making sense on any level, but they think they're supposed to make sense on some level they can't get to. It's like a Marxist with an idea that his writing is supposed to be social for the people, except he can't think of anything social for the people (laughter) and so he stops writing because he never understood what "social for the people" means to begin with. It's such a generalization; it has no real, immediate, practical application. But if someone is dominated by the conditioned reflex in that phrase and criticizes every immediate reaction he has according to this phrase he doesn't understand anyway which is supposed to be an idea ... Like, "My ambition as a writer is to be elegant." Who knows what the fuck "elegance" is? Everything you write, nothing is elegant; so you feel that your writing is terrible or you stop writing. So "letting go" meant letting go of an arbitrary idea that didn't make any sense.

■ *Where did you get it?*
From the teaching of poetry at Columbia and the community around Columbia.

■ *Your students have been to a lot of schools. So when they*
  hear, "Write down your perceptions as honestly as you can,"

they have probably learned that they ought to have certain
kinds of perceptions.

Oh, so how do you get them to locate their own perceptions rather than imitating mine? How do I get them to write in a style that's different from *Howl*? By demonstrating in the classroom how those perceptions are arrived at by me, by arriving at such perceptions during the course of the conversation in the classroom so that we all arrive at the same perception together or by pointing it out to them when inadvertently they've let loose with a perception that's native to them, by checking out the perceptions of other poets and texts and pointing them out as examples, particularly Charles Reznikoff and Williams because their basic method is "ordinary mind," then checking out the student's own writing, then in personal conversation and contact, or by lovemaking with the students in bed when appropriate . . .

■ *Are you serious?*
I'm totally serious.

■ *OK.*
I believe the best teaching is done in bed and I am informed that's the classical tradition, that the present prohibitive and unnatural separation between student and teacher may be some twentieth-century wowser, Moral Majority, un-American obsession. The great example of teaching was Socrates, and if you remember "The Symposium," the teaching method there involved Eros. So Eros is the great condition for teaching. It's healthy and appropriate for the student and teacher to have a love relationship whenever possible. Obviously the teacher can't have a love relationship with everybody in the class and the student can't have a love relationship with every one of the teachers because this is strictly a human business where some people are attracted to others; but where there is that possibility, I think it should be institutionally encouraged.

When you read the *New Yorker* or other accounts of the academic or poetic circuit, it's commonly accepted that it does happen, if not universally, at least more often than not. So we're just opening the discussion of normal, average behavior. That such a teaching relationship as an ideal would be considered reprehensible and scandalous, although it's universally practiced in the academy, means there's some basic lie as to educational method that's been universally accepted for conscious talk.

If you don't acknowledge the actual conditions, you can't, in class, point to ordinary mind, you can't point to epiphany, and you can't point to the recognition of one's own nature. It makes teaching almost impossible because one of the bases of poetry is frankness. So that's a fundamental insight to which we should relate.

It doesn't mean you have to make love to your students; it doesn't mean you have to talk about it all the time in class; it just means that the teacher has to consciously relate to that situation in a creative and open way. Even if the relationship is an avoidance of it, it's got to be conscious. If it's subliminal, then the entire nature of intelligence becomes fogged and if you have foggy intelligence, you have imprecise poetry.

The reason I'm going on so is that you seemed surprised when I said the best teaching is done in bed.

■ *At most universities, it's the only thing you can be fired for except gross incompetence.*

Yes, of course that's it. It's the one thing you can get fired for. If you look at the great teachers, you'll find all the gossip and scandal and humor of Coyote, the American Indian god, who is a trickster hero and who's beyond the law but isn't beyond human nature. It's not perfectly normal for students and teachers to be afraid of each other erotically. It's just a social convention and if someone can't tell the difference between a dopey social convention and universal nature humor, the whole discussion is hopeless.

If you open up the notion of teaching to the philosophy of the boudoir, you have a different angle. My own experience is that a certain kind of genius among students is best brought out in bed: things having to do with tolerance, humor, grounding, humanization, recognition of the body, recognition of ordinary mind, recognition of impulse, recognition of diversity. Give some basic honesty, some vulnerability on the part of teacher and student, then trust can arise. Mutually acknowledged vulnerability leads to mutually acknowledged trust—erotic vulnerability, scandal vulnerability, social vulnerability, the fact that raw human nature is vulnerable anyway, which is characteristic of great poets like Keats and Hart Crane, that raw open heart that's so useful in poetry. Given a conscious acknowledgement of vulnerability, you have a basis to begin teaching poetry.

Most of the people I've spoken with think it's important to read work out loud and you've explained why that's valuable.

Well, probably I've talked enough about vocalization in other interviews. Just one sentence—poetry and language exist in the dimension of sound as well as ideas and letters, so in order to have unobstructed intelligence, you have to be apprehending and hearing sound.

Some people have run into trouble with English Department colleagues.

It's the same thing like you're not supposed to make love. The poets who don't think you're supposed to make love and don't think you're supposed to read verse out loud are also the ones who have a limited idea of what's classic and what's traditional and don't like open form and don't like blues; they only like the closed forms that were practiced one hundred years ago. They only like the dead, closed forms like the sonnet; they don't like the rhymed, triadic, five-foot line exhibited in the blues, which is also a classic form, but they never heard of it as a classic form although it has a name, a nomenclature, and a practice and created what may be the largest and most sophisticated body of literature produced in America:

> I'll give you sugar for sugar that you'll get salt for salt
> I'll give you sugar for sugar that you'll get salt for salt
> Baby, if you don't love me, it's your own damn fault.
> Sometimes I think that you're too sweet to die
> Sometimes I think that you're too sweet to die
> Other times I think you ought to be buried alive.

That's Richard Robert Brown's "James Alley Blues." So there's this tradition of texts which will be classic in a couple hundred years but which would be avoided as literature by the same people who don't believe in lovemaking or reading aloud (laughter) or talking frankly.

A number of people have said it's important for students to receive exposure to lots of cultures, but that blues is excluded from the academy, American Indian Literature is excluded from the academy, Chicano Literature is excluded from the academy; so there's no American Literature being taught in the academy. It's all derivative European Literature.

Or American high literature like Pound, Williams, Marianne Moore—which is great, but the actual community literature which in ancient times was considered the important thing, the Homeric community literature, is ignored in contemporary letters.

There may be some argument about American Indian Literature because it's a minority literature; Chicano Literature because it's a minority literature; but blues is a majority literature that every white and black person in American knows by heart, has feeling for, listens to and does. Everybody hears blues; everybody sings it; everybody that listens to Dylan, the Rolling Stones, Beatles, all rock and roll, as well as the people who are smart and go to the black originals. So it's a universally practiced form which is ignored as literature.

Right there is a case of neurotic amnesia—obliterating this whole area of literary practice as if it did not exist. The reasons for it are complicated. It has to do somewhat with racism, somewhat with rigidity of consciousness, so that spontaneous and oral forms are not brought to the notice of those few students who would pick up on the form—it would alter their perception of the phenomenal world because the blues are franker about human relations than most literary poetry.

■ *And you certainly know about all kinds*
of literature, not only the blues.
The idea that recognition of the body, recognition of Eros, and recognition of sound would exclude rational intelligence is an error of judgment that only someone locked into rational intelligence and nothing else, neither imagination nor body nor feeling, would make.

The difficulty with Urizenic thought is that it bounds the horizon—"Urizen," Horizon. It makes a boundary so you don't see beyond the limits of conceptual thinking. So you don't hear the *sound* of poetry, you don't feel the rhythm of poetry, perhaps you don't even imagine the vast implications of the poem; but you get pedantically hung up on some rearrangement of mental forms in the poem. The poem finally presents manners rather than the entire gamut of human feeling and intelligence and rhythm and prophecy.

That's Blake's classical division; there are four Zoas, four basic principles of human nature: there's reason, there's feeling, there's imagination, and there's the body. If reason dominates the body and imagination and the heart, it becomes a tyrant and winds up a bearded old man inside the cave of his own skull tangled up in the knots of his rationalizations. If the heart tries to take over and push too far, then it becomes a parody of sentimental gush. If the imagination tries to take over and exclude reason and balance and proportion and body, you get some nutty LSD head, jumping naked in front of a car saying, "Stop the machinery!" and getting run over. The body trying to take over, you get some muscle-bound jock. So you have to have them all in balance.

You remember Socrates was given the hemlock for corrupting the young and Socrates was *certainly* a great educator; he was the acme of the teacher, both of philosophy and poetry. Socrates slept with his students, was kicked off the campus, was driven out of society and made to take hemlock. Christ, the greatest teacher of all, was taken by the forces of law and order and crucified. Buddha was relatively successful, lived to a ripe old age. However, because he was a very great teacher, he had to deal with ignorance; so old Buddha was given bad pork to eat by a jealous cousin. Buddha did quite well, but there still is a certain recurrent unreasonable ignorance in mankind which might be resolved after a long, long time; but confusion has its crises and its aggressions and there's no insurance against it. Actual teaching in the most traditional forms has led to conflict with ignorance in which ignorance has taken violent action, so it should be kept in mind that though true teaching won't necessarily provoke a vicious counter-reaction, when somebody gets into trouble, it may be they are teaching well. Every scandalous teaching should be examined with that in mind as the background: that the classical teachers were scandalous or were perceived as scandalous by those who didn't understand their teaching; the ignorant thought it was something extravagant rather than something obvious.

March 21, 1981

WE SHOULD TRY TO BE AS GOOD AS SHAKESPEARE

Donald Hall argues that poets need immersion in the best literature to nourish and challenge their own work. But since poems present a healthy balance of thinking and feeling that can benefit any human being, he enjoyed teaching Poetry for Non-English Majors at the University of Michigan. In these classes, he coaxed his students to stop treating poems like riddles and, instead, enjoy their sensual pleasures.

Donald Hall's poetry collection The One Day *won the National Book Critics Circle Award, the* Los Angeles Times Book Prize, *and a Pulitzer Prize nomination; his children's book* Ox-Cart Man *won the Caldecott Medal; and his autobiography* Life Work *won the New England Book Award for nonfiction. Besides poetry collections, nonfiction books, memoirs, short story collections, children's books, essay collections, anthologies, and plays, Donald Hall has produced a writing text. His recent books include* The Painted Bed, Subjectivity, Willow Temple: New and Selected Stories, *and* Breakfast Served Any Time All Day: Essays on Poetry.

My teaching experience has not resembled [that] of many poets now teaching in the United States: most of the people teaching writing are *only* teaching writing. I think that's terrible for everybody. I taught literature three-quarters of the time, at least, [and] I brought to the teaching of literature something measurably different from what most of the people teaching English did. I taught a formal way of reading literature: close reading, great attention to the *sounds* of poetry. Intellectual paraphrase or historical relevance was tributary.

The course I enjoyed the most was an introduction to poetry for non-English majors. (The University of Michigan being a big, sloppy place, in fact there would always be about one-quarter English majors.) The whole baseball team took it one time, and nurses and French majors and physicists, *brave* physicists, would take it. I would pretend that they knew nothing about poetry; I would tell them to forget everything that they had ever learned before. I would try to persuade them to, oh, a number of things . . . I [would] tell them to *give* themselves to a poem, to try to take it literally at first until it forced them to take it figuratively. (People tend to leap to take poetry figuratively.) And to read for the senses, for pleasure—to develop a sense of poetic form. I do not mean rhyme and meter. Constantly, I tried to embody the poems by speaking them. I did a lot of reading aloud and I read aloud well and I think it is important to do that. Oh, halfway through the class I would give them a session on meter. For the most part, they didn't like to hear about it, but I got them to write some blank verse—just to get them to write something that scanned.

Every day we'd go through one to three poems in detail, trying to deal with the shapeliness of each—its sound, its whole organization, the metaphorical construction of it and, incidentally, what we might paraphrase as its content. That would always be part of the poem, unless it were "Baa, Baa Black Sheep." There are some rather simple poems by Thomas Hardy, simple to paraphrase, which I complicated for the students by talking about how each poem achieved its shape and what was beautiful in it. Most students are little intellectuals who think that one should *solve* the poem, make some general paraphrase of it, then go on to the next one. If you're going to do that, you're never going to read a poem.

I [can] read [a] poem five thousand times and love it every time I read it, not because of the intellectual experience but because I inhabit its senses or it inhabits mine. It is a continuing pleasure, like hearing music or looking at paintings. You don't memorize the color of a painting to keep it inside yourself; every time you look at it, you see that color anew.

Constantly, probably even into the last week of the term, I would encounter the assumption that a poem is a riddle to be solved and that the answer is in the back of some book someplace. I tried various ways to combat this notion. I'd get kids suggesting a new interpretation of a poem, and if it had any validity, I would say, "Well, I hadn't thought of that. I can see how that would work." Or I would say, "I can see how that *might* work, but I'm skeptical about it." Or, "That doesn't work because it contradicts . . . something or other." I wouldn't lie; I *might* act a little more enthusiastic about an interpretation than I really felt; but frequently, once a week anyway, I would be able to show myself corrected or enlarged in my appreciation. Continually and repeatedly, I provided an improvisational and correctable view of the content of the poem.

A poem is like a work of sculpture that's perfectly made in the round: as you walk around it, every six inches your eyes are going to see something a little different; but it's *all there*, it's all in the sculpture.

Mostly I tried to demonstrate that somebody really loved the poem. People who believed that I loved it might believe that maybe [they were] missing something and pay attention. I tried to carry enthusiasm to them, so that they would continue to read poems in later life.

That's the wonderful thing about teaching: you get to read a lot of literature closely. I learned a certain amount from teaching writing, especially at the beginning, by saying things I didn't know I knew; and I had pleasure in the shop talk of writing. But the *learning* was mostly from teaching great literature. Every year I would touch down on the great old texts again. Now that I'm no longer a teacher, I noticed, after five years, [that] I was reading new things, mostly; I wasn't reading the old texts. So I've gone back to them consciously now, and I'm reading things I never taught or I'm reading things I taught a hundred times. I just reread "In Memoriam" for the first time in thirty years. This reading and rereading is important to me as a writer. It's ridiculous not to touch down on those old texts.

▨ *Why is that so important?*

We should try to be as good as Shakespeare or Keats or Marvell. American poetry is beset by a dreadful provincialism that is, I think, a result of graduate programs that aren't serious enough. There's a petty and egotistical competitiveness within the workshops; one student wants to be better than another. But it's a waste of time to worry about being as good or better than the girl in the next row. To be the best poet at Iowa is *nothing*, absolutely nothing. You should be out there like Keats, deciding to do what Spenser did only better.

▨ *Some people say that comparing yourself to the masters makes no sense either, that the act of writing has inherent value.*

No, I don't think so. The reason for writing is to make great works of art. To want to make great works of art is hardly modest, but the egotism of wanting to write great works of art is superior to the egotism that wants to write in order to pick up girls or be better than its neighbor. I don't say you have to compare yourself minutely: "I am two inches to the south of Spenser and one inch to the north of Keats"; that's stupid. But if you compete with anybody, you compete with them; not to be better than they, but to make things *like* them, to be among them. "And I shall dine at journey's end / With Landor and with Donne" was Yeats's boast. He didn't say, "And I'll eat supper at the end of the road with George Russell and Patrick Pearse," did he? He didn't say, "I'll be the best damned MFA candidate in the whole of Dublin."

Another problem is a kind of careerism in poetry which is not serious enough. I hear people at readings say, "I was deserted in Berlin. I didn't have a dollar. I got beat up. But anyway, I got a poem out of it." "I got a poem out of it" reveals the acquisitive notion that poems are property. Good poems can derive from bad experiences; but the experience is one thing and the poem is another and the poem is supposed to be a work of art. Then I also hear people describing poems in terms of genre or technique: "This is a persona poem." It's not serious enough.

There's a poëbusiness today, like agribusiness, and there are house journals and trade organs for it. Various groups put out newsletters every few months that have to do with how to place your poems and how to get jobs and publication. It's not the real thing. I think a lot of talented people lose themselves in poëbusiness.

I mean to be ambitious. Getting ahead in poëbusiness is pure triviality. It's being satisfied with small gains and small triumphs, which are encouraged by the creative writing industry and its trade schools, the MFA programs. In general, the academy values the number of column inches in your bibliography rather than the quality of the things done. I remember a young poet who had written some good stuff sending out a printed brochure soliciting readings, and on it he said he had published four-hundred-odd poems in the last four years. That's ludicrous. In his long life Wordsworth didn't write that much and he wrote too much.

I'm American too and I love quantity. I try to be puritanical with my poems, ride hard herd on them and not publish them unless I feel good about them—and yet I will publish about forty or fifty prose pieces a year. I work hard on them and try to make them good, but I'm proud of the *quantity* of them. I've published sixty books. I'm proud of making a living on my writing—not much of it from poetry, maybe 20 percent—but I think the prose writing allows me not to rush the poems into print.

■ *You've said that writing prose about New Hampshire is easier than writing poetry. So why don't you write things like that all the time?*
Maybe it's more fun to do hard things than easy things.

I've published lots and lots of prose books. It is easier for me to write prose than poetry; it's not easy, but I will write a poem one hundred fifty times, and the most drafts I have ever written of a prose piece is probably a dozen. I can frequently publish a prose piece that's decent in three or four drafts; that's never happened with a poem.

It takes me a long time to do a poem, to get the poem the way I want it—and for all I know, they're no good anyway. But I'm sure they're better than they were in the fourth draft! It's been three years since my last book of poems was published. I've only published one poem in that time and that was because a friend wanted it for an anniversary issue. Typically, it is a poem that I probably won't print in the next book. It's finished, it's witty, it's decent, a couple of people like it; but I don't really care about it. I don't think it's serious enough. Therefore, it came quickly—in twenty, twenty-five drafts.

In my house I have a book-length poem I've been working on for nine years [*The One Day*]. I've got at least a book's worth of poems in draft. But I won't send them out to magazines because I'm still tinkering with them. If I keep them around, they're going to get better. I know that some people send out a poem the day they first write it; unbelievable.

Bill Stafford and Allen Ginsberg and two or three other people do it another way. Bill writes every morning, 365 poems a year. He publishes a good many in magazines, and then when he publishes a book, he will try to publish just the best. He writes as much as I do. I do it by drafting the poems over and over again; he does it by doing different poems. Allen Ginsberg writes every day in his notebooks and several years later takes out of them what he thinks is still lively.

But most of the poets I know—Robert Bly, W. D. Snodgrass, Galway Kinnell, Louis Simpson—write draft after draft after draft. Snodgrass takes longer than I do: he usually takes five or six years, I usually take three or four. Of course, I have many poems going at the same time. This morning I worked on three out of the thirty-five or so that I have around.

How do you decide which three to work on?

It's the three that feel current. I'll be putting them out of sight pretty soon. I've been working on four during the past few weeks, but I didn't get to one of them this morning. Two of them need a tremendous amount of work before they're even thinkable; the other two are nearly done. I will probably put the two that are nearly done in a drawer for two or three months and then surprise myself by looking at them. Then I'll find some things to do to them. I've got other drawers full of things I want to get back to. I think some will probably be ready to send to magazines in the fall, but I may be wrong; it seems to me that I thought so last fall.

I feel like getting back into print again, but I . . . I used to be much more impatient, more like what I deplore. I'm telling myself continually to be serious, but it's been gradual over many years.

I work every day. I don't have any trouble getting to work on them. I have had that trouble in my life.

Do you think William Stafford is right that the reason for writer's block is high expectations?

That could be one of them, sure. It could be laziness. It can be despair and too chaotic a life. There was a time when I couldn't write when my life was a mess and constant distraction. I couldn't get out of my momentary concerns and into a possible work of art. I had two years like that, couldn't do work, and it was a wretched time for me. I was unable to write poems. I was able to write prose. I could distract myself enough for that: I was writing outside myself. Some poets, like Robert Browning, could write poetry when they were depressed because they would be getting into some prince of the Renaissance. I was able to work on a book on Henry Moore, but the poems that had to do with my emotional life and so on, I couldn't get into. That's my explanation after the fact; there may be other reasons as well.

Why do you think the prose is easier? Because you don't demand as much from it?

I don't demand so much from it.

In a poem, I don't want to say the same thing twice, I don't want to use two approximate words in place of the exact *one*. And I'm thinking every minute about the *sound* I make . . . I can write a prose paragraph with sentences of varying lengths, and tinker with the rhythm of it, but it flows more easily, and the revision is easier. I have trouble with large structures but not with sentences. I can relax in description and use of many words, but in poetry I question every syllable. I'm likely to write ten or twelve lines and then spend a year or so figuring out how I can boil those ten or twelve lines down to a line and a half. With a paragraph, I leave it whole and tinker with it.

I'm writing longer poems these days with longer lines; I think more of the prose fecundity comes into them. They're a little less narrow; they used to be narrow, tight, and small. I used to demand that the poetry be packed and build to some intensity at the end—but that's a formula as much as a villanelle. When you first find something new, it's liberating. Different voices speak through the discovery, but then it becomes a form which is restrictive of change. Then I try to find some other way to move.

 Some people have said that a teacher instructs best by serving as an example. Do you think that's true?

In the introduction to poetry for non-majors, enormously so— where I think the example of enthusiasm and pleasure becomes transferable. To a degree in every course, but the more advanced the course, the less so. In creative writing, by example of patience, of seriousness.

In a more exalted way, I think one of the major functions of poetry is to provide models. [Poems] are moments of thinking and feeling appropriate to each other. Therefore, they're teaching you how to live. When we teach literature, the teacher may be a model or an example—but the work taught is far more important than the teacher.

May 19, 1981

A POET COMES OUT OF THE PEOPLE

Etheridge Knight defines poetry as "an oral utterance" because when presenting work aloud, the poet comes into direct contact with the community that Knight considers both poetry's source and its final judge. The poet writes out of individual experience but always strives to transcend isolation by using words in a way that connects with others.

Knight taught at the University of Pittsburgh, the University of Hartford, and Lincoln University and published eight poetry collections, including Belly Song and Other Poems, *which was nominated for both the Pulitzer Prize and the National Book Award.*

■ *Most of the writers I've interviewed see the university as a hospitable place for poets. I would guess that you have a different viewpoint.*

I think MFA programs are fine. I think any poet needs the discipline that protected environment [provides]. I worry sometimes that the poets [in MFA programs] are seldom directed towards the people. They're directed towards other poets and towards grants and publishing on the page. I have seen people come out of MFA programs who have never discussed the poet as sayer, as singer.

There were poets before there were printing presses; so I see poetry as primarily and essentially an oral utterance, the written word as an extension of the spoken word. A poetry reading to me is when art really happens; the poem and the poet and the audience are in communion and it's the poet's voice that's doing that. A poet comes out of the people, comes out of his or her own history and times and [his or her] main address is to that audience. You get too far from your audience, you're not using the common language and your work will become vague and misdirected. You have to be clear who it is you are addressing and listen well to the language of the people you're addressing. It requires constant contact.

I got poems back [from publishers] for three or four years and the editors kept saying, "Too prosy." I was using words that delivered concepts. Intellect belongs in poetry too; [but] when you're trying to say something specific, you've almost got to use a metaphor. Otherwise, you're just giving information. Metaphors come out of a particular people's experience. There ain't no universal metaphors. The message, the inside of the metaphor may be the same; but people who live near the ocean, their metaphors are going to be made up out of fishing; people who mine . . . The metaphors are generally made up out of the basic economy; [how] people eat. I am a sexual person, an economic person, an aesthetic person. Political reality causes passions too. Our language is formed by our culture. We take in those words and create a miracle.

Sometimes poets say, "Well, people don't like poetry," but I'll bet you if you walk down the street, damn near everybody you run into will know a poem or part of a poem. Poetry is living when it's in people. When a line or two of a poem is remembered, that's timelessness. Some critics talk about timelessness and I get the feeling they're talking about how long a book has been in print. (Laughter) Shakespeare's poems become timeless as long as they're said aloud. A book can stay in a library for twenty thousand years; it doesn't become timeless until some human being starts saying it. Art exists in people. Our main audiences are people who've got things to do: they've got to get to work, get the babysitter; they don't have time to mull things over. You've always got to be clear. As Baraka says, the duty of the poet is to say as exactly as possible what he or she means.

When I put a poem out, I expect criticism because what you're dealing with is so intangible, [you] can't get to it in that first creative impulse. When you're dealing with feelings, you fool around and bob and weave. (Laughter) Sometimes you put out words saying one thing and really meaning another. I might be operating from this passion, but I haven't said it clearly the first or second time I'm working with it. First you have a vision and then comes revision. And you cannot get revision until you run it past the people. When I put out a poem, if it's not received well, I say, "Well, I ain't said it clearly enough." I know very few professors who take their classes out of that protected environment and have them publishing their poems out. That's where they belong. The word "publish" means to make a public utterance. There are all kinds of audiences. There are many mountains for these various Mohammeds to go to: there are mental institutions, there are prisons, there are hospitals, there are schools, there are churches for the professors to take their students to and let them say their poems out to people. Most people who get into "creative writing" already know how to handle the language on the page. Young poets, all poets really, should publish their poems aloud first. Once you put it on the page, it's hard to take back. It's hard to revise then; you're kind of held to it.

How can the student learn to profess properly if the teacher ain't professing properly? It seems to me that a good teacher in this environment would take his students out. I can see maybe at first [staying] in that protected environment, especially getting into relationships, getting in touch with their feelings, getting their confidence; [but eventually] they [have to] take their asses out into the water. He can't take them out unless he's going to go out there himself.

I was doing this free people's [class] in Minneapolis and we went out onto the buses at five o'clock. Imagine trying to get somebody's attention: it's five o'clock rush hour, people are tired and going home.

■ *And you recited poems at them on the buses? What happened?*

Sometimes people'd listen; sometimes they'd turn them off. The exercise is supposed to get poets to understand the power of the spoken word and also they would go out there with prosy poems and a whole lot of literateness . . . (Laughter) They'd come back and you wouldn't even have to take a pencil. They'd do it themselves.

■ *Someone else I interviewed who teaches poetry workshops in prisons said that he thinks some of the same energy that gets people into jail can be diverted into poetry. He also said that the students he teaches in prison have less trouble getting in touch with their feelings than students he sees in the college classroom.*

Creative energy everybody has. I don't think dudes in prison have it any more. Sometimes it is more focused, either creative or destructive. It's the same energy wanting to be. Just wanting to be. I doubt if the creative energy in prison is any more direct than the creative energy in war. I've been in two violent situations, in the army and in prison— one is more organized violence. (Laughter) At war times more babies are born. The closer you are to death, the more that life urge is forced and you are close to death in prison all the time.

The difference I found in conducting workshops in prison and on college campuses: it's hard to get students to get in touch with real rage, real anger, or real fear because the environment is so protected and their lives are so protected, they don't know how to get in touch; so many cultural blocks have been put up that they can't get in touch. It's there! I think because of the violence there, people in prison probably get in touch with basic feelings quicker: anger and fear. Things are clear. I don't know if people in prison can get in touch with subtler feelings.

I like nonviolent environments. They're hard to find in this country. (Laughter) It's hard to be creative or to be free under the threat of violence—even emotional violence. I don't think art thrives under the threat of violence. When I go into prison [to teach a poetry workshop], I expose seven or eight hardcore dudes to nonviolence and plant a seed. Moses came down from the mountain, so I can go to prison. The first thing we have to do is stop people from killing each other.

In almost anything, the key to human feeling, thinking, and behaving is in the language—always in the language. Yeah. I believe that words are magic, that when you speak a word there are physical changes in you. The word "h-a-t-e" is used too much. That's an awful word. The activity you go through when you say that word . . . Watch a child when he says that word. We'll stop a child from saying "son of a bitch," or "mother fucker," but not "hate," and that's much more destructive.

Psychiatrists know it, preachers know it: everything is in the word. Yeah. It's in the language now: "post–Civil Rights": you hear that term all the time; as if . . .

■ *Everything is finished.*

Yeah. (Laughter) It's tricky, like a limited nuclear war. (Laughter) Once the debate was nuclear war or no nuclear war, then it shifted to limited nuclear war. It's like arguing capital punishment, yes or no; now the fuckers are arguing how to kill—whether lethal injection versus—Hey! I watch the language; I watch what people say since words are the tools of the poet.

■ *Where did you pick up that sense of language*
and of the importance of words?

Well, I grew up a shoeshine boy. My first job was in a small town in Kentucky. You can imagine a little black boy on Market Street, down near the river, down where farmers and townspeople buy their groceries and there [were] taverns and juke joints and when you're a black boy growing up in the South where violence is always . . . You pay attention; you listen to what people say because you can get kicked in the ass. You listen to every nuance; it's a matter of surviving—really. "Shoeshine, mister?" "NO!" You have to watch out for some who are a little perverted; they want to play with you and you have to pick that up quickly. You can have your head down shining shoes and you'll still be listening to how he's talking to you. If he's talking to somebody else, you just listen and be aware. A little black boy out there on a street with a shoeshine box, he's vulnerable.

It surprises me that you mention prison so often because it isn't a large part of your life in terms of years.

Yeah, people have said, "Well, why do you talk about prison so much?" In fact, my ex-wife would say, "You talk about prison too much. Why don't you talk about . . ." I'd say, "You talk about your college days and people talk about their army days": people talk about the period of coming to self-definition whether it's the army, college, whatever. And beyond that, I see prison as my major metaphor. The main pool out of which anyone makes art is the reaching out to communicate from one's aloneness—rather than loneliness, it's aloneness. You've got to become I alone and it's a prison. My major metaphor is just more physical and concrete; but I suspect that if you'd probe any artist, they use their art to break out of aloneness. Being a black male in this country, I still feel, I still *am* imprisoned in lots of ways just from the racism in the air in this country.

February 22, 1986

CLARENCE MAJOR

EACH ACT OF WRITING BECOMES
A WHOLE NEW EXPERIENCE

Since a constant interplay takes place between the artist's self-awareness and work, Clarence Major maintains that as the writer's consciousness changes, so does his or her art. But an author also needs to achieve objectivity. To accomplish this, Major suggests putting a project aside for a time and reading it aloud.

Clarence Major has published novels, poetry, memoirs, anthologies, a dictionary of African-American slang, and an essay collection. His paintings have also been exhibited around the country. The New York Times Book Review *has designated two of his novels Notable Books:* Painted Turtle: Woman with Guitar *and* Such Was the Season; *he won the Western States Book Award for* My Amputations; *and his poetry collection* Configurations *was a finalist for the National Book Award. His recent publications include the novel* One Flesh *and the poetry collection* Waiting for Sweet Betty. *He teaches at the University of California at Davis.*

◼ *You make a number of statements that seem to link finding yourself as a writer with finding yourself as a person. Do you believe that the two are connected?*

I think the two processes are integral and interchangeable and inseparable—the continual redefinition of self and the process of learning how to write every day. It's an endless lesson: you don't really carry that much information and skill from one piece to the next unless you're doing the same thing over and over. Each act of writing becomes a whole new experience, which is why it's so difficult. It's not like a nine-to-five job where you know what you're supposed to do every day, so I think, yeah, the self is involved in that process. You're different every day and if you're trying to do something that's worthwhile, then you're going to have to rediscover yourself, and rediscover a new approach, a new technique, a new way of getting at the same old things about life.

▓ *So every day when you sit down and write,*
you have to reconnect with yourself?

Yeah, I think so. That happens automatically and unconsciously; it's an instinctive demand on the self.

▓ *You wrote, "It was finally through the hard work I put into* All-Night Visitors *that I came (in Ralph Ellison's words) "to possess and express the spirit and understand with feeling the footnotes on who and what I was." Is there any connection between that discovery and the fact that you were able to write your next book,* NO, *so quickly?*

Well, with *NO* it was different because I had a concept; I had a vision of that novel. I knew what I wanted it to be and it came pretty close to being what I wanted it to be. So I wrote it on an endless sheet of paper, which made it a lot easier. The things that I learned writing *All-Night Visitors* really didn't carry over to *NO*. And I wasn't able to use anything that I learned from writing *NO* in the process of writing *Reflex and Bone Structure*.

▓ *So you go about writing each book differently?*
You wrote NO *on that long sheet of paper . . .*

Yeah.

▓ *And you never did that again?*

I never did that again. And also I never had a clear vision of a book like that. *Reflex and Bone Structure* was a mock detective story or a kind of murder mystery and that's all I had in my mind, that I was going to do this very, very strange murder mystery. But I never knew from day to day where it was going. I would just sit there and say, "OK, typewriter, here I am" and that's the way I took it from day to day. In the subsequent drafts, [it] became a lot clearer to me what I could do with it, but the first draft was a learning process, unlike it was for *NO*.

And then the same is true all over again with *Emergency Exit*. It took seven, eight years to write that and during the first two years there were some very bleak moments when I did not know whether I'd be able to finish it. I had a vision of the whole thing as early as the second year, but I did not really know that I could pull it off. There were times when I didn't believe I could do it. And so even with the vision, I wasn't able to do it the way that I did *NO*, which was easy and spontaneous. It was a struggle and I had to throw away a lot; I had to rewrite and revise and reshape and pull parts out and reshuffle parts and all those kinds of really frustrating and aggravating things. I'm not able to say I have now enough experience to go forward and write my books . . .

■ *Easily.*
Because I don't. I can't really use the experience. It's not like an automobile mechanic who works on Volkswagens and he knows Volkswagens, so he's able to really use that knowledge and it carries over from car to car.

■ *So it really is a matter of starting over every day.*
And starting over every day with complete innocence, with no tools. It involves discovering a new approach with each time, with each step. If you're a writer, if you're trying to make a work of art out of prose or poetry, you have to go with your instincts. Follow them and you can use that knowledge that is there. [They know] more than we know. I could write to a formula and write the same book over and over. Some writers do that and I'm sure it's a lot easier and less aggravating. Probably they make more money doing that; but in the long run, I don't think it would be satisfying to do the same book over and over with different names. I welcome the challenge and I think it's the only way to write anything that has vitality.

■ *Do you think that writing clarifies your sense of yourself?*
I'm sure that's true, but I'm not sure that it happens in the same way all the time; very often you'll look back at something you wrote, say, a year ago or two years ago or maybe ten years ago, and understand something about yourself that you didn't understand while you were making that piece of writing. Or you become very aware in the very process. So the learning process, for me, is never the same. I just finished a book about the late actress Dorothy Dandridge, who committed suicide in 1965. It's a fictional treatment of her life, but I discovered while writing the book a lot of things about my own outlook, about my own experiences, my own attitudes and prejudices, everything, through the process of trying to project myself into her, into her sensibility, into her mind, into her outlook.

You've said things that imply you believe in order to write anything original or interesting, you have to get as close to your perception of things as you can.

I don't remember saying that, but it sounds true. (Laughter) I would say that it's very complex and difficult because this whole idea of getting into yourself constitutes a problem because if you're writing from an intensive, personal, subjective point of view, you're also facing the inevitable problem of nearsightedness. You're likely to miss something. One example: I was living in New York. I was walking along the street and passing in front of the Laundromat and a dog was tied to the parking meter. A little girl came out of the Laundromat to pet the dog and the dog bit off her ear. Whack! Just like that. A lot of people gathered around and it was a very tragic moment. It was not the thing you would expect on a casual afternoon; people were feeling good in the city; it was one of the first warm days. I tried to write a poem about it. I wanted to say something about how it affected me and what the implications were: how unsafe I felt we all were, forever. To try to put that on paper proved to be extremely difficult and finally, impossible. I was just too close to it. I tried to do it that very day.

We very often need some distance, not just from the experience, but from ourselves, in order to write anything worthwhile. That distance can be achieved in different ways. It's possible to do a first draft, for example, and put it away. Usually that's my process. First of all, I put it on the paper to try to see what it is, because I don't know, and then when I can see what it's trying to be, I go back and I try to reshape it and impose a kind of order upon it and focus and direction. I'll do a first draft of something and won't know how I feel about it. I'll put it away and look at it six months later, three weeks later, sometimes two years later, and then I can start working at the thing in some sort of objective way, so that I can see what's there in a way that I wasn't able to see in the beginning. But that's my process. I tend to overwrite and have to cut a lot, so usually what I do is look for the essence of it and try to refocus the thing and glean out whatever vitality might be there.

But I don't necessarily encourage my students to write that way. We're all individuals and we're all different. There are many, many ways in which things can be accomplished. What I try to do is understand their processes and it's really interesting for me to see all those different ways that things can be made, watching the students work. I don't ever impose a group assignment, but I make assignments optional so that they can pick and choose because they work in different ways. It would be unreasonable to try to make them all in my image.

■ *Or encourage them to do anything in a certain way.*
Right. Except their way.

■ *That must be exhausting.*
It is, it is. (Laughter)

■ *Someone else I've spoken with said that his students think that all good writing makes an important point, and so they try to think up a significant thesis. Have you seen that problem in your students?*
Well, that's very true of my students, especially the fiction writers. They will have an argument that they need to give expression to and they will build the story around the argument. There are different ways I go at that. There is a student in one of my classes now who writes really excellent satirical pieces about political situations and you can see that the fiction is really there as a conveyor for this argument. Then you think, that's what the history of satire has always been, really. You look back to Swift; you look back to Nathaniel West. I think it's OK and probably works pretty well and certainly has a substantial history and tradition. But the other kind is a lot more aggravating, where the students really have some sort of muddled notion of what the point of view should be and try to decorate that idea with a few pages of careless prose. That's a lot more disturbing from my point of view.

■ *What do you do?*
I do several things, depending on the situation. (Laughter) I would try the positive approach, but I run into the problem of so many students being in workshop for approval rather than tough, hard criticism, and that's one of the more difficult things that I have to face in dealing with the kinds of manuscripts that are "not worth talking about." These people are paying as much as anyone else, so they deserve their money's worth. I try to find whatever is useful in these things to serve as an example for the whole class without alienating the person, but there is always that problem. And then there are people who feel like they want to spend the rest of their lives writing and they shouldn't do that. What do you tell them? Those are the difficult, sensitive

moments; but those situations don't present themselves very often because usually the student serious about writing will have enough self-knowledge, self-confidence, and talent to know whether or not he can expect recommendations, etc., encouragement . . .

I don't believe that I can always help anyone become a better writer, but I think I can always help them become better readers and then become more sensitive to the language and how it's put together. They take that writerly experience back to the reading process; I've seen it happen. They understand something of the process and therefore, they can read with greater sensitivity, and more pleasure too.

There are three or four, five perhaps, in each class that are really good. I've worked with students who have published books over the years and who are now beginning to make names for themselves. That's very satisfying and I like to think that I had some small part, anyway, in their development. There is so much talent, it's just incredible. I'm sure most of it will just go down the drain and will never develop and I'm sure that happens with every generation.

Why? Because they don't need to write?
Because they don't need to write.

I gather from some of the things you've written that you're not very enthralled about people writing to make money.
I don't think a writer should sit down and write a book for money; it's not a wholesome motivation for writing poetry or fiction because . . . All the worst things that Fitzgerald did he wrote for money. All of his slapdash stories for the *Saturday Review* aren't really taken that seriously; every once in a while, a critic will say, "Well, those stories are worth taking a look at again. They're not really so bad." But they really are bad because they were manufactured pretty much to a formula for money and compared to the kinds of things Hemingway did with the short story . . . If you compare the two, you can see how Hemingway allowed himself a greater sense of freedom and certainly he started with a healthier motivation. Writing for money, almost without exception, one allows one's knowledge of the market to dictate the form and direction of the work. And the marketplace is invariably wrong or shallow or mediocre; all those structures that have proven to be sellable are the kinds of structures that editors and publishers try to insist on.

What about the view that writing programs are irresponsible because they are staffed with people like you who don't want to teach people how to make money writing?

I believe in making money and I believe in making money from writing. I know she's not a good example of a moneymaking writer (laughter), but Gertrude Stein said something that is very, very fitting: she said that the writer should force the world to see things his way rather than adapting himself to the outlook of the world. It's possible to make money Gertrude Stein's way . . . Well, Hemingway certainly made a lot of money. I can think of a lot of excellent writers who made a lot of money; Dickens made a lot of money.

In the introduction to your collection The New Black Poetry, *you said, "Unlike most contemporary white poets, we are profoundly conscious of forces that ironically protect us from the empty patterns of intellectual gentility and individualism and at the same time keep our approach fresh." It doesn't seem as though the intellectual gentility produces that many writers. At least, I don't think many of the people I've spoken with would see themselves as products of the intellectual gentility, nor would they be seen that way by others.*

Well, it's probably true, for the most part, but it's also strange, isn't it, because writers always, until very recently, came from the upper classes. They were the only ones who had any time to write or even think about writing or doing any of the arts. There are few exceptions to that: Millet, for example, who was a peasant and on the doorstep of starvation half the time and I'm sure there are others; but, yeah, the social changes that have taken place since the French Revolution probably turned the whole world upside down. The kinds of suffering that people from the lower classes or lower-middle classes perceive became more vital in terms of their implications in art than the perceptions coming from the upper classes.

My wife is working on her dissertation and she has done a lot of research on myth, ritual, and metaphor, also on the early Spanish picaresque novel. By watching over her shoulder, I've learned that the early picaresque novel is almost without exception about the downtrodden, the vagabonds, or the outsiders. These books were written by people from the upper classes; even that early, four or five hundred years ago, the perceptions made from the lower depths, about thieves and prostitutes and so on, were considered more vital or at least more interesting. That was certainly the forerunner of the modern novel.

Reubens was a comfortable middle-class man in politics and did some remarkable paintings. William Carlos Williams was a baby doctor who never went without money. On the other hand, Modigliani was walking through alleys practically feeding himself out of garbage cans. So great art can come from any class, but it's a nice idea that one has to suffer in a garret somewhere in order to produce a great piece. It's probably true for a large number of people and it's certainly true for me. For many years I was living a dangerous kind of existence. I lived in New York for twelve years; I was not in the safe world of the university with a nice insurance policy and tenure and all those very nice things, so I was constantly working out from that place of insecurity. You can't argue with your own experience; it's there! But I don't think you can generalize.

A large number of the people I've spoken with talk about the importance of having their students read aloud and listen to their writing. Is that . . .

Yeah, I think so. Especially in poetry, but also in fiction. I will have certain kinds of prose read in class because they lend themselves to that kind of expression; it's not just a visual experience. I certainly learn a lot by reading my work in public; it's a way of educating myself in public, or not educating myself, but rewriting, which is an educational process. And a way of getting distance too, looking at my work from different angles. Very often right in front of an audience, I will make a mental note to change something I'm reading because I've suddenly had the experience of seeing what's wrong with it as I'm reading it. So I think it's important.

One article I read suggested having the students talk into tape recorders and then write from that material. The author said he thought that would make what they wrote more honest because people tend to lie when they write.

They only think of writing as an approximation of their speech and the extent of our normal experience with writing is to write a letter to someone and it's always the same tired, worn-out expressions: "Dear Betty, I'm sorry that I didn't write earlier . . . ," rather than doing it the way we would speak. We get into the habit of thinking that writing cannot be an instrument of the voice, but the most effective writing always has been an approximation of the voice. I'm always trying to get students to write in their own voices and also to write out of their experiences and to write about what they know, and part of that process involves using an approximation of their own speech, not the way Shakespeare wrote and talked.

▪ *That sounds good. I had a student last year who used inflated language, because he was scared, I guess. When he came to my office, I had him read his paper out loud. He knew right away what the problem was.*

I run into it all the time with students who will get fascinated with a certain writer and they'll be writing that writer's prose. That's fine as a learning process, but one should move beyond that and constantly think in terms of moving toward one's own voice and one's own speech and one's own rhythms. That idiom is a vital part of the experiences they should be writing about. Most students in college today aren't going to have an opportunity to be in touch with who they are and where they come from in such an intense way ever again as they will in a workshop. They will go into different kinds of things: business, engineering, the sciences; but hopefully, they will remember how important it was to create a wedding of that voice that was theirs and that history that was theirs. No matter how much television one watches or how many movies one watches, the kinds of associations produced by those kinds of experiences remain marginal and accidental and incidental; they won't be like the experience of writing and discovering one's voice and creating that bridge to an audience. That's an entirely unique experience that there is no substitute for.

March 18, 1981

JAMES ALAN McPHERSON

THERE'S NOTHING LIKE THE
LITERARY IMAGINATION

Like many other teacher-writers, James Alan McPherson values integrity, so he not only admires the student who walked away from the University of Virginia's writing program, he also predicts that "We'll hear from him some day." Although honesty has enormous value, McPherson points out that stating one's views directly not only invites hostility, but it also does not work, so he creates a classroom that coaxes his students to complicate their awareness by exposing them to work that presents unfamiliar perspectives and coaxes them to reevaluate their own opinions. McPherson's belief that awareness of reality's complication rests at the center of good writing probably helps explain why he learned more from watching the novelist Richard Yates function than from the techniques he collected in writing classrooms.

James Alan McPherson teaches at the University of Iowa Writers' Workshop. He won the Pulitzer Prize for his short story collection Elbow Room *and received a MacArthur Fellowship. He has recently published two nonfiction collections,* Crabcakes *and* A Region Not Home.

At the request of James Alan McPherson, this interview was not tape recorded. It is based on notes.

Your writing emphasizes the limits of established orders and common assumptions. How does that idea influence your teaching?

I try to have them read things which represent other traditions. For instance, I'll have them read something like Isaac Babel and then I'll make statements that disturb them and make them think. It's important for the students to become aware of and challenge their assumptions because this country has bought into a false mythology. Basic American values evolved during three hundred years of Southern history, but we've turned our backs on that and embraced the myth of the American

West. The West was a significant part of our history for only twenty-six years, from 1870 to 1896. We now have people whose imaginations have been conditioned by the false mythology of the West. They're blind.

▪ *A lot of the people I've interviewed have talked*
about encouraging their students to be honest.

I want my students to be cunning. We live in a world shaped by a fallacious folklore. If you're honest, you might get killed. Besides, if you make direct statements, you become an ideologue, not a writer. Indirection persuades people more effectively than direct statement. For instance, Lenny Bruce and Richard Pryor use humor to attack routinized behavior and it works.

▪ *What happens to your writing when you teach?*

I write less because I give all to my teaching. I have a tremendous number of office hours with students. It takes all my time because as long as I'm doing something, I don't like to do a bad job.

I have to back away from it every once in a while. Everybody has an ego and everybody wants to be remembered. A teacher can't help but hope that maybe one of the students will remember something from class. I think the temptation to become a god is particularly strong for teachers of literature. It's important to become aware of and resist that temptation because students have impressionable minds. The power to open young minds is dangerous.

▪ *What about the other jobs you listed in*
Railroads: *waiter, salad girl* . . .

Oh, I was fooling around then. I was just showing there's nothing wrong with saying you're a Harvard graduate and a salad girl in the same breath.

▪ *Were you able to write when you were a student at Harvard Law?*

Sure. I went to Harvard from Savannah, Georgia, and discovered that there were people at Harvard who were pleased to do something for blacks. One of those people was Thomas Crooks, the director of the Harvard Summer School. Every April and May, I'd go to him and say I needed to borrow money to go to Summer School and take writing courses. He'd always get it for me. He had no idea that I'd become a writer, but he was happy to do something for me. The danger of being someplace like Harvard is that you can OD on optimism. I kept my sanity by working as a janitor near Harvard Square at the same time that I was a student at Harvard Law.

■ *The kind of thinking a law student does*
seems different from what a writer does.

Well, I've used law in my writing. For instance, I see a close analogy between the legal forms I learned about in Civil Procedure and literary form and that idea is central to my story "A Sense of Story." But I didn't just want to be a lawyer. I learned things from going to law school, but I wanted to learn and see more things than that and I've decided that the literary imagination offers the broadest and most inclusive point of view. A few years after I left Harvard, I ran into Paul Freund, who was my constitutional law professor at Harvard. He said he'd been following my work and he thought I'd gone beyond the law. That makes me proud because Paul Freund has an amazing grasp of the interrelationships of things; he not only understands constitutional law, he understands the dynamics behind it. People at Harvard Law School are proud of John Casey and me because we went on to become writers.

■ *What about the notion that fiction is*
escapist and thin compared to nonfiction?

All I know is that when I want solace, I can always find it in literature. How many people are still reading Mailer's "The White Negro"? But people are still reading Cervantes. There's nothing like the literary imagination.

■ *Do you think people can become writers by going to school?*

Good writing comes from hard experience. In school, you learn Proust, but you don't get any experience. People at Harvard have gotten there by going through schools like the Bronx High School of Science or Andover. They know nothing about life. They know how to be poetic, but their poetry does not come out of suffering. [Universities] can turn out teachers of creative writing, not writers.

There was a student at Virginia who won a big fellowship, showed up for a month, and left. This money kept arriving each month, but there was no student to pick it up. Now *that's* a writer. We'll hear from him some day. That's a writer.

■ *Was the time you spent at the Iowa*
   Writers' Workshop helpful to you?

Yes. When I was there the camaraderie was good. The people in the department had energy and it was possible for the students to connect with that energy.

■ *Did you learn anything about writing?*

Sure. I had Richard Yates who's a practicing writer and he made useful suggestions, but I also think it's important and valuable to see a writer like Yates coping with life. The sense of reality that experience gives to the student is probably more valuable than technical devices picked up in the classroom.

■ *Some people argue that exposure to writers with integrity helps*
   students develop the kind of character you see in the student who
   walked out and left the fellowship money behind.

Character can't be taught. Your mother teaches you character; that's all that you're going to get. If you don't have a good mother, you won't have a good character. I had a good one. She told me, "Let them take your money—you can always get more of that—but don't let them take yourself."

December 1, 1980

N. Scott *M*omaday

I GREW UP IN A VERY RICH AND EXOTIC WORLD

N. Scott Momaday describes writing as a personal, even isolated, experience where he submits to the process and can merely hope to succeed. Still, a variety of community experiences nourish his work: shaping new courses gives him a chance to undertake new explorations; he suspects sharing ideas with students makes him more articulate; and, always, the insights he has gained as a member of the native community enrich both what he writes and what he says.

N. Scott Momaday taught at the University of California at Berkeley, Stanford, and the University of Arizona. His published books reveal the multitude of ways N. Scott Momaday has found to make art, for they include poetry, fiction, memoir, literary analyses, and drawings. His receiving the Pulitzer Prize for his novel The House Made of Dawn *helped create a broad audience for Native writing. Recent books include* In the Bear's House *and* The Man Made of Words.

■ *Even though you don't teach creative writing often, some of the remarks you've made, not about writing, but about other things, sound like comments people who do teach creative writing have made about the writing process.*
For example . . .

■ *Well, the story about your father and his friend getting together to paint.*
From *The Names,* is that? Yeah, I remember—Quincy Tahoma.

■ *That episode struck me because it was so full of elation; there were a couple of things about it. One is that they work together. A justification for writing workshops is that it's hard to go off and write poems by yourself and feel that you're doing something that has a point.*

There's a basic distinction to be made there. You can sit at a painter's feet while he's working at the easel and you can, by observation, learn a good deal about what he does; but I don't think that applies to someone sitting at a typewriter. (Laughter) I paint and I have spent very valuable time with Leonard Baskin, for example, watching him draw; I learned a lot from that. And I would love just to be in the same room with Fritz Scholder while he was painting because I'm sure I would learn a lot just by watching. But I don't think I could learn anything about writing by observing John Cheever sitting at a typewriter.

Sure. But they were saying that if you're part of a writing community you feel that wanting to write a story or wanting to write a poem is not a totally bizarre thing.

Yes, it is. (Laughter) Writing a poem is a bizarre thing. It's a brash and artificial act. I think it takes a peculiar sort of person to write a poem; there's a compulsion involved and a very creative one.

Maybe my temperament sets me apart from a good many other writers. I've never found any benefit in workshops or in communities of writers. When I came to Stanford as a creative writing fellow in poetry, I worked with other poets and we all wrote poems and exchanged them and talked about them. I don't think that was especially valuable to me, and I didn't have the sense at the time that this is how to do it. I think of writing as a very isolated business, a personal matter. When I was a student at Stanford, I was offered a fellowship at the Iowa Workshop, and Paul Engle was in charge of that program at the time. "We have a community of writers here and you will be able to exchange ideas," he said. The whole idea was that one writer stimulates another. That didn't appeal to me at all. In fact, it turned me off completely. I thought, "My good Lord, if I got myself into that sort of situation, I'd probably freeze instead of being productive." But I do understand that a lot of people feel differently about it. I guess it finally boils down to what enables you as a person to write and I find the best situation for my writing is isolation.

There's another thing I wanted to ask you about that story: do you see any connection between the process of making things and the elation that you all experienced?

Oh yes. *That* certainly would apply to writing too. There is an elation in it. There's a wide range of possibilities. And at the two extremes you have, on the one hand, complete frustration; that's when you sit down at the typewriter, and this has happened to me thousands, tens of thousands of times, you sit down with a good stretch of time in front of you, say a morning, and you have the best of intentions and nothing happens. You sit there for four hours and you have nothing to show for it. There are few frustrations greater than that. But if, on the other hand, at the other end of the spectrum, you sit down and after four hours you have a paragraph or two, maybe, or three, and you understand that you have done something well—there are few satisfactions greater than that. And I would talk about that in terms of elation, euphoria; you feel the way we did when my father and Quincy Tahoma and I went up into the mountains after one of those sessions. It was a great release, a great sense of having done well on their part; but it was so electric and contagious that I could share in that feeling, too. It was wonderful.

Many people talk of trying to get their students to do what you did when you got on that horse in The Names *and said, "Let me hold to the way and be thoughtful in my going." You said that if you were going to enjoy that day thoroughly, you had just to let it happen. And that's an attitude people often identify as important to writing well: they say that the writer has to cultivate an ability to be open to things that come up spontaneously. Does that make any sense to you?*
Of course. Yes, yes. You never know what's going to happen. You never know what you're going to come up with at the end of an hour of writing; at least, I don't. I don't plan it ahead of time; I don't set a goal for myself and then reach it or not so much as I work and invest myself in the work without thinking of a specific goal. And then, after a time, if there's something there, it is bound to be surprising.

Do you think that your teaching makes any difference to your writing?
I haven't thought about that, but it probably does. If I'm teaching books that I admire very much, it probably is an incentive. I'm constantly coming upon passages in books that, no matter how many times I've read them, impress me in a new way and I feel a kind of inspiration: "Ah, that's well done. I could do that. I might just do something like that." It happens all the time.

The intellectual encounter is probably helpful too. You trade ideas with students; you are forced to articulate your ideas. I suppose in all that, there is some benefit to your writing.

■ *What kinds of literature courses do you teach?*
I teach a course called The Autobiographical Narrative, which is an investigation of the first person voice and the viewpoint of the writer who is looking inward on his own experience and writing about it.

■ *That sounds like something you've done.*
The Names is an example of that particular form and I was very much interested in books of that kind when I was writing *The Names,* so I fashioned a course out of it. We read things like *Out of Africa, Speak, Memory,* and *Goodbye to All That* and Sartre's *The Words* and Lillian Hellman's *Pentimento.* I'm teaching that course this quarter and for the first time I'm using a book called *This House of Sky* by Ivan Doig about growing up in Montana. It's wonderful. Regularly I teach a course in oral tradition which is focused on American Indian oral tradition. And I teach a course called Literature of the American West from 1850 to the Present, a course on the landscape in American Literature and a course on Emily Dickinson and Frederick Tuckerman.

■ *Your courses sound wonderful.*
They're fun. Yeah. I enjoy them.

■ *I imagine that you designed most of them.*
All of those I mentioned.

■ *Which comes first, the reading for the course or your own writing?*
It works both ways. I guess I had the idea of writing *The Names* before I had the idea of offering a course in the autobiographical narrative, so the course probably proceeded from my interest in writing in that form. But I'm sure it works the other way too. Every year you're sent a questionnaire as to what you propose to offer in the next year and that's the time when you think, "Ah, what might be fascinating to explore? What will the students find fascinating?" And so you are encouraged to be inventive.

One thing that interested me in your writing was the idea that people are losing their sensitivity to words. Do you deal with that in your course on oral tradition?

We talk a great deal about that in that course. It really is a fundamental examination of the way we exist in the element of language. It turns out to be a comparison between the oral tradition and the written tradition. It's great fun because few people think about their existence in language at that fundamental level. So it's fascinating and I learn a great deal every time I teach it. I think the students do too because I'm sure most of them have never thought about language in the way that I force them to think about it in that course. And we do, as you say, spend time talking about what words are and what their potential is for us in literature and in conversation—in every way.

When I first offered the course, I had no idea how it would be received. I was hoping that I could get maybe ten or twelve students together around a table. Well, 150 students showed up for the first meeting. I didn't want to turn anybody away, so I had to adjust my idea of the course and it became a lecture course, which is not what it should be; but so many people are interested in the subject that I've had to give it as a lecture course most of the time. Every two years or so, I allow myself the luxury of limiting enrollment to twenty and then I call it by another name, The Storyteller and His Art. And we do sit around a table and we tell stories and we talk about what the role of the storyteller is, how he exists in the language. It's never the same thing twice; it's determined by the people in it. I've been fortunate in having students who really wanted to participate, who wanted to tell stories. I've given them the option at the end of the course of either writing a paper or making an oral presentation and a good number always opt for the oral presentation, and they've been extremely imaginative and inventive: there have been stories, people have put on skits, dueled each other at the level of language, and done other wonderful things. I try to simulate an oral situation; I try to make them believe that they exist outside the written tradition and, of course, they cannot do that. Nor can I. But to the extent that you can make the attempt, it is valuable.

Why?

Because the understanding of language within the oral tradition is much more intense. It's a much more valid understanding of language.

Writing separates man from language one more degree; writing creates a false security where language is concerned. But the man who understands that he must pass whatever it is he has to contribute to the next generation by word of mouth takes what he says more seriously: he's more careful of what he says; he's less wasteful of language; he relies to a much greater extent upon his memory; he relies to a much greater extent upon his hearing. All of this is what we try to understand about the oral tradition and it's difficult. It requires a great act of the imagination and to the extent that I can get my students to *want* and to try to make that act, it's all to the good.

How can they pretend they're in an oral tradition? Are there specific things you do, like forbid them to take notes?

That's right; that's right. I don't allow them to take notes and there are no texts when I teach the story-telling part. Sometimes I use texts as a springboard. We'll look at stories by Borges, for example, who is a very imaginative writer, or we'll use *Seven Gothic Tales* or some of Chekhov's stories, maybe, just at the beginning so we can talk about what a story is and what the storyteller tries to do and what his relationship to the reader is. And then from there, we do away with all the printed materials and we tell stories and talk about the storyteller instead of the writer and the listener instead of the reader and make that crossing over from one tradition to the other. In some ways, it's futile because I don't think you can make the transition entirely, but you can at least suggest it and point to possibilities and I think that's extremely valuable. It has been for me personally and if it has been for me, then I think it ought to be for students too.

Your background probably has a lot to do with your consciousness of language. Has it been valuable to you in other ways?

I grew up in a very rich and exotic world and I find myself constantly recalling things from that world. I loved it and I've written a good deal about it.

February 25, 1981

YOU NEED TO WRITE TO BE A WRITER

Kit Reed builds her instruction around two premises: everyone writes the most powerfully out of a central obsession; and although she can serve as a coach, finally, her students must write—and write—to discover their particular points of view. Reed recommends that authors support themselves with jobs that call upon other capacities than those sustaining their writing to protect their focus.

Kit Reed teaches at Wesleyan University. Her most recent novels include Thinner Than Thou *and* @ Expectations. *Her short story collection* Weird Women, Wired Women *was a finalist for the Tiptree Award, as was her science fiction novel* Little Sisters of the Apocalypse.

■ *How do you teach?*

I started with a workshop. I discovered when I took a couple of senior theses that I got more accomplished talking one-to-one with people, so I have done some "Intensive Fiction Writing" courses for the past few years where I take only six or seven. We meet as a group three times and then we split up. I see three of them one week and three the next for the rest of the term. We meet for half an hour or more, depending on how much time they want and need. We talk about the manuscript, trying to narrow the gap between what they thought they were doing and what they have on paper, and we also talk about their lives. It's not psychiatry exactly; we're trying to find out what they have to write about. It's not me asking a lot of directed questions. We talk about whatever we feel like talking about, which sometimes is the movies and sometimes is their love life; but at the same time, I have a sense of them as people, so I know what they're writing from. I can look at what they've written and see whether they're coming at all close to their central material.

If you look at any writer who's any good, you discover that he is writing out of some preoccupation or obsession and it's interesting for me to see what a student has for central material. I don't tell them. I have a graduate student who was a Stegner Fellow at Stanford and was in a graduate program at Brown. He's Chinese-American and I said, "David, you're sitting on a goldmine"; I will go that far. I had another student, a writer named Stephen Alter. He was all of twenty-three when Farrar, Straus published his second novel, *Silk and Steel*. I kept looking at him through the three years we were working together, trying to figure out the central obsession. He is an American whose family was born in India; he's the third generation who has grown up in India and it was apparent to me that that cultural dislocation was going to turn up in his work. I didn't see it coming in the stories he wrote as an undergraduate until I saw them as a group. The collection became his first novel, *Neglected Lives*, and I suddenly realized that it was there, it was showing in the work already.

It's interesting to figure out what drives them. It's not that we try to tell them anything. The important thing is to try to figure out what it is that they think they're doing and help them do it their way instead of . . . The worst kind of teacher of writing or painting is the kind whose students' work looks exactly like theirs. It was nice this year to get my evaluations and have one of them actually say, "Kit tries to find out what it is that we want to do and help us instead of having us all write the way she does." So I don't try to direct them at all. I try to make them rewrite; I try to make them write more; I try to make them write enough to find out what they want to write. They have to do it. I can't do it for them.

■ *It sounds like you make a big investment in them.*
You must get something from it besides the money.
When you write a book, it's months, years, perhaps, before you get a response. You tell one of these people something and you can see the change in their faces, you can see it in their work; there's an immediate response there. I like them; they like me. Several of them have begun to publish and are going on. One is in a graduate program here; another one is in a graduate program over here. I have successes: Alter, Peter Blauner, Suzanne Berne, Simone Zelitch, Daniel Handler and Cheryl Sucher, among others, including war correspondent Kurt Pitzer.

■ *Does teaching interfere with your own work?*
No. I've always worked three hours a day, five days a week, and

when I'm teaching, I'm doing that in spite of teaching. At one point I had two courses because we needed the money for college tuition, which meant that I was teaching two classes a week, one a workshop and one Intensive Fiction Writing. I discovered that I really only could work four mornings a week instead of five. It was also true that in the year when I was teaching the two courses, I found myself writing something that had to be totally rewritten the summer that followed. So my guess is that if the quality of my work suffered at all, it was when I was teaching two courses in one term; but for the most part I've tried to compartmentalize. If I'm going to see my students on Wednesday for conferences, I do not look at their work until Tuesday afternoon, which means that their work is in my head from Tuesday afternoon until Wednesday afternoon, but then it's gone. When I work on Wednesday morning, their stuff may be there but to one side; but the rest of the time I'm thinking about my stuff and what I'm doing.

So you really have to separate the two.

Yeah. It's a matter of concentration. You can't deal with their literary problems and your artistic problems at the same time.

Some people complain that teaching makes them intellectualize what they do when they write and that makes it harder for them to do their own work.

In the course of, especially, the workshops and then in the one-on-one conferences, I was forced to explain how I did what I did, which did not in any way get in the way of my doing it. Somebody who reads a lot of criticism is a lot more likely to get in trouble than somebody who is talking about writing from the inside out. I'm much more articulate about the way I do things and why I do them the way I do than I was before, but I am certainly not crippled by explaining. As for my rate of production, the first novel came out in 1961 and there are nine in all and two short story collections. I have always worked five mornings a week and I think the productivity is about the same—it's no better, it's no worse and my mortality rate is lower. I don't have as much stuff in the trunk that I can't get published as I did in the old days, but the rate of what I'm doing is about the same.

Do your students seem well prepared?

I handpick the ones I take and I don't take any that can't write, so, in that sense, my students are all prepared when I get them. It's hard to tell what they've read. Richard Price said, "I'm teaching people now who are so dumb that they think Leslie and Arthur Fiedler are a husband and wife screenwriting team." I was telling this to my group and they all said, "Oh, yeah, well, who are Leslie and Arthur Fiedler?" At least half, maybe two-thirds of the people I deal with have read an enormous amount of contemporary fiction because that's what they're interested in. People read what they want to write. But I like the person who hasn't necessarily had a college education or who doesn't have a graduate degree because I don't think, after a certain point, you need to go to school to be a writer. You need to go to school to be a person; you need to go to school to learn what is out there and how to find out what you don't know. But you need to write to be a writer.

■ *Do you think it's good or bad that more writers*
are becoming associated with universities?

It's nice that they can find a way to earn a living. I was talking to somebody who is thirty-eight and just beginning and I was explaining that my great triumph was a student who had two novels accepted over a two-year span. I prorated his earnings and I realized that he averaged out to about $5,000 a year. And he's a big success! His stuff has been reviewed in *Newsweek* and the *New Yorker*. With this in mind, everyone has to do something.

At least one of the people at the Clarion Workshop is a computer programmer and we agreed that was gangbusters because he can make $350 a week, which means he never has to worry about money, [and] he's using a different kind of energy from the kind that goes into writing. Thornton Wilder said that if you could either teach mathematics or work in a gas station, that's the sort of thing you should do. You shouldn't be in the newspaper business, you shouldn't be an advertising copywriter, and you probably shouldn't teach writing. But because I've done both, I know that it's easier to write fiction as a sometime teacher than it is to be a reporter.

■ *Why?*

Because when you're a reporter you're writing all day and then you go home and you're writing some more. If you have to be a writing teacher, at least you're not writing while you're teaching, so there's some sort of split. I'm privately supported by my husband so I only have to teach one course, but you can imagine what it would be like to have your full-time teaching schedule and to write fiction at the same time: tough. So you tend to get eaten up by it: it takes a lot of energy, the same kind of energy that you use as a writer, which is why it would be nice not to have to do it. But I also think that sometimes doing something is a way to put off doing something else.

We had an interesting case at Wesleyan. A novelist friend who has published eight novels, his ninth is now finally coming, arrived at Wesleyan about three years ago with two-thirds of a short novel. He had been in advertising and was able to work all day and then go home and write at night. He'd been doing that for eighteen years. Then he came to Wesleyan and he was swept off his feet by the academic life. He had the best time: he loved going to these lectures, he loved being in seminars, he loved going and writing about the modernists and delivering a paper on that; some writers are seduced by university life. He left two years later because his appointment ended, went back and became a vice president and finished his novel. So for some writers, the university thing is a siren. For others, it's a thing they've got to do and they don't have the energy to spread around, and for others, it's this reason to put off writing, which they know is going to be very, very hard. Until your novel is finished and out there, you don't know whether you've blown it or not and as long as it's in your mind, it's glimmering and shining. It's beautiful and it's there. James Agee was always talking about this wonderful book he was going to write if he didn't have to write book reviews or movie reviews for *Time*, and he suddenly realized that if he really had it to write, he would have written it.

July 10, 1980

$\mathcal{A}$LIX $\mathcal{K}$ATES $\mathcal{S}$HULMAN

I PLACE A LOT OF FAITH
IN THAT PRIVATE SEARCHLIGHT

Alix Kates Shulman believes that good fiction gives shape to previously unnoted experiences. To achieve a distinctive focus, the writer must find the courage to rely on his or her "private searchlight." In her writing workshops, Shulman encourages an "atmosphere of trust" and forbids criticism of subject matter. This approach clearly works for Shulman: the Oxford Companion to Women's Writing *called* Memoirs of an Ex-Prom Queen, *"the first important novel to emerge from the women's liberation movement."*

Shulman has published novels, memoirs, and essays. She has also taught at many universities, among them the New School, Yale, and the University of Colorado. She continues to offer writing workshops around the country. Her most recent books include Drinking the Rain *and* A Good Enough Daughter.

I think writing involves exposing your deepest insights, your obsessions, if you will, the things you know best, the way you look at the world and pick out what to notice and interpret. Since people usually write about what's closest to their souls, then negative judgments of their writing can frequently be interpreted as criticism of the person, as it wouldn't be in, say, a paper on Chaucer. It's much more important to keep people writing and to locate the valuable part of their work than it is to give what some teachers call "hard criticism." It's very easy with one false reading or one harsh word to make people stop writing. What people need, on the contrary, is encouragement to risk exposing what they think and feel.

I start any semester trying to establish that the most important thing is for us to trust each other. This is a workshop; we're all in it together. I insist that my students read aloud in the workshops in order to reveal their work to other people in the same vulnerable situation (rather than to people who don't write). In this way, they learn that nothing terrible happens when they do so. When nothing terrible *does* happen, trust snowballs, and very quickly, students get to understand each other, recognize their particular writing strengths and weaknesses. Because they're in the same predicament and have no reason to show off their critical acumen to me—I don't *ever* encourage that; in fact, the opposite from the beginning—they quickly learn what to pick up on, what to listen for in a given person's work. And soon the dynamics of the class develop in such a way that each person seems to have a certain function in the class. But the main thing is to develop this atmosphere of trust.

I discourage as much as I can criticism of the subject matter. We accept every writer's subject and only explore *how* it's treated. My whole education as a feminist has led me to that. Many students have come to me as refugees from other writing workshops usually run by men, with mostly male students, or anyway, with male students doing most of the speaking, who simply reject the subject matter of these women. They say, "Well, who cares about that?" They don't do it intentionally—they don't do it consciously; but that is the effect of what they're saying. That's why, when I teach writing to women, I frequently start out with *A Room of One's Own* in which Virginia Woolf discusses this very question, "What is the problem for women writers?" And more recently, I try to use Tillie Olsen's *Silences.* Although her book isn't restricted to the problems of women writers, she does have several chapters on that subject.

Again and again it becomes clear—it's certainly in my experience and the experience of all the women writers I know—that until a certain moment (and I'm not sure that moment has yet arrived), what was considered important and worthy of writing about was not women's experience, whereas every year you have some baseball novel or sports novel which purports to represent the human experience. It's the metaphor for the human experience; in fact, Philip Roth's baseball novel was called *The Great American Novel.* You don't have such novels acknowledged as the universal human experience when the metaphor is, say, domesticity, which is one-half of human experience, maybe more. And so I think it's important to set it out on the table from the start of the course that approval or disapproval of each other's subject matter is not what we do here. What we do is listen critically and try to understand what makes the story work, but we accept the subject.

I frequently assign readings, stories which illustrate various formal techniques of organization and so on, and then I discuss those. If there's time, we discuss them together; but I always try to point out my reason for the assignment: what the structure of the story is, how symbols are used, that sort of thing, and try to get them to make those observations about each other's work and their own. By this device people are able to make very useful criticisms that do not get personal.

First, the class responds to a student's reading, and then, I always take the paper and give written comments on it. But I always say from the beginning that my being a writer doesn't make me a better *reader*; the whole class is equally qualified to make comments on one another's style. Of course, there are things I know that they don't know because I'm experienced, like ways of organizing material and so on, especially for long works. I do have a lot of tricks that I've learned over the years that I try to pass on; for the rest, I don't think I have a great deal more to tell them than they have to tell each other.

And people do improve. Writing is one of the endeavors, like dancing, that the more you do it, the better you may get. They start to get their stroke, take more risks. I try to encourage risk taking and let the students know that a failed risk is better than a safe success.

■ *I agree. When my students begin writing longer sentences, they will make mistakes; but I'll tell them not to worry because they'll learn how to fix them.*

I remember coming into command of long complicated sentences. It wasn't something I started with; I wrote for some time before I felt completely in charge of my sentences, before I felt that there was no sentence, no idea too complicated for me to transcribe. It came at a certain moment. Also, my command of vocabulary. I see a progression, a building in my command of the language. Naturally, students will experience the same thing.

■ *Do you ever feel that you should discourage people?*

No. No one should be discouraged from writing, just as no one should be discouraged from taking part in speech, political life, love, any of the other universal human endeavors. I do believe that just as everybody, with a few exceptions, is able to speak—that's part of our natural human ability—everybody can learn to write. I'm not saying that there aren't illiterate people who haven't been taught or some people who have been so messed up along the way that they believe they can't write, but those people don't wind up in my classes, which are voluntary. And if they did, I would try to teach and encourage them.

It's true that some students come to me with major problems. Some write exceedingly subjectively without any form; some can't distinguish between what they know and what the reader knows. But problems can be addressed. With attention and practice, all students can improve their writing—at least to the extent that they can write a little better or more consciously at the end of the course than they did before.

You develop your skill and you take your chances. I certainly don't think that every student can produce a publishable manuscript. Not at all. And I don't tell them that they can. But that's not the only reason to learn to write. I distinguish between writing which is an expression of the self as communication to others, and writing for sale, which isn't to say that they can't coincide. Often they do coincide. But they aren't identical.

Of course, part of writing is to be read, just as speaking is to be heard. When you write, you usually have in mind some audience. In that sense, I think it's quite comparable to speech. People do talk to themselves, but it's a peculiar aspect of speech and I think writing is communication too and communication implies a hearer, another person.

I try to get the students to imagine their audience; the question of audience is an important one. You have to make decisions about what to put in and what to leave out of your manuscript on the basis of your imagined audience. Are you going to assume an audience which shares with you a set of values or one whom you want to convince of another set of values? You tell entirely different things depending on the audience you imagine, but I don't encourage them to think of the audience as a specific one, namely, the editors in publishing houses. If what you had in mind was just a fast buck and your audience the publishing house, then you might be writing formula works about things that mean nothing to you. I'm not interested in that kind of work. I don't read it and I don't write it. I wouldn't discourage people who wanted to write such works, but I would also try to get them to write close to what they know and care about.

I place a lot of faith in that private searchlight that goes on in every single person's head to scan the universe for what's relevant, what's meaningful. No two people experience anything in exactly the same way. What is it that distinguishes one from another? It's that peculiar combination of experience and interest that produces this odd focus and *that's* what people should be writing about.

> *When I said that I wished I had gone through a writing program, you said that there are too many other things to know in the world.*

It seems to me that's one thing to pursue as a supplement, but oh, for a writer there's nothing to replace wide knowledge just as there's nothing to replace broad experience. Both those kinds of education are invaluable to the writer. If I had to choose between learning about the world and studying writing, for myself, I would choose to learn about the world. You can always take writing courses; they don't have to be part of an integrated program that has requirements. The richer your experience and knowledge, the more you'll be able to bring to your writing. So I would travel, in books or in the world. And write, too.

> *Some people argue communities of writers are deadly.*

I disagree; it depends on the community. I've gone to the Mac-Dowell Colony, a place I love, and have had some of my most productive and happiest times there. I love being with writers. I can't stand being with a certain kind of macho, competitive writer. That's death. I don't go to literary parties of a certain type because they are too depressing and competitive; but among the women writers I know and certain young male writers, that doesn't go down anymore. There's a real sense of community that I get from a lot of writers in New York, mostly women. And it's inspiring and helpful.

> *What about the idea that a writing community is too isolated from common experience?*

You don't spend your life in one. Besides, that's sort of like saying, "Well, who cares about domestic experience?" Wherever you are, you're a human being. I know of a number of novels that have been partly written in artists' colonies that are very good.

I also think you can learn anything if you need to. I've just completed a novel about a shopping-bag lady, a teenaged prostitute, and a pimp, called *On the Stroll*. It took me two-and-one-half years during which I hung out with street people and studied those subjects. Two-and-one-half years is a long time to study something, and I did it twenty-four hours a day, in a sense; that was what my mind was taken up with. Now I suppose I have the equivalent of a PhD in sociology of the street.

And some people live isolated lives. Look how far Beckett went writing about the isolated soul, the unconnected human. I think it depends on your temperament—whether you like the city or the country, the night or the day. I don't think there's any setup inimical to writing unless it's that competitive environment that stifles honesty. That isn't good, no more in life than in class. You have to discourage and avoid it.

■ *Trusting that searchlight seems to work for you. When I teach* Memoirs of an Ex-Prom Queen, *many students report that they can't put the book down because it speaks to them so compellingly about their lives.*

I think the intention of art is to make visible what is invisible, to give form and voice to experience that didn't before have a voice. I see experience as a kind of fluid which doesn't yet have shape until some human mind gives it shape, which is done by theory making and art making. Certainly the important intellectual, theoretical endeavors do just that, like the work of Freud, Marx, Wollstonecraft, Beauvoir. But fictional shape is another way of giving form to something which was unformed before. This is what the novel—perhaps all art—does.

November 18, 1980

YOU'VE GOT TO MAKE THE DECISIONS YOURSELF, IF YOU'RE AN ARTIST

William Stafford believes the best writing comes from trusting one's insights and language, not straining for eloquence. Stafford acknowledges that his approach may not always produce great work, but it consistently provides its practitioners with an invaluable sense of themselves. As a result, he keeps his poetry workshops free of his praise or blame, so his students can learn to teach themselves and each other.

William Stafford taught primarily at Lewis and Clark College. The author of more than sixty-five books, he won the National Book Award for his first poetry collection, Traveling Through the Dark, *was the consultant in poetry at the Library of Congress, a post later renamed poet laureate, and won the Western States Book Award for lifetime achievement in poetry.*

■ *When you talk about writing poetry, you usually talk about letting things happen.*

It's a strong impulse of mine to put that into any such conversation about writing because I feel that it's important to let the process of writing bring about things rather than be just the writing down of things that are already brought about. Some people talk about writing as if it's penmanship: you take dictation from your psyche that has already done something. Well, I'm interested in the psyche that hasn't done something and then does something. What does it do in between? So I always try to get the people to relax enough to pay attention to the things that actually occur to them during the process of writing. Does this make any sense?

■ *That makes sense, but how do you do it?*

I do it in any way I can keep them from feeling that they have to be on guard about what they write or that they have to have it all formulated before they begin or that there are unallowable things in dignified discourse. I'd like to go all out on this and confront as squarely as possible those who make students feel that writing is something done with the fully conscious, already accomplished self. I think writing is itself educational, exploratory, and worthy of trust while you're doing it. So if you think of something while you're writing, that's fine.

I still feel the weight of your question, "How do you get them to do that?" It's partly by creating an atmosphere of trust in the classroom. It's partly by joining them in whatever reactions we have: they sometimes feel funny about what they write, so I feel funny about it too; but I don't inhibit it.

Well, there is one other thing I'd put in somewhere; I might as well put it in now: I think approval of student writers is scary to writers. I keep meeting teachers who say, "Oh, yes. I'm very nice to the students. I always find something to praise." I don't like that. I would rather be in neutral or the way I would be with a friend discussing something that neither of us has a fixed position on but which we are both exploring so that the friend or the student doesn't feel that they have to get that approval by doing something good again. That just extends the area of inhibition.

Oh, because they learn to write for the approval.
That's right.

Rather than for themselves.
Yes. It has the same effect as criticism, really, because even approval is the implied presence of possible criticism. So there's someone you give a lot of approval to, everybody else gets it from the other end, "They got it. Now how can I get it?" I don't see any way around that. I don't know why I have so much trouble with teachers about it.

So you just discuss what they've written and . . .
Yeah, and I would like our discourse to be about those things that don't have to do with praise or blame but have to do with more or less, or "Did you do it like this? Tell me more about why you did it like this," and not the automatic stance that is almost always imposed upon teachers of being the evaluator. I'm not evaluator; I'm participant.

Are you able to get away without grading them?
I have been able to get away without putting grades on the papers;

this is a little bit different from not grading at all. The teaching part I would keep as far as possible from reminding them that they are in this area where there are minefields they have to cross in which they might ruin their grade. So as much as possible, I would postpone, dilute, avoid, play down the idea of evaluation. They would, I suppose, always know that sooner or later I'd have to grade them. But that's not part of our daily life; that's not part of the learning. That's part of what the society has imposed upon us in this institution. That's what I tell them. I think the grading procedure endangers creativity. This isn't entirely easy on them because they've gotten used to being evaluated.

■ *Oh sure, or being told how to do it; that's much more comforting.*

Either told how to do it or praised. Some people have said, "Well, Bill, you're so soft-hearted." No, no, it isn't that. It's more scary than that. But it's not scary in the sense of being haunted throughout the process of writing by the need to tailor make what you're doing for the approval of the teacher.

■ *Is there anything else you do?*

Yes, a whole lot of things. One is I try to induce in the classroom an atmosphere in which it is possible for reactions to come from all directions, not just from me.

I've done it many ways. I have a box in which I put all their papers and say, "Here are the papers for this class. Take a look. Read it." And they either read it in their room or check it in at the reserved book desk; so when we talk about a paper in a class, there are many reactions. But they're the kind of reactions that come straight across at the writers—not from high down to the writer, straight across from the peers. And once that atmosphere is established in the room, I can even hazard a remark myself now and then. But mostly I don't, especially early. I learned if I start the term by being either the one who does the evaluating or, and this is even more insidious with the same effect, the one who summarizes the discussion at the end, I'm still doing it; so I don't want to be the terminal remarker on a paper. I would rather have a paper slip through with *horrendous* things in it than spoil the system of the class by saying, "The rest of you have failed to notice that . . ." or "Let me summarize what's been said here," and then sort of correct everyone. Oh no. Once I can enter in like a peer, which I really am, but the system has not admitted that, then I try to do it.

There are many other quirks because the atmosphere in the classroom is induced by many little things: body language, where I sit, the time I get to class, whether I have a list of things we have to do—all sorts of things. And I just kind of weasel in on the class, sit in on the class, don't have any announcements about tests, or anything like that.

■ *You teach creative writing, but you have
also taught composition and literature.*
I would apply this to all kinds of writing. And talk, as a matter of fact. So all the teaching for me was a term-long finessing encounter with a room full of people who were to be wooed over into telling me what they knew and what they didn't know and the extent to which they knew it and the extent to which they didn't know it. And I had to go past some obstacles that had been trained into them.

■ *A lot of obstacles.*
A lot of obstacles. You know, I got a long-distance look and I feel you did too because we're thinking about those times in class in which ... Well, the ideal I thought of was the time when there's someone who hasn't done well in school who hands in a paper and you know it wouldn't pass one of those other courses, and you don't either praise this person for that paper or blame this person for that paper, but suddenly you're just in it together and your eyes meet and you look at certain things and those things that they are ready to have some slight adjustment to, they do half the adjusting and you do the other half. This is where I'd like to get. I don't want to be at a height, or holding them up, but just sort of looks of recognition between us. And if you get it right, it hardly makes any difference what you say. You can say, "It's terrible, isn't it?" It's OK, for they know it's terrible in the area where we're all terrible.

■ *Did your teaching interfere with your writing at all?*
Well, I sometimes thought wistfully about those who didn't have to do any work at all. But if I was going to have to work, I didn't feel menaced by teaching, partly because of the point of view I had about writing, that I wasn't learning techniques that were going to turn me to automation as a writer, that I was continuously learning from this lowest person in the class as well as from others. They had all sorts of ideas and I could roll my eyes as much with them as with anybody. So

that's what I'm looking for, that ongoing encounter, and I thought teaching was always full of richness. Any job that tired you out so much or discouraged you so much or dulled you so much would be a hazard to other activity. But I don't quite understand how teaching, in which you have all these level encounters about books, about ideas— all these lively people—I don't see why it's a menace to associate with lively people. If you get tired of lively people—I suppose you do sometimes—well, you can always go home and I often did. My dog would be duller.

I notice that you've had other kinds of jobs and I wonder if any of them were particularly useful or not useful to your writing?

This is sort of the obverse of the other: is teaching a hazard? Well, I say I don't know why it would be hazard. So I turn to the other jobs and think, "Are they a special help?" Oh no, they're sort of like teaching. I remember all the conversations when I worked in the oil refinery and lots of lively people there. And forest service; I liked that. And sugar beet fields; it had its own kind of heroism. Stoop crops are front-line productive activity; it's sort of fun to do that: survive the sun, be able to make a living at something that hard. There were many others too, like construction work and electrician's helper and things like that; I would have done more things too, if I'd had the chance. The jobs are full of encounters, people; even the dead periods, hoeing weeds around the oil tank—that's a nice, repetitive, vistas-over-your-shoulder kind of job.

Once when you were talking about what "allegiances" means, you said, "It's like assuming good will on the part of people—I tend to do that. It's like a kind of level look at every day's experiences as it comes at you and welcoming it. I feel that." When I read something like that, I see a connection between your point of view and the way you write poetry. For you, the process of writing poetry is a process of accepting and it seems to me that could easily become extended to other things.

I think what I'm trying to locate is that condition of a being who has not been distorted from the receptive, accurate encounter with experience. It's possible to overlearn fear or overlearn confidence. The conditions of life are such that make survival depend on the organism's ability to come back level again and be ready for the conditions of life as they are on the earth. There are people who are oversensitized. The intellectual position is to be a good—let me see, what am I after, what instrument shall I use? What they use to measure earthquakes: seismograph. An individual's intellect and emotions should be like a good seismograph: sensitive enough to register what happens, but strong enough not to be wrecked by the first little thing that happens. And so human beings have to occupy that position between being so steady and dumb and dull that they can't register and being so sensitive that they're wrecked by anything they register. So I just try to get into the readiness and be receptive, not stampeded, not overly trustful. I suppose we're all looking for that, but I feel the formulations that some people use disguise the necessity for avoiding both extremes. It's very easy to make powerful poems out of suffering all the time. It's all right, but that makes you a casualty.

■ *What did you mean when you said, "So I try not to learn, disengage, because reasons block the next needed feelings?"*

It links partly to this idea that for some people writing is done by fully preparing the being to come out with nothing but totally worthy utterances. And the only way to do that is not to step off the path. You've got to step off the path if you're going to explore new places; so I don't want to learn so well that I'm not learning from the encounter of now with the language. And if I had a wish to express at this point, it would be, "Save me from actually having or assuming I have the fully trained ability to write whatever is assigned to me." The person who assigned it may not have seen something that a more stupid person would enable them to see. You could both be programmed so well that nothing would ever happen to you but around and around. And that is what does happen to some writers: around and around. It's the equivalent of officialese in encounters; you get a clear, well-worked-out, and often totally irrelevant response.

■ *In another interview, someone said that "contemporary poets often seem to be super-neurotics in a neurotic world," and you said, "You shouldn't have neuroses. You ought to be on the level."*
(Laughter) Well . . .

■ *I'm very confused about where the cliché that artists are neurotic comes from. It seems to me that doing the kinds of things you're talking about takes courage. As you said, it's scary for your students to let go of patterns and virtually everyone I've interviewed says that's central to writing well.*

Analyzing someone who does something unusual, maybe people need to have locutions to use, so they say writers are neurotic. They operate in a different way from a carpenter, but carpenters are neurotic, of course, as everybody knows. In fact, when I was getting ready to put windows in our house, the glass person said, "We people who work with glass are really neurotic." (Laughter) He said, "You'd better not try to do that glass yourself. You'll find out why."

Well, I'll put it this way, in a positive way: I'm willing to take all sorts of tentative classifications about what we're like, we writers, but there's something I'd like to cling to and that is the essential thing that we're doing. And the essential thing we're doing is we're having enough faith in our own perceptions and decisions to make them paramount. You've just got to do it, if you're an artist. So you can say it's arrogance, or you can say it's neurotic, you can say it's humility in the face of the pattern the words want to take, you can have all sorts of myths about it; I don't care what myth you have, you've got to make the decisions yourself, if you're an artist. And I would like to have students realize that as soon as possible. They come into class and the first thing they want to say to me is "How am I doing?" "What do you think?" is the rejoinder, with body language, or raised eyebrows, evasion . . .

■ *Once you said, "It would be too much to claim that art, the practice of it, will establish a 'good,' a serene, a superior self. No. But art will, if pursued for itself, bring into sustained realization the self most centrally yours, freed from its distortions, brought from greed or fear or ambition."*
I remember that.

■ *I don't quite understand the distinction you're making because a self that is more centrally yours and freed from greed, fear, or ambition sounds pretty good to me.*
I probably ought to tone that down a bit, but I forgive myself for saying that partly because I was coming out on that skate from avoiding the other skate. The early part of that is I didn't want to claim that one should assume that one is creating something worthy of the ages. Not at all. So the product is expendable, but the process is precious.

THEORY

This is what I'd like to say. I keep meeting poets who say something like, "Well, I'm going to try to do something that is worthy and lasting and beyond my lifetime and so on." I think that's just frivolous. That's something only society decides and I don't see that it makes any difference anyway. But the process is the process of living centrally and paying attention to your own life. Surely that's worth doing. If you don't, who will? That's what living is about and you can be distracted from living by trying to create things that will last in the terminology and the mode of society that may or may not be harmonious to your life. So I want to shrug that part off.

I think it is a big claim and if it hadn't been an interview, probably, if I had been carefully phrasing it, I would have tried to accomplish the same thing without making such forensic claims for art. I don't want to make claims for it, but I'd like to recognize what I think I see in it and that is a real art, genuine art, comes not from hammering out something for posterity but from making the discoveries that are yours to be made because of your unique constitution and the unique encounter you have in experience.

Are there ever any days you can't write?
There are no days I can't write.

Are there ever any days you don't write?
There are days I don't write. For instance, I'm headlong from somewhere to somewhere else and full of distractions, and I forgive myself for those days; it's not a fetish, I think, but most days I do write.

Does that change the day at all?
Yes. It changes the day a little bit. For me, for analogy, it's sort of like jogging. If I've done my jogging, it's an OK day. If I've done my writing, it's a really OK day. It's a confirming, satisfying activity to do. And it's almost devotional. Maybe that's too strong, but it's as if a day of my life deserves a little attention from my life. It's my kind of attention to stop long enough, to let the evaluative, the speculative, the exploratory impulses that are native to that portion of my time be manifest in a sustained way so that I can recognize them and get sustenance from them.

One person I talked to said that you're a totally natural poet
and another said that everything you write is poetry.

Is that right? (Laughter)

■ *And I wonder how you got that way?*

Well "How I got those words" is the way I'd phrase it. I think that these people you talked to were generous people and I don't lightly dismiss their words. I take seriously what they said, so I try to figure out, "Now, what does this mean?" I think they're locating a kind of writing that grows out of my perception of what writing is, so I'd like to say a little bit about that.

Poems and stories and helpfully enhanced discourse of any kind, I think, are results of a trustful, undistorted entry into the language that's natural to yourself. And I suddenly glimpse the possibility of conceptualizing language as something that can be exactly congruent with your mental life. That congruency is menaced by many things: competitiveness, systematic educational distortion toward prizes, maybe even being bullied by those around you so that you just don't have the bounce that it takes to get into your thought and language. And so I hark back to something and that is, in our home, our parents were receptive to what we said. I never felt it necessary to distort my language or even in any serious way disguise my plans. Maybe my mother didn't want me to go fishing on Cow Creek, but we knew we were both operating in an area of general acceptance. And I think maybe that's important. So I hark back to the way I'd like to have a classroom so people can let that congruency between thought and language have its way with their discourse.

■ *Someone asked you when you found out you were a poet and you said that you wondered more about when everyone else stopped.*

Yes, yes. The kind of process we are talking about is native to everyone, kids with their hopscotch and so on. Everyone. Everyone I've ever met, everyone, has what to me is the essential element of what we're talking about. They may not write what they call poems, but they make remarks they like better than other remarks. They have that lip-smacking realization of differences in discourse. But then later they may feel, "I'm a salesman. I'm not allowed to have any lip-smacking impulses about things. I'm going to give it the way it is in the book." And so they quit, as far as I'm concerned, at least that part of their lives.

So I don't think it was just a cute way to keep from saying a time, although it is hard to say a time for me; I don't know a time when I wasn't enjoying language. And I guess that's what a poet does. But I think everyone shares in this and it's artificial to think there's a life without it. They're asking the question from the point of view that poetry is something that you have to nerve yourself to do. I don't think that's true. Not to do poetry is possible, I suppose, but it's hard and I've never met anyone who didn't do it in some sense of coursing sounds, of being either delighted or discouraged about how the sentence comes out, by responding or not responding to what somebody says. You're really in a tough spot if you don't have any of those responses. And so they're asking me to enter a universe in which the values I hold dear are reversed when they ask that question. I just don't want to go into that world, so I stop.

How do you feel about workshops and the fact that
there are more and more poets all the time?

I feel all right about workshops. And I don't know what they mean about more and more poets all the time. Maybe there are. In fact, I think, maybe there are; but what's this viewing-with-alarm bit? I feel that this process that's so rewarding is a right for everybody. And for those who teach workshops thinking that they are going to sift out a few gifted individuals and turn them into Miltons and Shakespeares and that the presence of other people is a problem for Miltons and Shakespeares, I say they've got it wrong. (Laughter) Maybe I shouldn't elaborate, but I feel strongly about that. I feel that point of view about the desirability of only a limited number and those only of the elite engaged in an activity as rewarding as poetry is almost like treason of the intellectual realm or the cultural realm. I'll do it the positive way by saying, if I go to a class, I feel I'm meeting a succession of people to whom I owe individually total allegiance and succession. I'm not looking for the ones who are going to enhance the school or my reputation or their own. That's nice, but as a teacher I believe that if there is such a thing as the lowest one in the class, they deserve the same level reception and cordiality as anybody else. I think as human beings, insofar as we cherish each other, we cherish that trust that it's all right to live your own life and even to have your own thoughts and occasionally in a mild way to express them.

February 3, 1981

IF YOU'RE ONLY A COPY OF A PERSON, YOU AREN'T GOING TO WRITE VERY WELL

Wallace Stegner considers writing whatever one wants the best way to develop as an author because good books grow from integrity as naturally as plants emerge from rich soil, so he recommends that anyone who hopes to publish books read widely and work hard.

Stegner founded the creative writing program at Stanford University in 1946 and directed it until 1971, when he retired to concentrate on his own work. The awards followed: the Pulitzer Prize for Angle of Repose, *the Western Literature Association's Distinguished Achievement Award, the National Book Award for* The Spectator Bird, *National Book Critics Circle Award nominations for* Crossing to Safety *and for* Collected Stories of Wallace Stegner, *and the Los Angeles Times Robert Kirsch Award for a body of work.*

■ *What was your goal when you taught writing?*

If you aren't a person, if you're only a copy of a person, you aren't going to write very well. And most people who come to university writing programs are gifted; they're people, or potential people. The ideal is to give them every possibility to realize their potential in their own particular way—not by way of imitation.

■ *How do you do that?*

It's a difficult, slippery, Socratic business. You can't assert your own beliefs too strongly because people are impressionable. Whenever I was teaching writing, I let them go in their own way, even when I felt they were failing, because I didn't want to stir up a bunch of little carbon copies of myself. On the other hand, a lot of wind and nonsense goes on in the head of a young writer just finding out what he wants to write about and who he is. That has to be laughed away without destroying his enthusiasm. It's not a teacher's function to turn people on; if they aren't self-starters, they don't belong there. It *is* a teacher's function to avoid turning them off; it's an easy racket to get discouraged in. So you work differently with different people. Some students you couldn't discourage with an ax and some students—not necessarily the worst ones—discourage very easily. The teacher's job is to keep them writing, keep them enthusiastic about what they're doing, and keep them believing in what they're doing. When someone has no proof that he *can* write, it's easy for him to feel that this is not the way to spend his life. So you abrade rather than abuse the work students offer.

Did you conduct workshops, distribute copies, and so on?

More and more, in later years, I had people read their own stories. If they were too shy to read them, I read them because reading aloud enforces a kind of attention that reading silently does not, and it gives the victim a much greater sense of how his stuff sounds to somebody else. Any piece of writing reveals its excrescences a bit more plainly when read aloud. It may be even better to have somebody else read it aloud to the author because then he's not worrying about the impression he's making; he's listening to what he wrote. It takes time, but it does more for the manuscript and for the writer of the manuscript than other methods I've tried. Prose ought to be written for the ear as well as the eye. You've got to hear it. I'm enough of a spoiled poet to think that if it doesn't have cadences, somehow, it isn't prose. There are good books that are bad prose, but I wouldn't want to write them.

Do you encourage students to make a habit of reading?

Oh, sure. And to read at large. If you're not a hungry reader, you're not likely to be a writer. Reading is one way you learn writing. You learn it through the pores, often without knowing you're learning it. People who have read a lot are likely to have some kind of reasonable style and some notion of how to tell a story and some notion of form without ever having thought about those things.

You've said, "There is never any question whether a book is there, only making it available to yourself." Do you still believe that?

I think so. Some people have means of finding stories and some people don't. I get a hundred letters a year from people who read *Angle of Repose* and write to say, "I've got my grandmother's diary and she lived a very exciting life. I've always . . . but I can't do it. Wouldn't *you* like to do it?" It's not for me unless I find it in myself. *They* feel it as a book, but they can't write it. *I* might be able to write it, but I don't feel it as a book.

■ *Do you have any idea how they might make that material available to themselves?*

One of the things you have to do is simply submit to the time in front of the typewriter or desk every day. The number of hours spent writing a book is quite incredible. You write every page of every book seven or eight times—every page probably represents a day's work, at eight hours a day—and if you've got a four hundred or five hundred page book, that's thousands of hours. Most people don't have that much time or won't spend it writing. So you have to reassure yourself every morning that what you're doing isn't insane; only then would you go through all the trouble of making a book. If a book could be made in two hours, like a watercolor picture, lots of people would write books; but the plain duration of writing a novel discourages most people.

In The Writer in America *you say that since almost every cultural force pushes your students in the direction of commercialization, "Let the colleges stand up for art."*

Many of the people who went through our shop wound up in advertising, publishing, or movies, and all of those are commercial aspects of writing in which someone gives them an assignment and they turn it out. But it does seem useful to young writers, for a year or two, to be in a completely uncommercial atmosphere where they can write anything their minds suggest to them. That's the best way to develop as a writer. People learn much writing to order, but they learn more writing what they want.

Most students in a writing program are not going to be important writers, but many of them look back on those years as a time when, for once in their lives, education was exactly what they wanted it to be: when they got none of the dictation from without that they might have resented, when only help came from without. So we give fellowships to ensure that some of these people can write exactly what they want for a year or two and still eat. And over the now more than thirty years, the policy has justified itself.

Every year former students come to me for blurbs, and I generally have to beg off: I can't read that many books. I read for the National

Book Award the last year it was given. We read over two hundred books and of those two hundred, twenty-two were by my former students. That's one-tenth of American Literature. There aren't any Saul Bellows among those people, but there are National Book Award winners and Harper Prize winners and Pulitzer Prize winners: Scott Momaday, Bob Stone, Tom McGuane, Ernest Gaines, Evan Connell, Ed Abbey, Larry McMurtry, Wendell Berry . . . There's a whole string of them through the years, and many of them go on producing steadily.

We didn't ever try to make publishing a condition. Nothing should be written for a specific audience—its vocabulary reduced to six hundred words for the sixth-grade audience, or whatever else. School-teachers often make the mistake of trying to limit vocabulary to accommodate bad readers with the result that they limit it for every-body. If you read Dickens when you're seven years old, you're going to be stretched; he didn't limit his vocabulary. And stretching is useful. Aim-ing a manuscript at a particular audience is never justifiable except on commercial terms, and those are the least useful guidelines for writing well. I suppose if you're writing true confessions for some lurid maga-zine, you have to do them in a certain way; but real writing is not done by mass production out of interchangeable parts. That's the way they make automobiles, not the way they make stories or novels.

On the other hand, if you're a writer, you're a man or a woman in search of an audience, and when you publish something, that means you've found your audience. So in our classes, everyone was greatly cheered whenever anybody in the class sold a story to a magazine or a novel manuscript to a publisher. That's somehow what it was all about, even though it wasn't cued to those cues. It was written in what the writer felt was the right way. Then when somebody likes it, that's fine. The writer hasn't prostituted himself at all.

■ *You've suggested that the most fundamental*
instruction in literature takes place in writing classes.

I'm not sure that literature classes—I may be speaking heresy here—fully justify themselves. Anybody with brains can read and understand a book, and if he doesn't understand it, he knows where to get the books that will help him understand it. I've seen students learn more about literature by hearing Frank O'Connor read a chapter out of *Portrait of the Artist as a Young Man* in his rich Irish brogue than by all the analysis and exegesis and lectures that scholars have devoted to that book. When it's read like that, it's alive, and a manuscript is still alive and still malleable when you're working on it, or when you're trying to help someone else make it the way he wants to make it. If you just read literature and never have the experience of trying to make it, it's a monument; but a writer knows that when it was being made, every word was debatable. Literature can be taught in different ways, but the routine grinding out either of literary history or of *explication de texte* is not as much fun or as rewarding as trying to make literature yourself in a congenial group, with a teacher who is neither too soft nor too hard, and with enough to eat.

You've written so much. Everyone who knew I was going to talk to you said, "I read the most wonderful book by Wallace Stegner," and it was always a different book.
(Laughter) You live a long time, that's how . . .

And they were all different kinds of books.
They ought to be different; you ought to change. But some of them are kind of alike. Two, for instance, are written about and around this hill: *All the Little Live Things* and *The Spectator Bird* use the same character, the same setting, and some of the same ideas. But *Angle of Repose* is different in that it's partly historical. And there is one novel about New Hampshire which is quite different because it exploits a different area and lingo than any of my other novels.

Editing DeVoto's letters and putting together Wolf Willow *are different again.*
Wolf Willow has the same relation to *The Big Rock Candy Mountain* that *Life on the Mississippi* has to *Huckleberry Finn*, to put myself in good company. It was a nonfictional treatment of much of the same stuff that the novel used.

What's the difference between expository writing and fiction?
For one thing, expository writing has to contain a body of information. But that body of information doesn't have to be blunt or obtuse. It doesn't hurt any writer of expository prose to try his hand at writing a story, because control of place and character and evocation of sensuous impressions and so on are all things that can be used in expository writing. You shouldn't write fiction when you're doing

expository writing, but you may use many of the devices and shapes and implements and weapons of fiction.

■ *Do you do different things at once?*
Oh, no.

■ *Or do you float from one to another or get interested in one and . . .*
Either way. I don't know how books grow, but they have a seedtime and a growing time and a harvest time, like other plants. Sometimes you have to dig up a subject and sometimes you don't know where you're going when you start. You start it and it wants to go another way; you resist, and very often it goes its own way in spite of you. But it had better not go entirely its own way, because then you're out of control. For instance, I wrote *Wolf Willow* as a bunch of chapters, magazine articles, because I got the feeling that I ought to become the Herodotus of the Cypress Hills; nobody had ever written a history of that country. Now I find that I *am* the Herodotus; I'm required reading in Canada. (Laughter) Finally, having gotten a whole mess of chapters together, I began to realize it was a book; but I still didn't know how to put it together. It ended ineptly and inconclusively and I couldn't tell what was wrong with it. I gave it to Malcolm Cowley and he said, "Why don't you just move this chapter from the front to the back?" That's all it took! That story "Genesis," about the cowpunchers running a fall roundup and getting into a succession of blizzards, was written because I didn't want to write as pure exposition stuff that I felt and remembered so vividly. So I chose to write it as fiction, which screwed up the book and made it a librarian's nightmare.

■ *Why?*
How to catalogue it. (Laughter) But I couldn't finish "Genesis." I got the cowpunchers to the place where their sled is broken down in the rapids and they make their way to a line camp, and I couldn't take it on. I put the thing away for at least a year and then I took it out and realized that I hadn't been able to finish it because it *was* finished. It didn't want to be a novel about the whole winter; it just wanted to be an episode about the making of a boy into a man. An ordeal story like that never wants to be as long as you think it might be; it has to be long enough to be a real ordeal, but not so long that it becomes excruciating. I wanted to make it excruciating and I couldn't do it.

■ *It must be hard to let books happen like that if you write for a living.*

When you write for a living you have to write a lot of things that didn't get generated in your own head. I've written travel articles on assignment, but I've never done it with fiction. I don't think I could. Writing for a living gets a little easier as you get older and have more things in print—unless your past writing disappears from sight. But making a good living from writing means writing best sellers and following them with best sellers, which is very hard to do. Or it means writing for the magazines—to a degree, putting yourself in the hands of editors who tell you what to do. Or it means writing information or think pieces, or, in my case, travel or environmental pieces which express something of what I think, but are more saleable to the magazines than other kinds of things. So I write many pieces about the public domain. I'm writing one now. I retired from teaching ten years ago. I've written for a living ever since. A complete living. It's a very speculative life.

■ *In* The Writer in America, *you said the fear universities would smother writers has been shown false.*

It depends on the writer. The universities have smothered some writers; they've made academics out of some writers, and that isn't always the best thing for a writer, or a critic. The New Critics got tainted by the academy too; they were a little too remote and monastic and concerned so rigorously with the text that they forgot texts come out of contexts. Books come out of contexts too, and if the experience within the university is the only experience a writer has, it's going to be a little narrow. On the other hand, there's Jane Austen. (Laughter) You can find plenty of people who have written well out of narrow experience, so it's not a uniform reaction. Some writers have been in teaching more or less all their lives: Saul Bellow, Red Warren, myself—there are all kinds of us. We haven't stopped writing and I don't know that we're any worse writers for having been in the academy; some of us may be better.

■ *Are you getting more writing done since you've stopped teaching?*

I don't think so; I just write a little more steadily. I tried to spend the morning writing and do the university's business in the afternoon and evening, but that wasn't always possible. So I might get in two hours instead of four; but now that I'm not doing anything else, I can do my own business for four hours or more a day. Four is about enough. I do it seven days a week, and that eventually adds up to some pages.

Frank O'Connor was always half hinting that I ought to quit teaching, and he was probably right. He and I agreed that when we got more excited about someone else's story than our own, we were in trouble.

■ *Because you get too involved?*

You *do* get involved, particularly when they're good students and you like them. You're very concerned to see them succeed with what they're doing; but you do, then, lose your own single-mindedness.

■ *And writing travel articles does not interfere as much because they flow out of your own interests?*

Travel is not unrelated to fiction; it's the place of fiction without the fiction in it. Sometimes you add a little fiction, a little autobiographical travel account. When I get broke, I can always write a travel piece; a lot of travel pieces turn into ecological and environmental pieces because so many places one travels these days show the marks of human carelessness.

■ *In* The Sound of Mountain Water *you say, "As a novelist, I may perhaps be forgiven for taking literature as a reflection, indirect but profoundly true, of our national consciousness; and our literature, perhaps you are aware, is sick, embittered, losing its mind, losing its faith."*

That was written about 1960, when almost every novel you picked up was concerned with aberrations of experience instead of the real lives of real people. It was a literature of perpetual losers, and everybody who wasn't a loser turned out to be the villain who made the loser lose. I don't believe that. So I was disturbed that fiction portraying psychological alienation seemed to take precedence over that describing lives which had some stability in them, and which arrived somewhere, did something—not much, maybe, but something.

February 16, 1981

RUTH STONE

WE ARE CREATIVE CREATURES

Ruth Stone believes that authenticity rests at the center of all good poetry and recommends reading one's work aloud as a good way to test whether one has strayed into pretense. She regrets that male domination of the literary world has made it difficult for women to honestly express their concerns in their work and still get published.

Ruth Stone has taught at Brandeis; Old Dominion; the Universities of Wisconsin, Illinois, Indiana, California, and Virginia; and the State University of New York, Binghamton. She won her first poetry prize in 1954 and has continued to collect them as the decades have passed. Most recently, she received the National Book Critics Circle Award for Ordinary Words, *the National Book Award for* In the Next Galaxy, *and the Wallace Stevens Award, which pays $150,000 for "outstanding and proven mastery in the art of poetry." Her latest poetry collection,* In the Dark, *just appeared.*

I have written while I was working, cooking, cleaning, driving, riding buses, raising a family—nothing kept me from writing. I didn't have to go off and sit in a quiet place; I was trained very young to block out noise. My father practiced drums in our house and I learned very early that I could have a quiet place right in my head.

I don't have any trouble writing. I came out of a family of women creators and everyone was well pleased that I was writing. They expected me to write. I couldn't not write anyway. It wrote itself.

▪ *I was interested in your remark that you didn't realize all poets are male until you got to the university.*

I did live through an interesting period because women participated in the modern movement and were given a lot of respect—even though Ezra Pound made a lot of fun of Amy Lowell. I don't hold any great brief for Ezra Pound and I think Amy Lowell did a lot of marvelous things. If she had been a man, she wouldn't have been the humorous figure that she was, the homosexuality included. But there was this nice fresh time during the early part of the century when a lot of women were among modern poets and were taken seriously.

In the late forties and early fifties there was a much more academic critical angle in poetry. It moved out of the realm of pure poetry into academic poetry even though people like Dylan Thomas could sweep the world for a while with emotional, lyrical poetry. Then the Beats were an anti-female movement. Did anyone notice that? I suppose they have. It put the women back in long skirts and long hair and having babies and serving men. Very few women were accepted into the projective poetry movement. Male adulation was going on with a lot of other good things.

I came smack up against all of that even though university men would compliment me by saying that I wrote like a man and not a woman. I wasn't flattered by that; I didn't know what to think of it. I didn't ever think of myself as a man, so I knew I was disadvantaged even though I was well treated and I've never been badly treated by the university system or the critical world.

When you arrive at the university and it hasn't been so blatant that the poet is male, and that the poet has traditionally been male, and that only male poetry is of the genius level, it makes you wonder what happened to all the wonderful woman poets. After going through that, you come out scarred. You can be greatly harmed. I didn't write for six months after a young man gave me some cruel criticism. It wasn't merited. He just flung out at me. He wrote me years later from Europe and said that what he had done to me had haunted him for years, that he wanted to confess that he had been jealous.

Women have been trivialized. I took a course at Harvard that started with Emily Dickinson and she was considered cuckoo—this strange little lady. It has kept [women] from daring to go ahead and do what they could. Now it's all changed. Women are running in all directions and that's good. Some of it will be fantastic. Some of it *is* fantastic.

Some people have said that it's still hard for women to get published.

Oh, I expect it is. I never pay any attention to, nor do I subscribe to a magazine which is 80 or 100 percent male. I'm tired of it. I've had years of that. I'm interested in magazines that are fifty-fifty, or even all women or mostly women and with women not doing just the shit work on the magazine, but in an editorial position. Frequently 50 percent of the population is left out of those magazines. Many fine writers who happen to be women can't get into them or have a hard time getting in them partly because we've all been trained to see the world through men's eyes because that's what has been presented to us in fiction and everything else. Women are very empathetic toward men. Some men have begun to learn to do this toward women, but it's a time coming and that's one of the reasons women might have more trouble getting published: the men who read their work don't understand it or think it's trivial when it isn't from our point of view. You look dismayed. Am I too vehement?

I'm probably looking guilty because before doing these interviews it had never occurred to me that women had special problems writing or getting published.

I don't think you have to limit it to publishing, writing, or anything else. The male world is frequently deeply insulting to women, deeply. Rape itself, all the things that go with the insults to the woman; it's all aggression. They try to say that they're just afraid of women, of their power.

Women jolly well better be afraid of men because men have threatened them. They mean it. Each time women have come out, they've been put back. They let [women] out during times of crisis when they need them, and then women have been shoved back into their restricted areas again; only this time it seems as though they are really creeping out. The educational system has made a lot of that possible. It's not over, but more and more women are occupying positions which were closed to women and so forth. Women are feeling better about themselves, even ones who are not in the big swim. Role models are making a big difference to everyone, even the old.

I accepted that I had to work harder than any man to get even near the place he could get so easily, but all of a sudden your eyes open and you see what's going on is an injustice. That's not right. Why should women be second-class citizens?

I never thought of not fulfilling my role as a woman either, the traditional role, I suppose, although I wasn't hung up on it. When I fell in love, I married, I had children, and I'm delighted with my children. I love them dearly and they're all artists too because that's what I value. They're three daughters and they're all married and they all have children and they're all still artists—musicians and writers and painters.

■ *I was struck by the imagery in your poetry.*

I'm just a natural seer, I guess. My family were all painters. We're all crazy about the visual because it's been so extended with possibilities. The visual experience has become greater than the verbal, I suppose. I can't see it ending up thinking visually. We do not think with pictures; we think with words. We think visually peripherally, but our main thinking is with language. Language goes through our heads all the time. It shapes us—language is what we are. We are language.

I almost hear the weight of words when I'm writing. I'm not the same person I am when I'm talking. When I'm writing, it's as though I move into a different space. It may possibly be something to do with that alpha wave, I don't know. All I know is that I have always moved into this other space and it is *there* that you're conscious of the weight of words, the stretch, the distance, every tiny bit that the word is made up of, the sounds and the emotional weight and the meaning—these things all work together to create the poem. Your ear will tell you when you have gone astray.

When I was at the Radcliffe Institute, they asked me to give a seminar on my writing, and I thought that I had written very rapidly. It was such an odd thing for me to have thought it didn't take any time to write these and that they just popped out because when I went back to my farm in Vermont and went through my boxes and boxes of papers, I would get twenty and more worksheets on a poem out of the boxes and the changes would be so many it staggered me. I couldn't believe it. I learned a lot about myself. I was concentrating so strongly when I wrote that almost a whole day would go by and I wouldn't notice. Then I would think afterwards that it hadn't taken me any time at all and yet the facts were there that it had. That surprised me. But of course anyone who is a compulsive artist, writer, can't not be a perfectionist. You can't reach perfection, but you strive toward it.

You're always turning towards a new facet of something, a new design; it's like looking at something and then looking at it again: it's minute observation and examination of experience. Poems say a great deal because they balloon out from what they say, but they're talking about a small thing, a moment. One of the problems with some political poetry is that they are trying to say too much. How moving a poem can be if it is hemmed in on a very small thing. Poetry has the essence of music and drama in it, and philosophy can be included, even ideas, but any one of those can ruin a poem. It has to somehow not be any one of those things at the same time. The language has to capture some specific images on which the person who hears it can hang all those things.

I'm not closed off to myself. The door to my unconscious was open almost all the time and I had a lot of rapport; I didn't even know it. But after my husband committed suicide, the trauma slammed the door. I felt the bird in me had died with him. I died with him. I had to make myself over and be reborn. Slowly the door began opening. It isn't open the way it was before. It opens and it closes. I'm not afraid of myself or what I might think. We all think all kinds of crazy things, but I am not afraid of myself. I must have had a wonderful mother. I did.

In my teaching I have treated each person individually. I don't drag myself, my poetry, or how I do things into it. I consider what is coming from them because the creation has to come out of that individual's experience. Everyone walks around with this enormous universe in their heads. They've got plenty to use, but it's not going to be exactly the same for each one of their emotional attitudes. Each person is in the process of teaching himself and you offer everything you can to help that person.

People who write and also teach creative writing know that you can't teach creative writing. Writing, writing, writing is how you learn to write. The person is in the process of teaching himself, but you can act as a catalyst. You can hold up a mirror. But no one can teach anyone to write; it's a process that must be developed inside of the writer. You can give him all kinds of methods, tricks, and so forth. It's a matter of getting the people's adrenaline propped up.

I have urged them to keep journals and to take notebooks with them in their pockets and to write it down when they get a flash. That becomes a good habit if you want to write. In class I insist that people read everything aloud themselves because you can't fool yourself so well if you're reading aloud. You can hear where you've gone astray, where you are sentimental or mushy, if you've got any critical sense at all. You have to develop a critical sense, although too much of a critical sense is detrimental to writing; it blocks you if you're constantly stopping yourself and criticizing it. I had a very brilliant, gifted student who couldn't get going. I think maybe she had been given a little too much praise, so she got frightened. That's a funny thing: a little bit too much, then you're afraid that you can't do it again.

I accept students. I don't question whatever they tell me about themselves, and I am responsive; consequently, they trust me and they go ahead and do. All students who take creative writing are not going to continue with it. I don't think about that. That isn't part of it. At this point in their lives they are doing it, and whether they go on or whether they don't is a matter of chance. I also do not think of students as horses in a stable for me to develop. All human beings are creative. We are creative creatures. The expression of your inner self or your responses to the world are important to each of us. It's important that people learn they can do this. It's a wonderful thing to do.

I'm loving, but I'm honest. They can rely on my criticism and they get good criticism from me. It's useful. And I think I'm authentic. You get rewarded when you're authentic by this longtime relationship with people. The danger in teaching creative writing is not being authentic, allowing your ego and a sense of embarrassment about your relationship with the students . . . you can get confused. It's very important for you to be open and have a deep morality towards them. You can misguide and mix up people whose minds are open to you in this way and it's a trust.

I love what's created. Making things is fun. Imagination and the world and the response to everything; it's all delightful. I don't feel I have any private purchase on it. It's open to all of us. It's wonderful to see a poem in the process, how excited people feel about it . . . It's fun. And I like the writers. They're warm and open. They're a little like me. I feel that they're my relatives. (Laughter)

■ *I've used up all my time.*
All right, darling. I hope we've said something sensible.

December 28, 1982

GOOD WRITING ISN'T ABOUT EASY THINGS

Diane Wakoski's comments correct the delusion that writing authentically means completing poems quickly and easily. She explains that producing good poetry requires a ruthless honesty about oneself and one's work that some students would understandably prefer to avoid. Wakoski's work reveals that she demands no more of her students than she does of herself: she has published four essay collections and more than forty poetry collections. Emerald Ice: Selected Poems 1962–1987 *won the Poetry Society of America's William Carlos Williams Award. Since 1976, she has taught at Michigan State University, where she holds a distinguished professorship. Her latest poetry book is* The Butcher's Apron.

The only writers that interest me are the ones who are original and I think their originality almost always comes out of an organically honest expression of [their] involvement with the world, so I am most interested in writers who are honest creators of their own myth. Even if you're not going to become [a] great writer, you'll become a better writer if you become a very, very honest perceiver of the world and I don't see any way for doing that unless you're a very mean and honest perceiver of yourself. I'm always urging searching the self and trying to come to terms with what you find there.

■ *Do you urge your students to do that?*

Oh yes, and I encourage the kind of writing that does that. I will not let my workshops be therapy sessions, no way. I'm a brutal critic precisely because I don't want people to do it just for an ego trip. The writing should be an ego trip and coming to terms with it should be an intellectual one. I don't think it's enough just to honestly record your emotions. It's important to look for the most important and deep emotions you have. It's important to look for the conflicts. Good writing isn't about easy or easily accessible things, so it means digging down. One of the ways I come to terms with this for students is by being very hard on them for writing clichéd or sentimental things because, as far as I'm concerned, things you don't have enough experience with are going to be in other people's terms, thus clichéd.

I have many kinds of students, but I'm more successful dealing with the kind that has read a lot and has [a] rich vocabulary and a good sense of language, but still hasn't learned a personal way of using it—hasn't learned how to get rid of clichés, sentimental speech. I mainly work with students who need a tutor or model to constantly be pointing out where their sense of language is deserting them.

In advanced workshops I almost always require at least one piece of writing [a week] and encourage two. I have the luxury of very small classes and we meet once a week for a long session, three to four hours, which means I can talk about everybody's poems or poem in detail. My first comment on a poem may be about the idea behind the poem. We may talk for fifteen minutes about the various ways people have used that idea, of how impossible it is to use in the twentieth century, where it comes in terms of other literature. I don't see how you can have a poet who loves language, who has nothing to say; whereas, I do see how you could have a poet who has something to say even if his language is limited. The nature of language changes so quickly . . . What we're all searching for is immortality and immortality of language has to be deeply wedded with content or the language has no meaning.

▨ *In* Toward a New Poetry, *you say "a lot of just plain bad language and adolescent or old-fashioned ideas have to be written through to get to the place where the slow process of revision will make a poem better rather than just different." How does that idea influence your teaching?*

I do think writing your way through a lot of junk is very important, and I don't have any good advice about how to handle that in the classroom. Let me give you an example of a problem I've had this year. This student makes a television news commentator sound like he has brilliant, original ideas. Why this boy wants to write poetry, I don't know; but I don't feel it's my business to discourage him from it. It is my business to try to get him to write something more interesting. His one saving grace is that he really wants to write poetry and he wrote more than the required poems. That's a sign of an ambitious, serious student.

Now it's true that he writes them in five minutes, but many of the other students write theirs in five minutes too, but they only turn in one every two weeks, and so this boy does have something on his side.

This boy came to two classes and got lambasted for five poems. He was absent from another class—I later found out because he was "so discouraged"—and then came to the next class and had about three more poems. One of them had a glimmer of hope in it. He used specifics. So I praised him highly and then went on to say that the beginning was terrible and the ending was terrible and the whole idea, if he really meant what he said, was ridiculous; but those specifics were really nice.

He asked if he could see me in my office, which he did the next day, and he said, "It was so wonderful. At last you praised me. At last I begin to feel that maybe now I can send something out and get published." So I said, "Well, you wouldn't want me to praise you if it were a lie, would you?" And I could see that he wanted to say, "Yes" (laughter), but he didn't dare because he knew that would provoke great anger from me. So I said, "Look, you're out of touch with reality. Your poetry is no more ready for publication than I'm ready to go to the Olympics in high diving; I can't swim. I tried to praise something you were doing because you were on the right track. Your problem is that you want instant gratification." I talked to him for a long, long time about this and it made him feel better. I kept trying to emphasize what he could do and how he could work and how he needed to take an idea and develop it and that he was kidding himself if he felt that all his best ideas came when he was walking along the street and didn't have a pencil. I said, "If that's the case, carry a pencil and a notebook, but I think you'll find you'll jot something down and won't have any idea what it means, that your problem is you don't take the ideas you have and develop them using these very simple specifics."

The next class session, he had a poem that was praiseworthy. And I praised it. It wasn't a great poem, but it was a nice beginner's poem. I pointed out what he did that succeeded and also, somewhat painfully, what he had done that didn't succeed. He glowed all through class and I thought, that's nice; maybe that pep talk helped.

The next week he came to class and he had no poem because he said he didn't dare risk having something fail after his success. And he never wrote anything for the rest of the term. (Laughter) It made me have great faith in my technique of telling people how terrible they are because, while they rant and rave, I feel more and more and more and more and more that we sell our *souls* for these educational ideas of encouraging students out of fear that they'll go away and never come back. My experience has been that the good students go away and never come back because they've proven to themselves they can get praise. I see many of the most talented students I've had in class a few years later. What are they doing? "Oh, I'd like to make a movie." "Oh, I'm working for an advertising agency." "Do you write poetry?" "Oh, no." Maybe the thing that keeps people going as students is the desire to accomplish something. Maybe that easy success is as much a cutoff of a person's life of learning—especially if it's false or it means something very small—as someone like me who's always being accused of discouraging people.

This student is very, very typical of the creative writing student you get in all beginning courses. He was really laying it on the line to me what the average student wants from a writing teacher: "Please praise me. Please praise me." And their excuse is, "I'm doing this for pleasure. Why should you make it painful?"

I gave a one afternoon workshop this spring, and one young woman said she had taken a poetry workshop in college and the teacher had been so harsh, she hadn't come back to poetry for years. I said, "Maybe you needed that time to come back to a place where you were ready to write." She said, "Oh, no, it just discouraged me so much; it took me this long to get my courage back up." I said, "I don't know anything about you or your writing, but I'd like to give a big hooray for your teacher because your teacher probably stopped you from something that, if she had praised you, you'd still be doing today and it probably was very bad writing. Sometimes you have to go away from something in order to learn to come back to it with intelligence and skill. You may have been way off on the wrong track or you may have been stupid; you may still be." She stared at me. And I said, "I know you think that teacher did something terrible to you, but she may have given you a gift. She may have turned you into a real writer." There was silence after this and I decided I'd better change the subject and I did. But there is too much of this sense we have to make everybody love everything.

A young woman I had in a writing class kept saying to me, "How can you give me a 1.0 and mark up the whole page: 'clichéd,' 'sentimental,' 'bad writing,' 'awkward.' I have always been told that I'm very talented as a poet. I won poetry prizes in high school and my teacher thought I was the best student she'd ever had." This girl was too diplomatic to say, "You're a bad teacher" (laughter), but her complaint was all saying, "What right do you have to say these things?" This was the third week of her complaints about this; I was sick of them and she's intelligent so she could learn to write better—but you don't learn to write better until you become dissatisfied with what you're doing. I said, "Look, don't you know by now that 90 percent of the world *hates* poetry? They not only don't read it, they dislike it when they read it and they will tell you anything to get rid of you. As soon as you understand that the only standards in poetry are those held by the few of us who really love it and probably write it, then you'll be ready to write good poetry." She looked as if I'd vomited all over her, which I had, in an intellectual sense. I hope this girl won't write any poetry for ten years. I hope she'll come back to it as an intelligent reader who through something in her life has really come back to poetry and not this ghastly, nauseous, adolescent, roses are red, swooning violets, worse than Hallmark cards stuff.

■ *Do you require your students to read?*

It's not fair to ask students in a writing class to do a lot of reading, but my theme song from beginning to end, every day, is that you will never be a good writer unless you read a lot. I have what I call my literacy list of twentieth-century poets that everyone should know; I read contemporary poetry and talk about it a little in my classes. In no way do I feel that I'm trying to give a remedial reading course because there's not time, but I keep pointing out that if you read more poetry, you couldn't write like this.

I have taken to assigning one oral book review that I give them no models for and don't grade them on. It requires that you read one whole work by a contemporary poet on my list. If you want to do serious writing about poetry today, you're better off writing book reviews than critical articles because there are plenty of places to publish them and they can do more good because they might help somebody sell a book. My rule of thumb is that you should try to be as literate as if you were writing a critical article, but you're permitted to make judgments that come out of the fact that you've only read one book. Sometimes it makes me squirm when I realize they don't have any idea what a book review sounds like. I toy with bringing in book reviews and giving them oral book reviews; I am constantly struggling with the feeling that if they don't learn how to do it on their own, then all I'm doing is giving them one model for behavior that helps prevent them from using their minds.

■ *So you don't think the primary issue is getting
your students in touch with themselves?*
I think the primary issue is getting one's deepest self in touch with that most outside the self, what poetry is. I don't think that by searching through the history of poetry you're going to come to any good poetry any more than I think that just by searching down into yourself . . . One of the reasons I talk about honesty is that I think you have to strip away everything except your real attitudes both towards what you read and your feelings about yourself and life before you can start making some harmonious connection between the two. I *would* rather work with a student who has read a million poems and isn't in touch with himself because it seems much easier in this society to help a person get in touch with himself (laughter) than to get in touch with literature. On the other hand, I think they have to be an equal process. I'm no more hopeful for the person who just wants to grub around in his interior and has no sense of art and language than I am for the person who's way out there in some lofty, ethereal, linguistic realm that has nothing to do with humanity. It's a problem of trying to get the interior and exterior in touch with each other and this is where a lot of teachers fall into the trap of wanting to be therapists because, in a sense, it's the same job: helping to integrate personalities.

■ *I was interested by your remark that writers shouldn't
need therapy because that's what they do all the time.*
I don't believe writing is therapy; I think writing is therapeutic in the sense that good writing is an act of balancing, harmonizing, understanding, putting things together, creating a whole, understanding the incomplete in order to be complete. We don't live our art, so probably your art is more whole than you are. You're in total control of your art and you're not totally in control of your life. There are all those other people in your life—from the income tax person to your wife or children—who have heavy holds on your life, and you have almost total control over your poems, which is such a wonderful reality. But I would think just being in touch with the wholeness would give you a kind of wholeness in your life.

■ *Then why the myths about writers being temperamental and selfish?*

Anyone who is an artist has trained himself and also simply allows himself to keep his senses and his emotions on top of everything else because that's how he records what he's going to use—whether he's a painter, musician, poet—and I think that on one level makes him very vulnerable, and on another level, gives him a privilege that many people envy because he's allowed to be a child in the sense that he's allowed to live for his emotions and his feelings. Well, when you look at it, he isn't really allowed to any more than a banker is allowed to live with money. He's made that his definition of his life and he's going to fight for it.

November 14, 1979, and May 31, 1982

HAVE POETRY BE A PRACTICE

Anne Waldman recommends making poetry a practice and reports that Buddhism serves her well as a parallel ritual, for it helps tame the ego, opening her to the world's influence. When she teaches, she uses a variety of exercises to help her students join her in writing from their "spontaneous, original minds" while passionately engaging the rest of the planet.

Waldman's approach has worked for her; she has produced fine poetry, nonfiction, anthologies, and recordings. Her early poetry has often been associated with orality and with music, such as her book Fast Speaking Woman. *Critics have praised her later work for its power on the page. Her most recent books are* Civil Disobedience: Poetics and Politics in Action; Vow to Poetry: Essays, Interviews and Manifestos; Marriage: A Sentence; *and* In the Room of Never Grieve: New and Selected Poems 1985–2003. *Waldman was a co-founder, with Allen Ginsberg, of the Jack Kerouac School of Disembodied Poetics at the Naropa Institute, where she is a distinguished professor of poetics.*

▓ *You've said that it was good for you to be taught by professional writers at Bennington. Why is that important?*

Professional, meaning "active," writers who take what they're doing seriously and hopefully take their students seriously, take their students to heart. It would be boring for them if they were simply turning out dilettantes. At Bennington, Bernard Malamud was most attentive, concerned, and helpful, giving advice from his experience and from his heart. Sometimes you could see right away that Howard Nemerov had been in some intense creative state, had just written a poem. There was a reading program at Bennington with many so-called academic poets visiting. John Berryman, although inebriated much of his visit, gave a brilliant, raggedy lecture on Pound and ended up passionately reading Elizabeth Bishop's poem about the man who "lies in the house of Bedlam," her poem about Ezra Pound at St. Elizabeth's Hospital. Seeing Berryman, for example, in a very fragile state was touching and inspiring. When I went out to the Berkeley poetry conference in 1965, it was much the same: mixing with poets and seeing their fragilities, seeing them in the process of living their work; there was no separation there. It was a sense of not compromising, of doing something outrageous for the love of the words and the music. I'm probably being too romantic; I was seeing it all with younger eyes.

■ *What's the value of seeing that fragility?*
You see that poets aren't fakes, aren't entertainers or politicians. They aren't manipulating language for devious ends. They've made a tremendous commitment to the life and spirit of the language—the beauty of the language. And there's a marvelous range of temperament amongst the poets. I first heard Robert Lowell in 1961 or so, and his stance, his "music" is so different from John Berryman's or Allen Ginsberg's, which is why I don't like the labeling "schools." There is no method or system for how you get to be a poet; it is very individual. You learn to rely on your own mind, your own instincts, your own intuition, and your own relationship to the language. Somehow seeing that passion, that inspiration in other people was important to me. When I first heard Allen Ginsberg's vocalization of his own work, I was very excited. His encouragement when I was starting to read my work out loud was so helpful, his telling me to push to the limits and let go, trust my own sound and rhythm. Kenneth Koch also gave me encouragement.

■ *In an early interview, someone said that the most important thing he got from his teachers was not technical advice, but validation.*
Right. It's one thing if they come to you with technical questions. Often I just want to affirm their commitment and demonstrate my own. Here at Naropa on the poetics faculty all of us work very differently as teachers. Allen Ginsberg and I agree on what should be taught, but we also diverge at certain points in terms of what we like in a poem, and some students will work better with me and others better with him. It becomes an apprenticeship situation which is very, very particular.

We all might use William Carlos Williams to cut through the unfortunate haziness about what a poem is, and as a way of working with what you see in front of your nose, getting grounded in what's right here, right now, and forgetting how your mother mistreated you decades ago or whatever. All of that can come back later if it really must be told, and probably in a more interesting way. Larry Fagin has all his students write a short autobiography first thing to get that need to tell one's personal history out of the way. Once you've gotten that out of your system, you can start fresh.

We set up a situation which can allow the poems to materialize in various ways but also allow the students to stretch their muscles, try things out. Try writing a ballade, a sestina, a term paper!

■ *What do you try to do?*

Pass on the pleasure I get out of poetry. My husband (who also writes poetry) and I don't own a television, and since we've a baby, we don't go out excessively; so we frequently read aloud to each other—Homer, Shakespeare, James Schuyler, Laura Riding, Helen Adam. Attention to poetry of all kinds, ancient and modern, is very much part of our lives. I try to present the work that has inspired me, hoping it will do the same for someone else: lift off the top of their heads a little.

I have an idea that there is some kind of muse or energy field that some people can tap into. You can allow and create a space or atmosphere for those things to happen. "Words are forces the breath lets go," says Robert Duncan. So you organize your life and have poetry be a practice, a study, a discipline, as necessary as food, light, etc., and you give it back to the world.

I'm very interested in getting people working spontaneously; I want to start from a fresh place. You might have an idea that poems have to include the blue sky and the clouds and the waves and the gulls and how great you feel that day: a lot of gush, usually. One sees that sentimentality a lot in early work. There are a lot of silly ideas about how you write a poem and not enough looking at your original mind. There's a way of cutting through that by experiments where you are brought into the moment confronted by your crazier or more interesting mind, and you are also more alert to what's around you—the world's more vivid.

Working with dreams can bring some of that out, although having everybody tell their dreams can be boring. Diane di Prima and I both use an exercise based on a Navajo ritual. You have one person sitting in the center of a room tell a dream and people walking around the person and absorbing the dream as it's being told, and moving, if they want, in a particular way inspired by the telling of it. Then you have them pick up on certain images, write them down, and use them in a piece of writing that can be "about" something else entirely. It's an interesting way of starting a group working together, but it's also starting on the spot; one isn't bringing in preconceptions from years back, and you are using a common ground. Another thing I've done is ask students to bring in objects that are relevant to them and have some history that they can relate. Everyone else takes notes and can ask questions about the objects and many stories come up that transcend the personal because the object keeps it away from "This is how I feel about that." Ego-centered work is a problem because everyone feels, "I'm a poet too and I have my story to tell."

■ *So there has to be a balance between connecting to yourself and having a sense that someone else is out there?*
Yes. Or being able to put the work outside yourself and look at it objectively. We often put the actual object on the table and so it removes the person in a way. It's almost a psychological exercise, but a lot of the writing is quite interesting. A student will come up with a detective story where these objects are clues toward some elaborate denouement. So then people are getting something out about themselves without going into a lot of psychoanalysis.

William Burroughs has one experiment he's done with students at Naropa frequently, called "The Walk." One takes a walk, comes back, and then does writing using images of what one has seen. If you see a street sign or the name of a store, you may use that, but you also use what those things remind you of—other places, other "sets," words out of dreams. If you see an elderly woman who reminds you of your great aunt Ruth, you flash on that and use it. You try to use all those things that come into your mind as material. It is a way of tuning up your mind, noticing what's in front of your nose rather than relying on what you feel. Another thing is going out and noticing all the red— a red hat, a red car, a red face. That's wonderful to do whether you're writing or not. It heightens your perceptions.

The marvelous poet Dick Gallup, who has taught at Naropa for a number of years, has very interesting ways of getting poems to happen: he'll suggest a poem where each line has a color in it or a season—and also working with forms. Some students work wonderfully with forms. They come here thinking they want to be experimental and get away from the sonnet or the haiku or whatever, and then their minds can do it best with some kind of gorgeous structure.

Sound has turned out to be important to a number of people I've talked with, but you seem to have been conscious of its importance from a young age.

I always was an avid reader and my parents were constant readers and had a good library and so on, but it was somehow hearing poetry out loud, reading it oneself out loud so that one can almost feel it physically, feel the vibration in the language. This is the effect too, of mantra. It awakens parts of your body and brain. I had that experience, so that was something I was after in my work. Not all of my writing is consciously chant work, but it's important and natural to me. My own sound made me stronger.

Many people I've spoken with say they have never had an experience of poetry until they've heard it read aloud and I think one can bring alive Shelley's poems or Shakespeare and Sappho by trying to present them orally. But I also think the boundaries between art performance and poetry are a little thin at times; one isn't quite sure: "Is it a poem or is it a performance? How much is the person presenting putting into it?" You might read it later yourself and it would be less powerful.

Many students come to the Kerouac School obsessed with the idea of poetry being primarily oral and I have to make them pay attention to what they're doing on the page as well. The page is like an artwork; the shape of the poem is exciting sitting in blank space and can conjure up things. There are things that haven't been done yet on the eight-and-a-half-by-eleven sheet of white typing paper. Many writers can present their work in an exciting, dynamic way, can get away with endlessly presenting *themselves* and be sloppy on the page. So there should be a happy balance.

You've said some things that suggest you see Buddhism as a way of encouraging a state of mind that is useful to writing.

I think that's true. If you become a serious Buddhist, there are going to be periods when you are so involved with the practice, looking at your mind in ways you hadn't before, it could block or inhibit writing. It's like anything you delve into deeply: you can handle only that at the time. Writing for me has always been a practice and it's something that is with me all the time. I think Buddhism is a parallel practice. Buddhist practice should ideally infiltrate your whole life to make you a more awake, alert, functioning person and a saner being on the planet. A lot of experiments we do, especially with beginning students, are trying to reverse neurotic psychology, bring people into the moment, get them awake to what's in front of them. One might say the best writing is by the craziest people, but in that moment of creation, the craziness is channeled or transmuted into something absolutely enlightening. Use your rage, use your jealousy, your passion, but put it out in front of you and don't be lost in it. Use those states skillfully.

In the Buddhist practice, when you look at your mind, you see your neurotic patterns. "Buddhism" isn't the best term because anyone can sit still. When you're doing sitting meditation, you aren't meditating on the eternal flame or the white light; it's looking at your mind and what comes up. The fantasies, the emotions, the projections, etc. You see them and you say, "Those are just thoughts" and you let them go. Craziness comes from having those thoughts become solidified so that you might think you're John Lennon and go kill the other John Lennon or whatever. That is an extreme example, of course.

At the root of the Buddhist practice is the likelihood that you'll make friends with yourself. You look at your mind and stop playing games. It cuts a lot of those patterns where you're trying to put one over on others and consequently, yourself. When you see your ego is an alien parasite feeding on you, you can work on it, transmute it. You can see how slippery it is and how manipulative and how it controls your thinking, your actions so much of the time.

When you sit in front of the typewriter and a blank white page, anything is possible. It's so refreshing when you come to that in a sane way. Not all the time. I will certainly come to it anxiety ridden because I haven't written a poem in so long, or the poem I want to write is not coming out right. I find my life is saner with having my poetry be a practice and not worrying about my next book—the maintaining of my identity as a poet, etc.

What's been nice about the poetry world has been the tremendous support one gets among one's male and female confreres. The stakes are low in poetry; it's not like the art world, for example. There you might make a great deal of money on your work. No one is going to pay thousands of dollars for a piece of paper; maybe when you've been dead hundreds of years and it's handwritten in indelible ink. (Laughter)

■ *You said, "At school I was reading the classics, had a solid education, but if I let the masters take over—one would give up if you had to compare yourself with Yeats, Rilke, Shakespeare—especially a young student female poet!" It sounds as though being a woman is freeing.*

In the middle of one long night, I realized the women right now could seize the artistic power or energy, as poets. Most of my teachers have been male and the poets I've gotten much from have been male; I think I came at this lucky time when the male poets who were my peers were able to transmit their knowledge in a way that they weren't doing ten years earlier. Diane di Prima once talked about how so many of the talented women that she knew in the so-called Beat scene were not given the technical information or the sources or the lineage, so they dried up, committed suicide, destroyed themselves out of frustration . . . Diane, of course, was a fighter and survivor. She has always been an inspiration to me. She's a tough woman, not personally, but in terms of her commitment to her work.

I've been very lucky. It's hard in the beginning: you have doubts and often men seem to be deciding your fate. But I do feel I'm on the crest of a new wave of exciting women writers.

March 23, 1981

I DON'T KNOW WHETHER YOU CAN DO JUSTICE TO YOURSELF WITHOUT DOING JUSTICE TO THE WORLD

Richard Wilbur encourages his poetry-writing students to engage the rest of the world more intensely by having them present work to each other, by exposing them to classic literature, and by having them try translation. His conviction that the writer must know a great deal in order to create substantial work makes him hope that aspiring poets will study subjects other than writing.

Wilbur's poetry, translations, prose collections, and children's books constitute such an accomplished body of work that he has won some prizes twice: the Guggenheim, the Pulitzer Prize, and the PEN Translation award. His many other awards include the Bollingen Prize, the National Book Award, the Gold Medal for Poetry from the American Academy of Arts and Letters, and poet laureate of the United States. He taught at Harvard, Wesleyan, and Smith and has received a multitude of honorary degrees. Richard Wilbur recently published Collected Poems: 1943–2004.

■ *You said that "Birches" "is happy in all the ways in which a poem can be happy" because it "does justice to world, to self, to literary tradition, and to a culture." What do your poetry students have the most trouble doing justice to?*

Like all young people, they are better at doing justice to self than to the world. I don't know whether you *can* do justice to yourself without doing justice to the world, but in any case there's a lot of self-absorption among young people and, most of the time, what one is doing in writing courses is pointing out moments of self-absorption.

I have all my students get involved in the act of criticism. We present the poem of some student anonymously—twelve or thirteen copies, so that everyone can be staring at it—and everybody talks and *always*, unless it's the utterly successful poem which disarms criticism, *always* somebody says, "What were you trying to say in line six?" And the writer answers, in effect, "I did say it." And then the original critic, backed by perhaps two or three others now, says, "No, you didn't say it. No, it didn't come through to us. You were nudging your closest friend, maybe, but you weren't conveying it to the general reader." I suppose that's the most valuable thing that gets done in a half year of writing-teaching: people come to learn that they have to go to extraordinary lengths to compel a trained and willing reader to see something of what they want to show, think something of what they want thought. I remember Allen Tate saying in *The House of Fiction* that the commonest failing in the writing of amateur fiction could be called the "unwritten story." People think they have told the story; they haven't, they simply haven't told it. The love of small vocabulary and incoherence that accompanied the sixties has made it harder for young writers now, even though everyone is trying to recover from that.

All of this is reflected in writing courses and in a feeling among the students that it would be embarrassing to be too eloquent, too literary, too clear. It wouldn't be honest, in a certain debased sense of that word, because it would be showy. I suppose all of that is distilled in the familiar expression, "You talk like a book." (Laughter) You'd think that it would or could be a compliment, but it never *is*. (Laughter)

▪ *Do you attempt to correct that attitude when you teach?*
I'm not very coercive; I guess I'm going to get more coercive this fall. It is, after all, 1981. I do want to encourage my students, not necessarily to understand scansion theoretically, but to try their hands, at least once, at some simple formal structure. I'm not complaining bitterly, but I think that I shouldn't let anybody get through the semester without brushing with that kind of discipline. I have in the past allowed people simply to try to do well in the manner that came easiest to them. And I can't explain why I'm now going to be a little more authoritarian, but I am. (Laughter) I guess I'm just fed up. (Laughter) I'm damned if I'm going to let any of my writing students be utterly ignorant of the literature of the past, or their work be utterly irrelevant to it.

▪ *Do you give your writing students reading assignments?*
I pick different books in different years, sometimes an anthology containing a good deal of work from the past; but, in any case, I keep presenting them with mimeographed poems of the past and asking

them to read in all ages and in as many languages as they can manage. To further that a little, I'll give them an exercise in translation: a French poem, accompanied by a literal translation and by a critical commentary borrowed from somebody, all of this to be worked up into a translation. I've even asked people to translate from less familiar languages because, with a sufficient amount of apparatus, I think it can be done. If the right sounds are made aloud, somehow that's a penetration of the poem's spirit. If they hear what kind of meter it is, that helps too. I do think that there's a swing back now toward some sort of core curriculum and so students are more and more picking up a sense of literary tradition. The period of disruption caused by the Vietnam War was disastrous in that respect. Many students got the idea that the past was indeed dead and that all they needed to learn was themselves. Oh, of course, they needed to learn also the things which they had appropriated to themselves, or decorated themselves with, such as William Blake and Hermann Hesse; there were certain things you were expected to have in your pocket, as you had a guitar in your hand during that period. (Laughter) But I was most annoyed by the teachers who went along with it all and, indeed, fostered a great deal of it, told students that the past was irrelevant, accepted that nonsense word "relevance" as a way of acquitting students of making the acquaintance of humanity throughout its whole temporal range. Such a primitive notion: that you can ignore the past as a mob of strangers. Those people represent what one might again be, or what one still is.

■ *Some people say that their writing students come into class believing that the most important aspect of a poem or story is its theme and that they have to think up something significant to say before they begin to write.*

I can recall student poems which seemed not to have arisen from the genuine concerns of the poet but simply from an effort to sound weighty. One student, way back there when I was first teaching at Harvard, said to me, "Mr. Wilbur, you're not an easy person to write for." And I said, "Great God, have you been writing for me all this semester?" I guess that many people do come into your class with the feeling that they are to some extent writing for you, and if they think that the English teacher wants them to adopt a theme of proven weight, there it comes: a poem which has been misconceived from the start. I often quote to my students that well-known bit of Auden's where he says that the most promising thing in a young writer is a hankering to play around with words, and that the most unpromising thing to hear from a young writer is, "I have lot of ideas I want to express." (Laughter)

■ *But you don't have any system for handling that.*

No. I think that if I ever say anything about the matter in class, I do so in the particular case. I might say, "We know by now that this writer is capable of something better than this. This appears to be a high-minded propaganda poem, or a poem on a supposedly obligatory weighty theme, and that's why it isn't any good." Not that one shouldn't start with some sense of a subject, but one shouldn't start with somebody else's subject.

■ *Your poems are very rich, but you sometimes wait a long time for them. Could you wait that long when you were twenty?*

Oh, yes. Yes, I did. I suppose I wrote a little faster than I write now, but I've always written very, very slowly and that's one reason there tends to be, for better or for worse, quite a lot in the individual line, why paraphrase would be hard. If you picked up the latest issue of the average poetry periodical nowadays, you'd find for the most part a density of language which is approximately that of prose. It is sometimes good in an affectingly sincere way, but because I'm a product of my time, it lacks for me the excitement that I look for in poetry. I look for the unparaphrasable; too many poems are now being written which are their own paraphrases.

■ *Most of the literature classes I had emphasized what you call "paraphrasable meaning"; I imagine that you focus on something else. What do you do in your literature classes?*

When I teach Milton, for example, I deal with him in all respects, spending a lot of time on matters of technique. You have to with a great technician, with the greatest verse architect in history; you cannot understand that "L'Allegro" and "Il Penseroso" are serious poems unless you worry the structure to death and discover the ideas implicit in the structure. And so I and the students wrestle for several days until we've found the structure of the two poems. You have to talk about theology too and to some extent, history.

■ *Do you read aloud in class?*

I do that a great deal, both when I'm teaching literature and when I'm teaching writing. I think there's no substitute for it. You read something aloud as well as you can, and I think you thereby give a new sense of its measure as well as of its meaning. If you're reading a student poem aloud to your students, they all know that you're going to do as well by it as you can. And if it doesn't quite work, they have a fresh sense of where and why it doesn't work. I read things as long as "Lycidas" aloud to my classes when I'm teaching literature; the musical and emotional dimensions can't be got in any better way, and also a feeling of the poem as a whole. If one is talking at it and explicating little corners of it, one can lose what they call "the big picture"; one can simplify wonderfully by reading. I try to get students to read aloud too, a thing they're often scared to do because they haven't been asked to do it in any primary or secondary school. I wish that that were done more in the earlier stages of schooling; everyone should have a competence in that.

■ *What part of your education was most helpful to your writing?*

Certain of my literature courses presented me excitingly with writing which made me want to "do something like that." The same is true of the courses I've taught. The courses most useful to me have been the ones which excited me by putting me into the presence of things which I wanted not so much to copy as to equal in art and vitality.

■ *If there had been a lot of writing programs around*
when you were a student, do you think it would
have been a good idea for you to go to one?

Probably not a good idea at all. I went to Amherst. Amherst is a place I'm terribly fond of, and so I shall probably exaggerate its virtues, but the air of Amherst is full of approval for poetry and for writing and always has been. You can't solve the matter by saying, "Oh, Emily Dickinson lived in that town," or "Oh, Robert Frost was on the faculty for a while." It's no one thing, it's no number of things that you can add up, it's just there. There was a great deal of extracurricular excitement about writing when I was a student there, and all of one's teachers were glad to look at anything in the way of a poem or a story and criticize it. They were always very encouraging, and with all that encouragement, it wasn't necessary to burrow into a writing course. A number of my friends did take the one writing course then offered at Amherst, but I didn't see the necessity. I visited it once; it seemed OK, but I felt I would learn more somewhere else.

Some people have said that it hurts literature to have so many people become writers by going through writing programs.
I think it's hurting a lot of people, and that it's hurting the whole scene. I'm not alone in having this cranky feeling. Too many people are failing to study what they should study by concentrating too much on creative writing courses. There are so many schools in which people are allowed to major in creative writing, right through to a BA. They go through impoverished, knowing, as Yeats said, "nothing but their blind, stupefied hearts." And so often, having become defective and specialized in this way, they go on to graduate school in creative writing, and then drift on out into the MFA market looking for jobs, not too many of which are there. Until recently, the government has been providing them with poetry in the schools programs, occasional fellowships, and subsidized little magazines in which they can publish. It's a lamentably "supportive" world in which far too many people are encouraged to imagine themselves poets beyond the point at which they should wake up and decide to do something useful. One consequence of all this over-encouragement and subsidizing is that we have quantities of little magazines full of bad poetry, depressing poetry, around us. Standards are lowered as soon as you have a whole lot of creative writing courses, because you can't ask for the highest performance of young people who have not had much experience as writers and have no strong calling. Insensibly, you lower your standard. And standards are lowered on the graduate level, because there are so many people going to these competing schools of writing. I have no desire to make anybody stop writing poetry, but I think it would be a favor to many people and to poetry if some people stopped thinking of themselves primarily as young poets and kept on writing on the side.

It affects everybody if a whole lot of bad work in any art is being published and supported. If there are magazines all around us full of poems which start, "I turn off the television," and so on—that sort of loose-jointed, prosaic, supposedly sincere poem that says what you have done in the last five minutes—it's going to affect the general sense of what poetry ought to be doing.

■ *I'd like to ask about "The Writer," the poem you wrote
to your daughter. What did you mean by "It is always
a matter of life . . . and death"?*

Getting oneself off one's chest, writing. I'm wishing her a lucky passage, and it's a passage both in the sense of making connections with the world, getting out of oneself, and of writing a good paragraph. When one is dealing with young writers, one almost always has both those feelings going: you're hoping that the young writer will do well, will write a good story or a good poem; you're also hoping that the doing of that will be a successful coming to terms with the world by way of the common means of language.

■ *Is there anything you'd like to add?*

Yes. Since many of my remarks have been a bit negative or tart, I'd like to right the balance by saying that there is, in fact, much good poetry being written these days, that year after year I encounter students who are truly gifted, and that a course in writing can be stimulating and salutary. As for anyone's taking two such courses, or three, at the cost of neglecting geology or Latin, I have my doubts.

May 25, 1981

RICHARD YATES

THE HARDEST AND LONELIEST PROFESSION

Although critics repeatedly praise the authenticity of Richard Yates's work, in this interview he focuses on craft, urging writers to remember that they have an audience. Indeed, he calls the pleasure of writing well the whole motivation for persisting in the loneliest and hardest profession. At his request, this interview was not taped. It is based on notes.

Yates's first novel, Revolutionary Road, *was nominated for the National Book Award. He followed it with five more novels as well as two short story collections. Widely regarded as an underappreciated writer, Yates received praise from many fellow authors, including Tennessee Williams, William Styron, and John Updike. He taught at Columbia, Boston University, and the Iowa Writers' Workshop.*

■ *How did you like Iowa?*

I taught at Iowa for six years—too long; I got stale. The first three or four years were fine, but I hope I never go back to full-time teaching; although when I first had the opportunity to teach, to get paid for talking about what I loved, it seemed a munificence to me.

Whenever I taught, I stopped writing. I don't know what the connection is, but there has to be one. My first two books were copyrighted in '61 and '62; then my next book was copyrighted in '69, and the next one in '75. There are thirteen years lost in there and they were the years I was teaching. I can't say teaching took too much of my time because college teaching does not take that much time and at the Iowa Writers' Workshop, things were arranged to leave time for us to write. I think teaching used the same energy that I might have used for writing. I would write regularly—once that's a habit, you just keep going—but I couldn't keep anything I wrote.

In spite of all this complaining, I'm glad I knew all those people in universities. There are a lot of nice people in universities.

■ *In* The Easter Parade, *John Flanders says that teaching*
makes one's writing academic. Do you agree?

Oh, there's this thing that the rough and tumble of the real world somehow nourishes writing, but it makes no sense. That distinction between the real world and the academic world is ridiculous. Even the words are ridiculous: everything is the real world, including the academic world.

■ *Some people have said that the most useful part of being*
in a writing program is seeing how writers function.

I don't know what you mean. People in a writing workshop—both writers and students—know no more about each other's private lives than telephone operators who work together or clerks in the same dime store. They may make guesses about each other, but finally they don't know what happens to each other after they go home. Everyone keeps one's privacy.

There were generally two groups of students at Iowa: one group that got together, drank and shouted and another group of people who went home to their apartments and drank instant coffee. I tended to hang out with the first group because I like to shout, and, of course, people who got together frequently like that would share secrets, but both groups produced the same number of writers. I don't think you can make any connection between being or not being in a group like that and writing or not writing. Sharing and caring was a big thing in the sixties, but there's no more of it in writers' workshops than there is anywhere else.

■ *In an interview in* Ploughshares, *you said that anyone doing*
autobiographical writing has to avoid self-pity and self-
aggrandizement. How do you handle this with students?

Well, I warn them against those two traps: self-aggrandizement and self-pity. I still stand by that statement. And I'd also tell them what Kurt Vonnegut said, "Never forget that you're writing for strangers." You wouldn't walk up to strangers on the street and confess your intimacies to them. If you're determined to confess your intimacies to your readers, you have to give them a reason to be interested.

■ *Is part of the pleasure of writing, the pleasure of getting it right?*

Yes. You put together a couple of nice words, then a phrase, then a paragraph. That's very satisfying. That's the whole motivation for going on. Mastering the mechanics of writing will give you a basis for going further.

■ *If writing is so satisfying, why did you say*
it's the hardest and loneliest profession?

It's the hardest because you're self-taught, because each story implies the ending of its own craft and you have to start over. It's the loneliest because no one can help you. Even the sweetest, most understanding wife can't help you more than a pencil in a telephone booth. What would be harder?

■ *Carrying bricks, working in a factory,*
being president of the United States.

All those things are easy. All a president does is eat jelly beans, talk on the phone and read things that other people write for him. Even if he makes difficult decisions, sixteen people help him.

■ *How about carrying bricks or working in a factory?*

They work, they get a lunch break, and when the day's over, they can go home and watch TV.

■ *Writers can eat lunch and watch TV all day.*

Yes, but most kinds of work leave your dreams alone. Writing doesn't.

May 14, 1981

A WRITER WORKS TO GIVE THE READER
A TRUE EXPERIENCE

Although Helen Yglesias notes that the successful writer needs compassion and strength along with rich life experience in order to have something substantial and meaningful to say, she also believes that in order to touch readers, the author's perspective must vanish into an utterly lucid writing style.

Helen Yglesias began her first novel, How She Died, *at age fifty-four; it won the Houghton Mifflin Literary Fellowship. She followed it with two nonfiction books and four more novels, most recently,* The Girls. *She has taught at Columbia University and the University of Iowa Writers' Workshop.*

■ *I was sorry that I couldn't get a copy of*
Starting. *Is that an autobiographical book?*

Starting is nonfiction, about doing what you really want to do; especially women, I think, get sidetracked. It does have a section on myself; as soon as I started to read, to be able to tell a story seemed to me the most wonderful thing to do, but I did not get to do it until I was fifty-four. I was editing and working on newspapers and magazines and even that work was interrupted because I had three children I wanted to raise myself, so I didn't go back to work full-time—I did things in between: I did freelance editing and freelance reviewing and so on—but I didn't go back to full-time work in the field, I'm not even talking about *writing* full-time, until my youngest child was ten or eleven. By that time I had pretty much given up the idea of writing fiction. I was a book editor on a weekly magazine. As a reader, I had been reading only the top novels. When you're a book editor you see everything. A lot of mediocre stuff is published. That was a big revelation: all this material was being published, being hailed, in some cases, as wonderful, as works of genius—some works that I thought were pretty bad. It leveled my sights. I said to myself, "Write the best book you can and see what happens." I wrote *How She Died*. And I was very, very fortunate.

My oldest son, who was then in his early twenties, picked up the manuscript and read the first chapter without my knowing it because I don't like to show things that aren't finished. He suggested that it would stand alone as a short story, which was something I couldn't have seen because I was too involved in it as a whole book, and that I should send it to the *New Yorker*. My husband had published in the *New Yorker*, and so it seemed natural to send it to his editor. It was taken, and its editor, a marvelous woman, Rachel MacKenzie, sent it to Houghton Mifflin to another wonderful editor, Dorothy de Santillana, who immediately offered me the Houghton Mifflin Literary Fellowship. That was overwhelmingly encouraging. I trusted myself then.

I wrote *Starting* because I felt my own experience could be encouraging to other people, and in *Starting*, I also tell stories of other people, not necessarily all late starters. As a matter of fact, I tell the story of my son who was a very early starter: he had a book published at seventeen.

▦ *I came to these interviews with prejudices about artists that I picked up from reading Freud and Jung: that you all create because you're neurotic and so forth. You all seem so much healthier . . .*
(Laughter) Than you expected.

▦ *And than most people. I think you're better able to follow yourselves.*
You have to be very strong to be a writer. This quote is from a wonderful Czech writer, Vaculík: "Writing is always somehow an expression of powerlessness, or the fruit of frayed nerves. It betrays complexes, or a bad conscience." I think that's true; but to write also takes a lot of ego strength and ego health. Otherwise, it's just too hard to pull it out of yourself.

Fiction, for me, is an immersion in the world I'm creating. It absorbs my total energy; I'm lucky if there's anything left over for the people who are closest and dearest to me. My reaction to a student's manuscript on my desk when I'm involved in my own work is, "I don't care about this, I don't want to read this." I don't even care to read published fiction when I'm writing. I will reread, or I'll read some classic that I haven't gotten to, but I won't read contemporary fiction. In fact, I get so crazy when I'm writing something, everything seems to relate to what I'm writing. My reaction to almost any book by almost any other contemporary woman writer is, "Oh, she's writing exactly what I'm writing!" It's that syndrome you experience when you learn something new and then see the new thing everywhere.

I find it very difficult to teach and write at the same time: I have to feel the entire day is mine for my own work. At Columbia it was set up so that [I taught] only one day in the week, and even then it was as though I had opened myself up to inroads on my own imaginative energy. Once I had done that, I couldn't turn off the rest of the week. I also have to feel I'm in my own space; even though this is my private office, in my mind, it's associated with the teaching.

■ *Why do you teach?*

I didn't know why the first time. I taught at Columbia after I wrote How *She Died* thinking I could start to write *Family Feeling* while I was teaching. I don't think I wrote three lines during that spring semester.

■ *Then why did you come here to teach?*

I had just finished *Sweetsir,* a novel which was very draining. After I complete a book, perhaps not everybody goes through this, but I need a period of recuperation and filling up again. While I was still working on *Sweetsir,* the request to teach at Iowa came in and I thought, "I'll be through with this novel and it will be nice to do something that won't take anything out of me." I had totally forgotten how demanding teaching is. I taught the other class in the mid-seventies. I like teaching and I enjoyed that experience. I made good friends among the students; I was instrumental in getting one of them published and I was very happy about that. I remembered it through a haze of good feeling as having been a lovely time. Now that I'm in the situation again it's coming back to me [that] I get very wound up in teaching.

I like young people very much; I have three children and two grandchildren. I don't mean that I relate to the students as a mother or a grandmother; I don't. I relate to them as someone who has the same difficulties they have. It's as if there's almost no time span between me now and me at age twenty thinking, "Oh, I want to be a writer; I want to be a writer; I can't wait." I don't feel separated from that person. I still feel something wonderful and miraculous happened to me that I pulled through and got published. So I identify very strongly with the feeling of a beginning writer. I think you have the sensation of beginning again with each new book; you feel after you complete a book, "I don't know how I did that: I'll never be able to do that again."

I get very involved in student manuscripts and in conferring with the writer. The students I've been in contact with are graduate students and they're screened and they're talented and they're serious. They're not all going to make it, but there are enough who could make it that I get very concerned for them and try to help them as much as I can. A very varied personality structure goes into making writers, naturally; they're like all other people. The single thing writers have in common is the desire to write or the need to write or the compulsion to write. And to be so closely involved with so many writers in the most basic relationship, judging what they're doing, affects me in a way that I can't throw off easily. I'm sure I would if I taught regularly. It would become routine, but I wouldn't particularly care for that. It is possible to read manuscripts absolutely coldly, but not if you're going to be of any help. To be of help, you have to immerse yourself in the particular imagination at work in that story; that's the only way you can see where it's gone wrong—or right. Writers project themselves into the feelings of others. When you are that sort of person, it's hard to be in contact with a roomful of suffering personalities. I project onto them how I would feel in that situation and I know I would be suffering agonies. I never took such a class because I would have found it too painful to expose a work that is not totally finished, that has not reached the stage where I feel, "Yes, I am ready to show this."

At the same time, you don't want to overprotect. You want to do your job, which is to show where the writer has failed, and where the writer has succeeded. But what you know that the beginning writer doesn't know is that your views are essentially meaningless individual reactions. After a writer has been accepted and published, he or she is reviewed across the board. One person is going to say, "It's great" and someone at the other end is going to say, "It's garbage" and the writer finds the way within that. The exposure aspect is very painful to a writer, but to a professional, it's part of the scene and there are other bolstering aspects feeding in. I worry about a workshop being damaging to a beginning writer. I would not want anyone to leave my workshop feeling, "Well, I don't want to write anything. The last thing I want to do right now is write another story for them to get their teeth into." That's not the purpose of a workshop. All of that grips me in a way that I can't throw off lightly.

*How do you teach? It sounds as if you lose
yourself in what they're trying to do.*

I try to stay totally within the text. On one level, a teacher operates as an example; you use yourself, your experience as a writer, your aims as a writer, and your work where you can, to illustrate what you're saying. But in a more precise way, I operate as an editor because I do have that experience. I work closely with the text and try very hard not to change the story. Very often the students in the class are saying to a writer, "Don't write that story; write this story; I like this story better." They make up a totally different story which doesn't interest the writer one bit. What interests him is, "How can I make *this* story a better story?" I stay very close to the text and try to demonstrate skills. There are real skills. It's not all inner wisdom. I don't mean you can teach someone how to become a first-rate writer or a great writer; I don't think you can teach that. We're not talking about that. We're talking about professionalism; we're talking about preparing the story at the level where it can go out to a magazine and be read and judged and possibly bought; we're talking about preparing the novel to a point where it can be considered by a publishing house. It is true that there are writers who never need that; they have read enough to have learned the trade without these crutches. Most people who turn to writing classes do so because they have some problem or another: it may be only a problem of not having the self-discipline to do the work. That's a perfectly valid reason for taking a writing course. Or simply a need to meet other writers.

You never took a course like this, but I assume you went to college.

No, I never went to college. I've taken the equivalent of what any college student would have taken in English Literature courses which I monitored without credit. When you pick and choose that way, you're probably getting better instructors. I don't think writers need formal education as writers. It's very good for writers to be something else in their lives; it's wonderful that Chekhov was a doctor, for example. Even though living my life and working at what I worked at and having children and raising them kept me from writing, it also made it possible for me to have something very solid to write about when I did begin to write. One thing I don't like about a lot of contemporary writing is that it isn't about anything; there's a lot of emptiness at the center, particularly the writing by very young people that comes out of writing workshops. They want to be writers, but they don't have subjects.

A lot of writing is about writers in publishing or on magazines or it's about writers who teach. It's not about the people who are out there leading what we like to think of as ordinary lives but which aren't the least bit ordinary. They're very extraordinary. One of the critical reviews I got of *How She Died,* which was in the main praised, criticized it for taking what he considered very ordinary people and trying to make them extraordinary. He's a leading academic critic and his reaction is typical. If it couldn't happen in the back pages of the *New York Review of Books,* it's not worthy of our attention.

What do you think it does to writing when so many people who write are associated with universities in one way or another?

I think it's not good for writing. I think it's good stylistically; they're writing very well-made stories and their surface is very beautiful. A lot of them get into the *New Yorker.* I say that though I've gotten in myself at least twice. Nevertheless, there is such a thing as a typical *New Yorker* story, which I find empty in its core, and I don't think that's wonderful for writing. Or for readers.

Books should be well crafted and well written, but novels should be about more than the closed world of the university or the closed world of publishing; about only middle-class, privileged people; or about the older professor who is having an affair with a beautiful young student; or the older wife of the older professor having an affair. I don't want to read any more of those books.

I was struck by the power of the details you used in How She Died, *and since my father died of cancer, I know they were accurate. I was going to ask you how you did that, but I think you've already told me. You didn't write that book when you were twenty-five years old.*

It's a made-up book: the character Jean is not me and has no relationship to my life except in that every character you write is yourself. But the character of the girl who died is very closely based on a dear friend and on her actual experience.

Can you teach students how to select details that work the way yours do?

The Orwell essay "Why I Write" is wonderful; it's a plea for concrete language. It's a good antidote to the theory that it's all in the language; it's all in the surface; it's all the play of the language; it's all in the puns and the jokes. That is not even true of Joyce. There is solidity in *Ulysses*—there's reality behind the pyrotechnics and if you put it all onto the pyrotechnics, you come up with nothing. You come up with razzle dazzle.

At the opening session, one of my students said he had come to my class because he felt that I would stress feeling and concrete experience in writing, whereas other writing classes had stressed technique: structure, style. I reminded him that you can't do the feeling and experience without the structure and the style. They are totally interlocked and must be granted equal weight and space. A writer works to give the reader a true experience and, yes, to dazzle while doing it. Orwell aims for a style that is as clear as a pane of glass so that there is no obstruction between the text and the reader. That's the major lesson I try to impart. That it is clarity which makes for the purest, brightest dazzle: clarity—and content.

September 19, 1980

INTERVIEWS WITH AUTHORS ABOUT
HOW THEY WORK

$\mathcal{M}$ARVIN $\mathcal{B}$ELL

I WANT IT TO BE TRUE

After almost fifty years of writing poetry, Marvin Bell still finds it exhilarating because giving himself over to the process continues to teach him new things about himself, about life, and about making poetry. At the same time, he admits that even after so many years as a professional maverick, taking risks is still hard because like all human beings, he likes approval. But the rewards for doing things his way overwhelm the discomforts.

Marvin Bell is in the process of retiring from the University of Iowa Writers' Workshop, where his students have included Rita Dove, John Irving, Jorie Graham, James Tate, and Joy Harjo, among many others. His sixteen poetry collections include Stars Which See, Stars Which Do Not See, *a finalist for the National Book Award. His most recent book is* Rampant.

■ *How do you see the sequence of your books?*

For me, books for years were collections of the poems I had been writing and although I organized the book, I didn't organize it before I had the poems.

■ *But* The Escape into You . . .

Oh, well, yeah, that's a book-length project. I didn't know how many would be in it, but I knew I was writing poems that had over-lapping formal elements, an overlapping concern, a kind of buried narrative, and that it would be a sequence of poems, or a cheater's version of a long poem. But whether they would cover subjects A through Z and then end, or subjects B through W and then end . . . No, I didn't make decisions like that. Afterwards when I organized them, it seemed to me there were three that could go up front that formed a kind of introduction—I'm trying to remember way back now to the sixties—and the very last section is probably the most philosophic section because I was trying . . . it may seem foolish, but my idea was to try to make affirmations based not on fantasy or delusion or wishful thinking, but on the facts. In a way, I was already prepared to use that Zen admonition that I used as an epigraph to *The Book of the Dead Man*: "Live as if you were already dead." That's a version, of course, of living with the truth.

So it would be possible, I am sure, to say about me as I think it would be possible to say about almost every poet who ever lived, that the philosophy was probably ingrained and fully developed whether the person could say it or not when they first began writing. Philosophy is kind of a highfalutin word for this, perhaps, but it's a stance, it's a viewpoint, maybe it's even a vision, it's an attitude, it's a leaning, it's an idea—whatever it is, it has its abstract parts and its concrete examples and it's not that an idea was created into which the examples are made to fit, but the examples that seem to hold symbolic import or metaphoric import or a convincing reality about them for a particular sensibility prove by extension the abstract philosophy that they later hold, whether they can express it or not.

When I was a kid, I had an interest in writing already. And I remember taking a book out of the library . . . I'm pretty sure it had a black, cloth cover, but no book jacket and a kind of pulpish paper inside. It was one of those hack books about how to write fiction: *Can You Write Fiction?* There was a test in the back of it to see whether you could think like a fiction writer. So I read all the questions, answered them in my head, and then checked the explanations. And very quickly I figured out what the idea of the test was although it was never admitted by the author, as I recall. The test was to see whether you could be dispassionate to the point of cruelty. As I remember, one of the questions was about whether or not a woman should have an abortion. Obviously, in the plot she should have an abortion. He was trying to see whether you could make that answer. There were a lot that involved cruel circumstances in which the best decision from the fiction point of view and from the life circumstances point of view was to make the cruelest decision. And if you couldn't do that, he thought, well, you couldn't think in the minds of these characters and maybe you wouldn't be able to write fiction. I had no trouble answering the questions. I didn't like the answers necessarily, I didn't want my life to be like that necessarily, I didn't want to put anyone in that position necessarily; but I knew what the answer was in every case. And I knew that the answer was the cruel answer.

That unblinking view of the human condition exists in [William] Stafford, it exists in some of James Wright, it exists in some of Galway Kinnell, it exists in many poets; I think it's fundamental. This may just be because I'm a small-town boy and unless the performance has something to say about life and not just about performance, I'm not as interested. I want it to be true because I do believe the truth will set you free. It won't make you happier; it will set you free.

■ *How have you changed as a poet?*

Even though it might have been a young man's illusions, it was important to me to try to write poems that were not those that had been written before. I was always interested in art as an experimental expression, as an intuitive, and in many ways associative and spontaneous, expression. I had to start making a living early, so I can be practical, I can be rational, I believe in being civic and social and all of that requires rational attentiveness. I choose to let go of that in the writing because I think the results are much more worthwhile and certainly more interesting to me. Now, I never let go of it in terms of my attention to the language and what it stands for. No, no, no.

In the beginning, one is anxious to learn more and know more and use it all. And that includes writing methods, what people call strategies. It has to be absorbed to the point where it can never be extricated, and where it has become less a convention than a necessity, less a demand than a desire, and even to the reader, if one's lucky, it will be obvious that it is an expression of a sensibility and that the process is too whole to be broken down into elements of intelligence, learning, conventions, and so forth. I think it's possible to set up a teaching situation in which the young poet gets a glimpse of how surrender to the materials of an art makes for a richer art than absolute control of those materials. It does mean something in terms of writing to say the way out is through the open door; it does mean something to say that writing is getting emotional in the presence of language; it does mean something to say learn the rules, break the rules, make up new rules, break the new rules; it does mean something to say that sometimes the best revision of a poem is the next poem; it does mean something to say that behind the successes of a poem is the ghostly presence of the failures of the poem which if followed may produce successes of a new kind.

That's the problem sometimes with poetry workshops: they want to clean poems up and in the process reduce poems to their most publishable form. This is a disservice to the young poet because you can't expect the young poet to resist the lure of external approval for the sake of his or her art. Therefore, it is up to the teacher to have the conscience not to reduce poems to their most publishable and not to present external approval for more than it is and at the same time to analyze and describe the language at hand so that one can see what it's doing and not doing. But to say what it's not doing is not the same as saying "Cut it out," "Delete it," "Replace it with nothing." Sometimes I know how they could fix that poem, I do. And sometimes I can see it's going to help the poem and it's not going to hurt them to say, "Well, if I were God and this were my poem, I would take out line three and make that the title and I would chop off the last five lines." But most times it is going to hurt them to say that because there was something going on in those five lines that needs to be *done better*, that's all. It's the beginning of something.

They threw the ball at the basket and it didn't go in. Now what? Never take another shot? Move in closer so that it will go in? No, no, no, no, no. Take bigger shots. Shoot with your eyes closed. Turn around and heave it at the basket. Learn to shoot with your legs instead of your hands because actually that's the way it's done. It's not necessary for me to tell the young poet who's just thrown up his first shot what strong legs they're going to need later on. But it is necessary for me to trick them into running laps so that they'll have the strong legs later on. I need to try to convince them that getting into motion is important, that reading and writing [are] important, that learning the rules and breaking the rules are both important, that it's not a question of making this poem more publishable, it's a question of becoming a bigger and better writer. It's taking a chance so that twenty years from now, ten years from now, whatever, when he or she looks in the mirror, that person can say to themselves, "I've been doing it my way and it's been a lot of fun."

Also, it's metabolic. I get worked up inside in the presence of exciting ideas and exciting turns of phrase. And it is an *exhilarating* feeling. When I'm writing at night, if I'm really into something, if something's cooking, I am cooking inside. I have to get up and walk around. I gotta get going. So if someone wants to say this is just another form of drug, it just produces a metabolic effect in you, it's releasing endorphins and you are hooked, I would have to say that is possible; but it would in no way lessen the importance of the event for me because it's all electrochemical, is it not? For some people it removes the possibility of a spiritual life, but I don't see it that way at all. If it doesn't make your blood boil and your socks fall off, then you should find something that does.

That's one of the aesthetic problems that's so interesting about writing and it overlaps the issue of whether poetry makes ugly things beautiful: writing is such a joy in and of itself even if it has attached to it pain, even if it is about troubling subjects; it has such a joy, such a physical exuberance, such a metabolic pleasure to it that it's a high. It's a high. Maybe poets are just people who are addicted to that high.

And indeed, *The Book of the Dead Man* wants to insist over and over that writing is metabolic. (Laughter) If you sit around with students or other writers asking them when they write, what you find out when the conversation loosens up is that people often write when they have gotten themselves going physically. They've had to run some errands, for example, and they come home walking, and they'll throw everything down and . . . bang!; they feel like writing. Well, guess why? Blood is stirred up.

Suppose people find out what I look like and act like late at night jumping up and down and writing poems? If I were a jazz musician, they'd probably say, "Ok, great, terrific, yeah, work, man, work." But I'm a poet. That has to do with language. Most people feel that they use the same language that poets use and since they're using it to be informational and intentional and skillful and directive and organized, then that must be what poets are doing, too. And it's a great revelation to students to be set free from that. I almost always say to my students at the beginning of a semester, "If you'd all go home this week and write a hundred poems, you probably would learn more than you're going to learn in all the classes. I know what that means: you have to stay up all night and you get sleepy and you get deranged and you don't know if you're going to make it and some of them have to be really short and some of them have to be really silly." Now, I may be overstating the case, but there is a way in which the work is the reading and the writing, and the rest is talk.

There's this wonderful poem by Bill Stafford in which there's a little man crying inside him, yelling out "Faker!" And he keeps doing this, in his dreams, when he's awake, and at the end of the poem he says, "Awake or asleep, I am a little man myself crying 'Faker! Faker!'" Well, here's the punch line: the title of the poem is "The Title Comes Later." Readers of poetry who think that it's all written by plan, who don't realize that the title could come later or that the title could come from left field or that the title could be oblique or that the title could be spontaneous . . . that the title comes later might indicate that the poet's a fraud. If that little item might convince them that the poet is a fraud, what would they think if they found out how much is accidental, how much is free association, how much is imitation of someone else, how much is influence, how much is convention, how much is an assignment, how much is the occasion, how much is the mood, how much is the fact that Oliver Goldsmith needed to pay for the burial of his mother, how much of it is a dare? Now, I realize that this can be carried to its extreme so that one has nonsense verse and all language becomes is a series of minor and perhaps frivolous effects. Yes. Finally, it all comes back to the integrity and to the values of the artist. Yes. Does he or she stand on the ground or not?

Dorothy [Bell] was looking through the poems in *Iris of Creation* and she looked at that one poem I'd written which I had called "from: *The Book of the Dead Man*," though there was no such book; it just felt like it came from something bigger. And also *The Book of Life, The Book of Death, The Book of the Terminally Ill, The Book of Work, The Book of Labor*, whatever it is, it's sort of authoritative and complete. And she said, "Oh, I think you should write more of these." And I said, "Aww." And I probably never would have except . . .

You want to know the banal truth? At the Port Townsend Writers' Conference one year, I sat down for lunch with Jane Yolen, the children's book writer. And she said to me, "I'm doing an anthology of adult fantasy works. I wish you'd send something to me for it. That *Book of the Dead Man* poem, that would be a perfect poem for this anthology except I don't want to use published works. I want all unpublished works." And I said, "Well, OK" and I forgot about it. And then she said, "Well, I'm going to do another anthology, so this time maybe you can make the deadline." So I said, "Oh yeah." I went through all my unpublished poems and I grabbed everything that seemed fantastical and I sent it to her and she sent them all back. And she said, "Well, these are all wonderful poems, but they're not quite right for my project. But, boy, that *Book of the Dead Man* poem, that would have been perfect." And I thought to myself, "Well, you want a *Book of the Dead Man* poem, I'll write another one." So I did. I wrote the second one. And then I don't know what happened. I guess I began to realize what I had. And so I went on. It probably took a few before I

PRACTICE

began to make certain choices about how I would handle things, which direction I would go.

Once I got a whole book of them written, I didn't intend to write another book either. The last line of the last poem (#33) in *The Book of the Dead Man* says "The Dead Man is over the top," which I think is pretty good, myself, as a way of ending the book because it's an expression of—I don't want to say happiness, but at least acceptance or success or survival or triumph, and "The Dead Man is over the top," that's like coming up out of your grave. Although "Over the top" also means excess, doesn't it? And excess may be the path to knowledge, sometimes.

▪ *But you're always talking about poets being smart.*

Obviously intelligence is an advantage, but if intelligence were the crucial thing, then the most intelligent poets would write the best poetry. But I'm not sure that can be shown to be the case. It's one thing to be the court poet and to write poems about an occasion in such a way as to make your point without offending the source of your support. That requires all your intelligence and all your skill and you had better be Alexander Pope before you try it. But it's quite another thing to be writing the poems of a society based in part on individual freedom, or at least the illusion of it. And the decision to be a poet in recent times has involved a commitment to going against the grain. If it doesn't make one an outsider, it requires abandoning some convention or conventions that were useful. So there has to be a certain wrongheadedness about an artist who would be original. If the fool persists in his or her folly, he or she shall become wise. (Laughter)

And also, I would be less interested myself in writing poems about what I already know than about what I sense and don't know in the sense that I've already said it to myself. To me that's the great work of art, to go into areas of linguistic complexity beyond where we've gone before, to give us a new picture of ourselves or a new expression of ourselves. Schooling is all about doing it the way it's been done. That's why so many artists are people who have dropped out of school or been a little off to the side of what other people are doing. They've gone their own way in some pig-headed fashion. (Laughter)

I'm always saying and I really do believe it that there is no one way to write and there is no right way to write and that's true to the max in poetry. There are poets who write by poeticizing arguments that have been written down first in prose and they can be very good at it. And there are poets who write by planning a book which will cover an area of their biography or a theme or a number of speakers, and they're very good at it. And there are poets who write to explore a mystical idea or an archetypal form and they're very good at it. But that kind of planning would take the joy out of it for me. Now the truth is that I was a journalist and I love deadlines, I love assignments, I'll try anything. It's a kind of freedom when someone else makes the decisions for you. It gives you a chance to obey the rules and break the rules all at the same time. But in the absence of a deadline and an assignment, it would take all the joy out of the writing if I were to do it by brilliant planning.

■ *Why?*

(Sigh) Those of us who have had the fortune or misfortune to go to college and beyond and those of us who have made a world of books and of literature and of conversation and of ideas know so much about who we are and what we are and what the world is. So there's a lot we know, but we're aware that's not the whole of it, and we're aware there's an artificial complex to this knowing. Whether anything more natural is possible, one can never know. Too late for that. But I want to do something beyond convention, beyond accepted levels of skill, beyond the expected, beyond the predictable, beyond the wholly welcome.

Writing poetry has been a very wide door into parts of my being that might or might not have been explored otherwise. I think it is for everyone. Writing, when a certain attention is given to it, is a valuable and important and enriching experience because it involves extricating oneself as much as one is able to from expectations, conventions, reflexes, prejudices, and surrendering to the materials, or at least being overwhelmed by them maybe even without having intended to be and thereby surprising oneself, giving expression to one's inner life. That mix in inner and outer is what art expresses, not only expresses, but encourages, maybe even creates. No one knows. These are chicken-and-egg questions.

We deal on a level not as complex most of the time. We have to. We have to locate language within narrow borders in order to make it work. But we're often thinking two or three things at a time, we're often feeling two or three things at a time, we're often thinking about before, now and later all at the same time, and feeling it all at the same time. And we may be thinking what you might call scientific thought and aesthetic thought all at the same time, and these two thoughts may be so intermingled that they represent something else for which there are no words. And that's why poets backtrack and hedge sometimes when they're asked about their poems because they don't want to make them smaller.

I write late at night; I mostly always have. I *love* staying up very, very late and one of the reasons I write late is that once it gets late enough, the rational part of the mind lets go a little bit, one is able to be a little less sensible and proper. Functioning in society means being rational, deliberate, organized, intentional, careful; functioning poetically means being personal, reckless . . .

Now, look, I say all this when I'm enthusiastic, but I'm like anyone else. I get low when I think my work's being misunderstood or disdained, I get low when I think editors are so overwhelmed that they can't see something original; of course I do. It's not always possible to open up. We all have defensive strategies that are meant to keep us safe: emotionally safe, psychologically safe, physically safe. And it's very difficult to trust that one won't be hurt or one won't be made less able to function one's own way. And I can be as closed . . .

A friend from high school said it's easier to connect with people you knew as an adolescent because you were friends before you built those barriers.

Exactly. I feel the loneliness of this quite fiercely at times and probably the source of my low periods when I have them is that it's very hard to have good friends. It's just very difficult. [Dorothy and I] have been going back to Long Island between semesters in part because one of my close, old friends is there. You have an emotional overlap with those people. I went off to college. People don't do that where I come from. I became a professor, I moved to the Midwest, so we don't have anything in common, but still you have an emotional overlap with people you knew when you were an adolescent.

In *Letters to a Young Poet*, Rilke talks about solitude that you carry with you even if you're with people and I think that solitude can be hard on people who have moved away from the culture that gave birth to them. I understand full well the strength of the extended family even when not everyone in the family is behaving properly. I understand the strength in community mores even when those mores are debilitating to unusual characters. I understand full well that I would be harassed and perhaps driven to death by a conventional situation. But I also understand the strength of a conventional structure: whatever its drawbacks, which are substantial, you're always riding close to the center of the tree. You're not out on your own little branch singing a song you hope someone else will hear.

And one shouldn't be subject to other people's expectations in this matter, but we're affected. Fear of failure is about writing the poem in the first place. There is Dante and there is Emily Dickinson and there is Shakespeare: the models make a preemptive strike on you. Fear of success is even more pernicious because you become your own model; you have invested in an image. It's irresistible: everyone wants to be loved and everyone wants to be paid well. Now, I don't think I ever did this. But I understand why others might have because one does run the risk of losing the readers one had for the last book with the next book because you have gone your own way. When people have said, "Come and join our club?" you have said, "Well, I'd like to come to the party, but if you don't mind, I won't join." Then they stop inviting you to the parties after a while. And I've never been a joiner. I do not have the ability to become a true believer.

I remember what great fun it was when I stumbled onto the Writers' Workshop, which was a faintly disreputable program then because MFAs hadn't sprung up everywhere and it was just an excuse for a community of young writers. And here we were, most of us a little older than other students, most of us slightly disheveled . . . Everybody'd meet at the bar every night and nobody was thinking about would they publish a book or how soon or when. It was just: here we are, a bunch of outsiders and we're all like each other in some way and, boy, this is really exciting and maybe what we're doing is even worthwhile and serious. But it's also fun.

May 26 and 27, 1995

GETTING IT AS RIGHT AS IT CAN BE GOT

Ivan Doig works extraordinarily hard at all dimensions of his books, but he seems especially committed to accuracy. If he describes a forest fire, he will ask those who have actually fought them to appraise his rendition. Doig aspires to convey the lives of relatively obscure people committed to decency and hard work. His efforts to precisely and fully describe them underlines his determination to accord his characters and the history they represent total respect.

Doig's memoir This House of Sky *was a finalist for the National Book Award;* English Creek, *the first novel in a trilogy about Montana, received the Western Heritage Award for best Western novel;* Sea Runners *was named a Notable Book by the New York Times Book Review; his second memoir,* Heart Earth, *won the Evans Biography Award; and the Western Literature Association gave him its Distinguished Achievement Award. His most recent book is* Prairie Nocturne.

▨ *It must have taken a lot of courage to put aside magazine freelancing and trust through the long process of writing* This House of Sky.

Carol had more faith than I. I was never consecutively convinced that there was a living in it as well as a life. It turns out that indeed there is. I'm now published by Simon and Schuster, and one book has had movie rights sold, and on and on. But it took fifteen years or so. And there was no guarantee, ever.

▨ *Didn't you begin* This House of Sky *as a play when you and your wife spent her sabbatical year in England?*

I had in the back of my mind some sort of book about the homestead generation of my parents. My dad was born on a homestead, and my mother grew up on the next thing to one. As early as 1968, certainly a solid four years ahead of sitting down a few blocks from Hyde Park (laughter) and beginning a play about a Montana haying crew, I had begun tape recording people in Montana, starting with my dad and my grandmother. And I pecked away at that. I went back to Montana several times while my grandmother was still alive and I accumulated material without entirely realizing it was going to be *This House of Sky*. So I suppose the material was in slow germination. Then the increasing preposterousness of the economics of being a freelance helped turn me to working on the book more fully. And ever since we've been in Seattle, I've had the safety net of my wife's job. A working spouse is not a bad idea for a professional writer of any kind. I do mention too in the forward of *This House of Sky* and should underline a bit, the presence of a friend — still our oldest friend, Ann Nelson — who was acting as agent for me at the time; that got a third mind working on the book process besides the two in this household.

The play attempt ended up with nothing at all to do with *This House of Sky*. Bits of it did find their way into my second novel, *English Creek*; the name of the central character, Jick, and some of the bunkhouse material originated in that play.

■ *Why a play? Did you think a play would be more profitable than a novel?*

No. None of this was keyed to any estimates of profits, because they are so unpredictable. If you're a magazine freelancer, you're accustomed to doing things and seeing if there's going to be *any* profit. I'd just always been interested in drama. Didn't take very long for me to see that my subject material, (laughter) Montana's immense landscapes and people's lives against those, were better rendered in something else I'd been tinkering with: poetry put into prose.

■ *In the forward to* This House of Sky, *you mention looking at your journal and realizing that the book began to move when you started focusing on your father's voice. Have you always kept a journal?*

I can't tell you exactly when the journal started, but sometime in the late sixties or early seventies. I'd long kept various kinds of notebooks, and on the trip to Great Britain, I began keeping a diary as well. That's long been my habit — not dailiness of grace but at least weekliness of grace in getting words, ideas, down into a journal.

■ *Is it about writing or is it about everything?*

The diary is probably mainly about writing since that's mostly what

I do. It has other material in it, though, jumbled in. But in the other journals I keep, there are separate categories. There's one here [indicates a shelf] called "Phrasing," another called "Comparison and Description," "Anecdotes," "Technique," "Lingo," and "Ideas." Into them go turns of phrase that pop into my head, or ideas, or good stories I hear.

■ *Do you sit down once a week and grab the right notebook, or . . .*
No, it's oftener than once a week. I always carry a pocket notebook, so these are often the typed transcription of that. The stuff grows and grows out of that. Behind me here you see the file cards which are the iceberg of the book I'm on now, a novel called *Bucking the Sun*. These are research cards, but many of them, too, are turns of phrase, or possible snatches of dialogue. One thing I'm doing in this book—sometimes I wonder if it's worth all the damned effort, but—there's a lot of description of how people speak at the moment.

■ *How do you find out something like that?*
Well, I watch people. As you just now looked at me, a little crimp came between your eyebrows. That's how I find it. One of my characters is already doing what you just did; I won't swipe it from you (laughter) but I need a lot of ammunition of that kind in a book. So I swipe some from how people behave, and I make up some. This is the storehouse of that material.

But, back to your earlier question, there are generations of notebooks on my dad. When I began accumulating the material for *This House of Sky*, I would sit down and type what I could remember of details and circumstances onto lined notebook binder paper, because sometimes I'd handwrite instead. Into that would go, perhaps, turns of phrase my dad and my grandmother had used. Details of lambing, what some of the technical phrases were: where we put the ewe and her new lamb was called a "jug," a little thing like a jail cell, and so the lingo came from that mock jailing of them. Or the wonderful phrase the "gut wagon," (laughter) which was the maternity wagon for the sheep.

Ultimately, I found file cards easier for me to handle. A *New York Times Book Review* piece about Anne Tyler mentioned that she was using file cards for small details she was going to sort into her manuscript. "Cobb wears knee socks when she dusts the house," I think was

Tyler's example. I thought, "Well, hell, I can do that. I've been to graduate school." File cards turn out to be a pretty good idea for someone of my habit patterns and so there are now tens of thousands of them around here through the soon-to-be eight books.

You were asking about my journal habits. I don't know where I got the stamina, but on my first book of fiction, *The Sea Runners*, I managed to keep an almost day-by-day journal of what I was doing in the writing. I'll show you a couple of those entries:

10 March '81—the month's name is apt so far; the past 7 writing days, I've marched on schedule, averaging 5 pp/day as intended. Most of it is choppy, written by the graf [paragraph], sometimes just a sentence lifted from the file cards; it's the effort to get a critical mass accumulated, so I can get the revising and adding-to underway.

Today during the [daily midmorning] walk it occurred to me to add the couple of proverbial bits—'Paper is the schoolman's forest,' etc.—to the Rosenberg [governor of Russian America—Alaska—in the 1850s] scene, and to say something here about the effort I'm making to put a proverbial sound into this ms. [manuscript]. The aim is to tap into the interest proverbs hold for us; they're nuggets of idea and language, and we all respond to their gleam. Thus, the proverbial tang of M's [the character Melander's] dialogue; and I'm considering whether to put biblical flavor into W's [the character Wennberg's] monologues. Have ransacked a number of books of seamen's slang and the like, to pattern M's talk on. Also, I trust that my proverbs aren't diluted too much by the fact a number of them, I've made up.

3 Dec. '81, 9:30 A.M.—This morning, and for the most part the days of this week, at last are the point at which the ms. begins to knit itself together. With no intention at all of it, I spent Monday and most of Tuesday on the Makah whaling scene, which has become one of the longer and stronger of the book, I think. At once this morning I set to reworking the ShiShi scene, and in not much more than an hour had refashioned the 3 pp. of K [the character Karlsson] at the seastacks into 4 pp., including a couple of new interior monologue grafs. Then went to Edmonds for coffee break, and while driving, 3 new bits for the ms. came to me:

—B. [the character Braaf] suggesting milk cow etc. to W's notion of wintering where they are;

—the men as chilled as if cold water had been poured into their bones;

—for the Vancouver I. [Island] section, the line 'Three times it snowed, swarm of white from out of the gray.'

▪ *Those journal entries remind me a bit of the intuitive process you followed when setting up* This House of Sky. *Did you follow the same procedure for your later books or were you more organized?*

(Laughter) Well, let me try to parse through book to book and we'll see whether it adds up to organized or not. My next book was *Winter Brothers*. Max Shulman once wrote in a humor column that I read in college in the *Daily Northwestern*, "God never told nobody to be stupid," so that's a watchword around here. I knew when *This House of Sky* had been accepted, enthused over, and nominated for a National Book Award, that was the time to get on right away with the next book idea—time not to be stupid, right? I had wanted to do something with the diaries of James Swan. My friend who'd been acting as an agent was 1,000 percent pregnant then and had to drop out of the picture, so off I went to New York. Over lunch in New York City, I told my then editor what I had in mind, and got no static. It's one of the few points in a career when you can go in and say, "I want to write about elephants" and they'll say, "OK." Out of that came in some ways my oddest book: in essence, a diary of a diary. *Winter Brothers* has always been difficult to explain, and it's always been difficult for cataloguers. Do you call it biography? No, it's partly *auto*biography, it's partly history, it's partly something else. But the book is still in print, still sells a few thousand a year—it's ended up making quite a little money for the publisher and been done on public television out here.

▪ *Did you grope your way towards that or did you understand what you wanted to do?*

I understood what I wanted to do, and I understood that I wanted to do it in one winter and day by day. So I was back there negotiating a book contract with not a hell of a long time to do all that research and all that writing, almost simultaneously, and then spend another year or so polishing it up. All that was a logistical nightmare: to know enough about Swan's diaries, as well as be at certain places during the winter in real time and coincide with his experiences at the same points of the season. But I came out of that winter with the material to do the book, did I ever.

In looking up a sociologist's reference on Swan, lucky for me the sociologist was off a few issues of an old newspaper in his citation and in one of those wrong issues, I saw [the story that became] *The Sea Runners*. Right away I ran a photocopy of that ten- or eleven-inch newspaper story. Couldn't find enough about it to do it as nonfiction, and so, being kind of a flat-footed Scotch Calvinist, I thought: "Let's see, what are the other possibilities? Well, fiction." Indeed, that became my first fiction ever. I'd never even tried a short story, but I had been a professional writer of various kinds for quite a while, so I thought, "Well, why not?" And my next four books were fiction.

I want to keep emphasizing that all this writing career of mine has behind it the best guessing eye of a person who set out to be a professional journalist from the spring of his senior year in high school. I went off to journalism school at Northwestern and I went on the job track from there as quick as I could. I've always been aware of career hurdles. You write a first book that's well accepted, well, you've got to do a good sophomore book of some kind then, don't you? It didn't bother me, from that point of view, that *Winter Brothers* was kind of strange—so much the better. And that book did fine. Then, OK, you want to write fiction—well, now you've got to write a good first novel, if you're going to keep the career going, in terms of how the book's going to sell, of trying to build it up into a living as well as a life. And everything clicked through those first three books: the first two nonfiction, and then *The Sea Runners*.

Next, I'd long had in mind to try to write about the homestead period. I took my dad out of that and wrote about his life separately in *This House of Sky*, but I still thought the homestead period in the West was a big tasty kettle of history. I wanted the writing to be about Montana, where I still had the murmurings in the inner ear from people I'd grown up around. I also knew that the story of a quarter of a million people coming to Montana to homestead, mostly in the decade pivoting on World War I, exists back in the National Archives in their individual paperwork. Scholars haven't much gotten to it. And I was aware of Montana's centennial coming at the end of the 1980s and I got to thinking, "Well, there's a lot of history there to be used. What if I do a set of books, a centennial trilogy?"

With the homestead book idea as the gangplank to all this, I plunged into the generation *after* the homesteaders, and wrote *English Creek* first. I knew it was going to be the quickest book of the three, because I had the voices in my head. Even though it's set in 1939, much of that time in Montana was quite similar to what I remember well from the late 1940s; much of Montana small-town life was frozen into place by the Depression and World War II: horses were still being used in haying, for instance. Then came buckling down to imagining the homesteaders, in *Dancing at the Rascal Fair,* ferreting out a lot of the history on my own. For all three books (the last in the trilogy was *Ride with Me, Mariah Montana*), I ran classified ads in small-town Montana newspapers asking for people who had raked hay with horses or who had done laundry for hay crews or something of that sort, to tell me about it.

■ *A lot of your last book,* Heart Earth,
had to be from your imagination.

A lot of that memoir is pedestals of fact from which I imagine, or fill out the scene around a phrase in my mother's letters, or one of my dad's stories, or an incident in an Arizona newspaper of the time. It always does have these pivots of fact: we were where I say we were at the time, German prisoners of war did escape the night I say they escaped, and when we were spooked by 'em, that became one of my dad's favorite stories. We remember certain things from childhood, but to have any dialogue from your parents, say, you've got to refashion it, re-imagine it there on the page. That's what the great autobiographical works like Kate Simon's *Bronx Primitive,* and one of my real all-time favorite books, James Herndon's *Sorrowless Times,* do.

And in *Heart Earth,* I also went back to Arizona and to Montana again. Part of the process is always going and taking a look at what I'm writing about.

■ *So you always look at settings while you're writing?*

Very much so. One of these [notebooks] is settings: Carol's slides of Fort Peck and the small towns around it and the Missouri River—for 600 miles, actually. (Laughter)

■ *Do you do the research before the books or simultaneously?*

It's always a three-ring act. To me, a book is a circus rather than a one-trick pony, and so I do as much research as I can beforehand, but

I don't postpone the writing forever for the sake of the research. I end up doing some research to fill in things after I have a lot of the draft done. I'm facing that right now in the current novel. It involves the building of the biggest earthen dam in the world during the Depression, so one of my characters is a diver. You wouldn't necessarily expect, in essence, a deep-sea diver on the Missouri River, but indeed a large part of the daily work there was that this guy had to go under the river and work on the footings of the trestles and the railroad bridges. So I've got to have a rapture-of-the-deep set of research. I'm just now starting to face that. I know what the diving suit is down to the last detail; I've put on the diving suit, mentally, time after time. That's the kind of thing you come up against as you keep pushing your characters to the edge of their own spots in life.

■ *Some fiction writers talk about their characters taking over.*
Mine do when they start getting onto the file cards, actually. Some of it is with my help, of course. It turned out I wanted to have somebody talk a certain way, so . . . Beth McCaskill in *English Creek* talks with those capital letters partly because I wanted some character to do that. [The narrator Jick McCaskill in *English Creek* remarks of his mother, Beth: ". . . (M)y mother forever tried to tell the other three of us. That the past is a taker, not a giver. It was a warning she felt she had to put out, in that particular tone of voice with punctuation all through it, fairly often in our family. When we could start hearing her commas and capital letters we knew the topic had become Facing Facts, Not Going Around with Our Heads Stuck in Yesterday."] By the time I thought of that characteristic, she was the logical candidate. So you give her that characteristic, by God. And that begins to do a lot of personality shaping for the character, and changes how certain things happen. Putting a few capital letters on a character's viewpoint has quite a ripple consequence.

In *Sea Runners*, as I worked through that book, it kept having a nineteenth-century flavor in the language. I figured, "Well, then, somebody ought to know something about the Bible, in this book." I already had the other three main characters created, so Wennberg, the fourth one to show up — the least likely to be familiar with the Bible — I thought, "Well, let him *be* the least likely," because I like to work on complicated characters.

Readers seem to like my characters, even though I'm not sure I've ever been entirely satisfied with a character. I've always wished there was a way to show a little more on the page. So I'm conscious that I want them to be surprising. I think I'm getting more of that in this novel (*Bucking the Sun*) I'm working on now. There's a series of surprises through the plot, but some of the characters do startling things, too. Anyway, yes, the characters do take on some life of their own; they certainly take on some qualities I hadn't necessarily intended. Stanley Meixell took over more of *English Creek* than I ever planned, because as I got to writing his voice and how he looked and the way he could slope into any scene . . . all of a sudden, dialogue would begin going on around him. His Missourian-Montanan way of talking gave me a way to get a lot of lingo in. I was trying to write a poetry of the vernacular into the entire trilogy, so Stanley was often the bard of that.

■ *Is writing fun?*
Well, . . .

■ *What's the most fun?*
Editing my own stuff. The drafting is difficult and the research can be awfully hard. But I suppose that's another kind of fun when you spend one of those grab-everything days—mine are often research raids where I go back to a place, almost always with Carol, and pillage in as much stuff as I can in a short time. To come back from, say, Fort Peck, Montana, which is the setting of this book, and know that we went in there and in one day found everything that a diver wore in the 1930s, and photos of this and that about the dam, well, yeah, that's fun.

■ *When I interviewed Wallace Stegner, he said that he didn't write blurbs for his students' books because he didn't have time to read them. But he wrote you blurbs. I understand he was adamant that things be accurate.*
We didn't know each other very well; we only had a couple of times together. But, yes, I think there was a mutual accuracy-admiration society. We reached where we are by doing things right, by getting things accurate, by sticking with certain things and telling other things to go to hell. Getting it as right as it can be got. He seemed genuinely to like *English Creek* and *This House of Sky* for that reason. And I think on Stegner's *Collected Stories*, the only blurb is mine. I swallowed

pretty hard when that book showed up because I'm not a short story writer. I don't even much like the format. And so I did a blurb that in essence says: "This collected work of Stegner's shows a gifted writer moving from apprenticeship work to being a master of prose." The book came out and there was a little longer than usual flap-copy biography of Stegner, so I ran my eye down to see what they'd added, which was that Stegner had won all these prizes for short stories early in his career, that I hadn't known at all. Here he had things in *Best American Short Stories* and *O. Henry Prize Stories*, year after year. But, apparently, he had liked this blurb attitude of mine: "By God, learn how to drive the nail straight." (Laughter)

Probably the acme of my freelancing was writing travel pieces for the *New York Times*. I did half a dozen there in one year and so I was, I think, their second most productive writer. Barely made any money, but I got some of the best editing in the universe. An editor there would call and say, "It's a nice piece, it's a nice piece, nice piece, nice piece . . . just needs a few fixes." (Laughter) And then, I'd redo it by about 35 percent and, indeed, the piece would be much better. Those fixes are the kind of thing I still want. How does a forest fire behave when you're setting a backfire? Carol wouldn't let me go see for myself (laughter), so I had to ask the forest rangers. The forest fire scene in *English Creek*—four forest rangers of four different generations read that for me, and each one had a different angle on it. And the Russian lingo in *Mariah Montana*—my college Russian is pretty rusty, so a University of Washington professor fixed up my phonetic Russian. And there are going to be engineers to be talked to on this dam book.

▓ *Elizabeth Simpson's book about you*
suggests you like fiction to be moral.

Why I don't give a Goddamn about Donald Barthelme's work and yet think Russell Hoban's tricky book *Riddley Walker* is high art, I can't entirely spell out for you, except that to me there's not the breath of real life in, say, the fancy-pants attitude of Barthleme's work. Metafiction, I guess, is what I'm writing off. Minimalism, too. On the other hand, I deeply admire experiments pushing the edges in fictional *technique*. But I think you ought to be able to see in a writer's work something of that writer, whether it's his guts or his brains. Hemingway—it was sometimes his muscles, but so what? They were good muscles.

■ *There also seems a moral impetus for some of your work. I read that indignation over Spiro Agnew's book contract helped motivate you to write* This House of Sky. *You also seem concerned about the environment.*

Back when I was beginning seriously to work on *This House of Sky*, Watergate came into the open. Let's remember, it's not simply the example of Agnew; almost any co-conspirator, indicted or otherwise, got a book contract or a television miniseries out of one of the biggest cases of public corruption in our history. Agnew's was a fiction contract; there was no reason in the world for him to get that. Spiro T. Agnew writing a novel! Now there's a spur to a professional writer to show the SOBs how it's really done, to get on with my family's story that I'd been telling myself I intended to tell. And I told it. What the bastards do in public life indeed is part of my writing motivation.

Environmental concerns are major with me, too. Much of my freelance life here locally, much of the writing was for a regional magazine called *Pacific Search*, where we were trying to cover environmental issues.

I've thought of myself as a grown-up since about the time I was six, and so I think things count in life. What politicians do, counts. What corporations do, counts. What I do, counts—I and my family tree of writers like Stegner and Mari Sandoz, Hamlin Garland, people who came out of the outback of this country.

■ *When you say, "Writing is a living as well as a life,"* *what's particularly interesting about that life, as* *opposed to, say, a teaching life?*

Well, the chance to be creatively lonesome. And I'm semi-serious about that. The chance to sit around alone and make the language dance is what's behind all of this.

■ *Is that why you like editing best?*

I'm probably a more natural editor than I am a first-drafter, so, yes, the farther along I am in work on a manuscript, the happier I am. An entrancement with language and a curiosity and a kind of a lust to see what can be done with it, I suppose, must ultimately be behind all this. The freelance life, the book-writing life is a chance to do it on your own high wire rather than somebody else's high wire. You don't know how those other buggers put up the high wire. (Laughter) One of the books I've liked and thought most deeply through is Anthony Storr's *Solitude*. He writes about the work being the companion, and that registers with me. I'm from a line of people where that was always partly true, often pretty fully true of their lives.

■ *Really hard workers.*

Yeah, I am from a line of people who worked themselves to death, and from a part of the country where that was often the case. I can recognize that way of life, and Stegner did too. I hope people take various things from my books, but sometimes it's enough that they just savvy we're not alone in this hard business of life. I think it doesn't hurt that some of us are examples of not ending up in some trash bin of life just because things were tough.

Sad things do happen. Strange things happen. My writing contemporary Mary Clearman Blew (author of *All But the Waltz* and *Balsamroot*), who grew up in Montana not far from where I did, has had some tough things in her life, and I'm pretty proud of the fact that Mary and I have ended up as two of the writers pointed to in our generation.

It says something about human capacities that books, if they're worth a damn, have some moral quotient in them. People read books for sustenance. Some of that is intellectual, but some of it is a sustenance of life. What does the book's language do; how does this writer fit the language to the story; what story is he telling; "Gosh, is it anything like *my* life's story?" Or, "This is the kind of story I've never heard before, but, God, isn't it interesting?"

May 20, 1995

JIM HARRISON

PEOPLE WITH CURIOSITY ARE ALWAYS RIGHT OUT THERE

Jim Harrison demonstrates what he means when he describes the writer as a hero of consciousness: He spends years recording notes and images before becoming deeply enough immersed in the reality of his novels to begin them. At the same time, he seeks out situations that coax him beyond the limits of his "own brain," producing work that meets particular formal requirements, losing himself in characters totally unlike himself, and doing botanical research. When Harrison declares that "people with curiosity are always right out there," he describes himself.

Harrison has published poetry, novels, a memoir, and short story and nonfiction collections. His writing has won high praise from critics and fellow writers like Raymond Carver, who said that Harrison's novella, Legends of the Fall, *"can stand with the best examples the form has to offer—those by Conrad, Chekhov, Mann, James, Melville, Lawrence, Isak Dinesen."* The Beast That God Forgot *was named a* New York Times *Notable Book and was on the* Los Angeles Times Book Review's *list of the best fiction of 2000. His recent publications include a memoir,* Off to the Side; *a novel,* True North; The Raw and the Cooked: Adventures of a Roving Gourmand; *and* Braided Creek: A Conversation in Poetry *(with Ted Kooser).*

■ *An editor suggested I interview people about their writing processes, whether they write with pencils or pens . . .*

The things that get people going—that's very strange. So-and-so has to have seven sharpened pencils and somebody has to have a Bic rolling writer, needle point. It's all very crazy. It's got something to do with magic, so the process always has all these little secret reasons. I can't stand computers or anything like that because I don't like electrical noises. It's that absurd. For years, I couldn't write anywhere except at my cabin and my house and then my office in the granary, but two years ago I got liberated and wrote a novella in a motel in Montana. I felt splendid because then I wasn't locked into those places.

All that stuff is primitive. Writers are one beat from the tom-tom. It's got something to do with tools and hunting and gathering; it's a ritual they think begins to open the door. The first thing Dr. Weisinger, who was my mentor, pointed out . . . this was before the Tang dynasty in China, a poet Wang Wei said, "Who knows what causes the opening and closing of the door?" for a writer. It shows you where we come from.

In the Paris Review interview you said a writer should be a hero of consciousness. What did you mean?

I meant in the amplitude and dimensions of consciousness he's willing to go. You can't hold back. You don't want to narrow the spectrum of consciousness for some political or religious ideal. I think Robert Graves said you can't have any higher fidelity to your art than your art, so you'd better keep loose and separate it from preoccupations and clubs and associations that might limit your consciousness. Sometimes, naturally, it's no fun; but that's what you're supposed to do. (Laughter)

You talk about Jung and Hillman . . . and I think of the hero in Jungian terms as also willing to face the underside.

Well, always. I never understood writers' aversion for psychoanalysis or therapy because the knots prevent the free flow of consciousness. Every culture talks about them. Buddhist writers, Tang poets, for instance, are always talking about having to deal with the demons.

You said you write from images and then you talked about dreams supplying you with images.

Well, sometimes they do. That's inadvertent. That's your nonlocal mind continuing to work while you're asleep. So it's not anything mysterious.

Do you write your dreams down?

Very, very rarely because I'm interested in the images that stick of their own accord. Some things are so powerful they cause dreams almost immediately. I've cooked bear stews and I invariably dream about bears that night, but that could be my own goofy head because they've always been a very powerful animal to me. It takes something as powerful as a bear . . . (laughter); when you eat applesauce, you don't dream about apples. (Laughter)

■ *You don't write your dreams down, so when you write . . .*
Well, sometimes I have a notebook that I record little images or just little . . . I published part of the notebooks I wrote for *Dalva* and that's the kind of thing. Sometimes they're just little philosophical nexuses of what I'm working on at the time; they can be totally peripheral to the thrust of the narrative. Once you properly set people in motion, they develop their own lives and you don't have total control.

■ *It's just an intuitive decision to keep a notebook or to write a poem?*
Yes. And then sometimes I'll go a month without writing anything because I don't want to, again, get another habit and I know people who got into tremendous problems becoming addicted to their notebooks.

■ *In the Paris Review interview you said you generally write best from two to four in the afternoon and from eleven to one at night.*
Yeah, that's the best. That's the *hot* period that I would like to defeat, but I haven't been able to. I just am a victim of this rhythm and lately up in the Upper Peninsula I've been able to write in the morning.
People have circadian cycles. I write fiction on about a two to two-and-a-half-year cycle between books and I cannot seem to change that cycle. I would like to be writing on some fiction all the time; but I just can't do it because what happens to me, . . . like this new *Julip*, I've thought about the essential story now for twelve years, and *Dalva* was four or five years, and I think *Woman Lit by Fireflies* was three years and, again, it's an accretion of images to understand character. And—UH.

■ *Did you keep notebooks all those years?*
A little bit, but you know, oddly enough, I take out boxes of notes on *Dalva* that I made and then never look at them during composition. I might look at them before I start again. They're up in a loft right over my head and I sometimes glance up at them.

■ *So it's just the process of writing down those images; it's not that you use them in any direct way.*

No, one will unfold another, one will unfold another, sometimes. That Neruda quote that seized me so much: "The heart is an interminable artichoke," that kind of thing. Yes. Or the inmost leaf of the flower, whatever goes for poetry. Rilke, what was that thing?:

Oh, Rose
Oh, pure delight
Contradiction of being
No one's sleep under so many lids.

You know how he can do it when nobody else can. But consciousness, . . . we're either lapsed or evolving. When we're evolving, images tend to flow without dams.

■ *Do you plot your novels?*

Very vaguely. It might have something to do with locations that are particularly poignant to me, the spirit of place. But just someone's story . . . say, in *Farmer* I liked that Greek form where everybody knows what's going to happen. I start with Joseph and Rosealee at the ocean; I start with the end of the novel, then I make them forget it. And when they get to the end, [they] say, "Oh my God, we should have known."

Wolf was an interesting situation because I plotted it out like a musical scale. I saw its shape abstractly. I used to try to memorize scores and then play them over in my own head and see how close they came out to the playing time. I used to do that with Stravinsky. I would listen to the music a lot, then I would take an old railroad watch, and I would go for a walk and play it and see how close I came. It's sort of an insane thing to do.

■ *Do you know why you did it?*

Because I love the abstract shape. My first novellas were all thirty-three pages, thirty-three pages, thirty-three pages, and a one-page epigraph. And I still know how on page 19, say, they will come out perfectly to one hundred. I like the play involved in forms. I like the artificiality of forms, or else I would become totally victimized by my brain.

Come to think of it—I forget this stuff all the time, mostly because I hardly ever do interviews, so I never have the occasion to think about it—I think some of the first suites were all that thirty-three, thirty-three, thirty-three, too.

Someone had noted all these visual images in my work and then I started thinking, "Well, that makes sense because I first wanted to be a painter." A couple years ago, a curator I know got me into the Gauguin exhibit very early in the morning before it opened and I could wander around there. Sobbing, I was . . . (Laughter) It's just . . . Oh, God. He was always my great hero because when I started I wanted to wear a turtleneck and paint nude girls, that kind of crap.

■ *Can you write poetry all the time?*

No. Like I wrote a poem last week and I think it was the first one in six months. Poetry, . . . you can lose your voice by behaving badly. I've been doing a lot of film work for years, just to make money, greed . . . I've had a screen nightmare for about two years I'm finally cutting out of my life—the usual Hollywood problems. That is more destructive to poetry than it is novels. Right in the middle of my worst Hollywood nightmare ever I wrote this novella *Julip* and didn't think about my problems while I was writing it. But a poem will tend to stay out of touch with you during those crazy times. A poem is just much more fragile. Dylan Thomas, for instance, wrote nineteen screenplays or something—not very good; I read a few of them. But he certainly didn't write "The force that through the green fuse drives the flower" during his screen meetings in London, I can guarantee it.

■ *Someone I spoke to said the problem is that*
writing films is writing for committee.

All the stuff about the *auteur*, that's garbage. Writers in Hollywood know it's a collaborative medium and it's really a director's medium. But that doesn't mean you can endure radically changing the nature of a story. They junk it up. That was the pathetic thing about *Revenge*. John Huston was going to direct, but Warner's didn't want him and then when it finally was made ten years later, they ruined it by junking it up—throwing in bugles, turtles . . .

This latest screen[play] [*Wolf*] originally came from Eliade and Jung's *Symbols of Transformation* and Inuit folklore and so on, about both men and women under extremist pressures. A traditional way of treating them, in hundreds of cultures, is for them to go into their animal, whatever their animal is, for a few days. You usually come out changed, physical and mental illness being thought to be the same thing with these people. Then, sometimes, you don't come out of the animal. I was trying to explain this to these Hollywood people—they're bright people, too—but this is the kind of information they *don't* readily take to. So, naturally, they're making it into somewhat of a fucking werewolf movie, which just drives me crazy, but there's nothing I can do about it.

I was trying to explain to them [that] in a Cheyenne bear ceremony, they're sitting around in their tepee, invoking the bear, they've been doing it for days, and they think, "Uh-oh, look at Frank over there," and Frank's jaw protrudes and hair grows on his face and then he disappears under the ground and they never see him again. He's become a bear. Well, there's just no way [for them] to deal with this kind of information and I should have known better. I'd been talking to Herbert [Weisinger] about it. Herbert said, "How would you have thought otherwise?" That's the wisdom of certain people, especially if they've been to the Warburg Institute, hung out with the Panofskys at the Princeton Institute, that level of iconography. So I'm not the first one who's been treed by this. These disappointments are hideously ordinary. I should have known from reading Blake: you don't give your heart to an institution. How is this different from all these men who are invariably six feet two—they gave their hearts to General Motors and now they're out?

I remember telling a bunch of Hollywood big wheels this great thing I discovered lately was on real moonlit nights to go way out in the wilderness in the UP [Upper Peninsula of Michigan] and walk around alone in the forest to frighten myself. They said, "WHAT?" (Laughter) Then they know you're different.

◾ *You write so much.*

You're back to Blake, "The cistern contains, the fountain overflows" and you wish to be a fountain and you'd better make yourself a fountain or you're going to be dead as a doornail as an artist. "Flow," that's what's behind *The Theory and Practice of Rivers.* Or that story of a Chippewa shaman who became a creek and, unfortunately, couldn't stop being a creek. (Laughter) It's that sense of flow. I got it again my last experience in LA. It finally became unendurable so I went over to a bookstore and got a book I loved but I hadn't read in fifteen years and I wondered if it would still do it: Pablo Neruda's *Memoirs.* And, WOOOOO; it's so incredibly powerful. It was very hard on the studio.

I made them cry. I didn't answer the phone. I walked around a garden smelling flowers and looking at colors at UCLA. I could have given less a shit. It made me dysfunctional. (Laughter)

■ *Could you please explain this passage from your poem called "Acting":*

When you wake in the night,
the freedom of the nightmare
turned to dream follows you
into morning, and there is no
skin on earth you cannot enter.

That's why I like being older, frankly, because I studied a lot of very old Zen Buddhist texts for a long time in Dogen, who's the classic from fourteenth-century Japan. He said this alarming but painfully true thing: "To study the self is to forget the self; to forget the self is to be one with ten thousand things." When you're released from your obsessions with banality and you get to be a tree or a creek or a bird or a woman . . . That's how you enter into character, by giving yourself up. You can't enter into character if you're carrying yourself along with you.

I started writing fiction in my mid-to-late twenties, but I only could write inner versions of myself. Much of the content of male American fiction is nifty guys at loose ends and that's what I lost patience with: that narrowness of vision. "I'm bad, but I'm really neat." That kind of bullshit. That became so tiresome, I couldn't stand that kind of persona either to read or write about.

It wasn't, say, until *Sundog* that I could really, totally enter different characters. Even in *Legends of the Fall*, well, I could in my own mind extrapolate Tristan, in *Legends*, or Nordstrom, in *The Man Who Gave Up His Name*, or Cochran, in *Revenge*, but . . . *Sundog* went much further. I could invent, enter someone totally unlikely for myself and then even further in *Dalva*, yeah, or *The Woman Lit by Fireflies*. That's fascinating to me . . . to let go of everything.

A novella I just wrote, *Julip*, which is a twenty-one-year-old girl and her three much older lovers, which is intriguing to me because, say, you're forty-eight and you have a lover who's twenty, twenty-one, only slowly it occurs to you, possibly, what do you look like to her. What is this experience for her? It's sort of startling, not altogether pleasant . . .

■ *There was an essay you wrote in 1982 about wanting to change your life and you were writing notes for a book. Was that* Sundog?

It must have been *Sundog*. That was called "Fording and Dread," I think. It was the dread you have of sea changes.

■ *You talked about the anima [Jung's term for the female component of male character]. So I wondered if writing* Dalva *in the voice of a woman was also part of that process.*

Actually, I didn't write the novel I intended. She entered. It was going to be about a great grandfather and her grandfather who sort of raised her and then she took over. I had a dream of what she looked like. That image of someone from the Sandhills of Nebraska sitting on a balcony in Santa Monica looking at the Pacific at night was very evocative to me. So then she just took [over].

■ *You said in the* Paris Review *interview that when writing on* Dalva, *you could work in the morning. You said, "She gets me up."*

Yeah, yeah, well, the curious thing with her is that I had to stay so attentive to her voice and her moods because it was so different for me that I really had to behave well. When I finished, it was a surge. When I finished the last sections, my doctor said both my eardrums were broken and I had no thyroid sign. I had just ignored everything. I'd had the flu and infections in my ears . . . the mindlessness. At that point, it really is a demon thing.

I hung up on some newspaper interview about the woman's voice thing. I finally realized, "This asshole doesn't even know who Flaubert is." I said, "Well, look, Flaubert, *Madame Bovary* or certainly *Emma* . . . Emily Brontë understood Heathcliff better than any man could because she could see that feralness more lucidly." So I said, "Writers are essentially androgynous." He said, "What's that mean?" I said, "Oh, fuck you!" BANG. (Laughter)

Of the two or three hundred letters or more I got from women about *Dalva*, there was only one that said, "How dare you?" So a lot of that harshness is gone away now, which is much a relief. I'm no longer a MACHO PIG, whatever that is.

But the power comes from that androgyny, I'm sure, because traditionally, if you go back, a writer is a version of a priest or a shaman. And those are all somewhat androgynous professions. I don't mean in terms of sexual practice, but it made Ernest Hemingway extremely nervous. That's the liberation that's gone on: "Who cares?" Just simply who cares except for the quality of the work and the experience?

■ *You said working on* Dalva *you did a lot of research. Had you done that before?*

No, I hadn't and I loved that. Now I've got a botanical monograph on the wild flowers of the great plains. I'm just no good at stuff like that, but I wandered around (laughter) and I finally got one I can identify.

■ *You clearly read all kinds of things. Is there any logic to that?*

I don't read much crap anymore, but I read widely whether it's botany or ornithology or history or psychiatry, just out of curiosity. It's what I gave *Dalva* and that's the thing that gets people through life: people with intense curiosity are always right out there. That gets you away from self-absorption or disappearing up your own ass, which so many people do.

■ *Do you read things connected to what you're writing or do you just read . . .*

Oh, sometimes, around, peripherally, and then, . . . like when I wander around the Sandhills, I stop in historical museums. The best one is the Nebraska State Historical Society at Lincoln [, which] has [an] immense photographic collection headed by this guy John Carter, who did books of early photographs of the West. For instance—I haven't used it yet—I saw a photo taken in 1912: a man in a suit and a chesterfield coat and a bowler hat in front of this enormous house and he had two wolves on leashes. Now there's something there, right? (Laughter) I love this book by Alain Fournier, *The Wanderer*, about a guy that finds this farmhouse back in the forest. He meets this lovely woman and then he goes back home to settle affairs so he can come back and he can never find the place again.

That's what I said about *Dalva*. The subject is the character of longing in American fiction; longing is everywhere.

■ *Last night you said writing is a guild, not a sack race.*

I didn't and still don't feel competitive at all. Everybody dies and nobody wins. And I'm not going to lose energy in this kind of thing. Competitiveness destroys the spirit. Either some of my books will be durable or they won't; I can't do anything about that. Someone said in the *London Times* that I was immortal and I thought, "Does that mean I can take out the garbage in three hundred years?" Things are moving so fast now immortality only lasts for a month.

November 7, 1992

$\mathcal{M}$ARGOT LIVESEY

WITH EACH BOOK, I'M LEARNING HOW TO WRITE THAT BOOK

Margot Livesey's modesty pervades this interview: she jokes that Brian Moore may have stopped instructing her out of boredom, not because her story was finished and friends had to persuade her that her novel Eva Moves the Furniture *worked. This humility undoubtedly helps explain the escalating quality of her work, since it prods her to not only keep perfecting her craft but also to test her perceptions and assumptions with research.*

Livesey's fifth novel, Eva Moves the Furniture, *was a New York Times* Notable Book of the year, *a PEN/Winship finalist, and an Atlantic Monthly* best book of the year. *Livesey grew up in Scotland, graduated from York University in England, and now lives in Boston, where she is writer-in-residence at Emerson College. She has taught at a number of universities, including Williams, Brandeis, Tufts, and the University of Iowa Writers' Workshop. Livesey recently published* Banishing Verona.

■ *You've said that after you produced a bad novel at the same time that your boyfriend wrote a philosophy book, you vowed to learn how to write fiction. You obviously succeeded. Did you teach yourself?*

Regrettably, I did largely teach myself to write. Growing up in Britain and going to a British university, I didn't have the concept that creative writing was something which could be taught or could be learned. So my role models were Charlotte Brontë, say: you sit in a parsonage in some lonely place and then suddenly you write wonderful fiction. I did study with two people. I saw advertised in the University of Toronto newspaper that the current writer-in-residence, the Irish-Canadian writer Brian Moore, had office hours. I was working as a waitress, but I made an appointment to see him and I took him the same story nine weeks in a row. Every week, he read the story aloud to me, imitating all the parts. On the ninth week, he declared, perhaps out of self-defense or boredom, that the story might be finished. I was so startled I said, "I'm not at the university; I'm not really meant to be here talking to you." And he said, "Well, I knew that all along." (Laughter) "None of the students wanted to talk to me." He was amazingly helpful because he showed me that I knew more about my work than I'd realized. Previously, when I was rereading my work, I'd thought, "This scene is boring to me because I wrote it. If I was reading it for the first time, I'd find it riveting." What I realized with Brian Moore's help was that if a scene was going to be interesting to the reader, it was going to be interesting to me; if it was boring to me, it was going to be boring to the reader. That made an enormous difference in how I continued to read my own fiction.

Then I was part, again for only a few months, of a workshop in New York taught by a Canadian writer named Linda Svendsen. Being with other people struggling to learn to write was very helpful in a different way: I suddenly thought, "Oh, there are other people trying to do this." And realizing how many different ways there were of reading things because of the different priorities people have. Those were my only two more formal educational experiences. Everything else was reading and writing and struggling on my own.

■ *Some of your comments suggest that you read experimental writing and then tried out the techniques in your first short story collection,* Learning by Heart.
Yes, Yes.

■ *Was that a way of teaching yourself?*
Very much so. Like many young writers, I was intrigued by the flowering of experimental fiction in America in the late sixties and seventies: Pynchon and Sorrentino and Barthelme and Barth come to mind, and Richard Brautigan and Janet Kauffman. As I've got older, I've leaned more towards William Trevor's view of experiments: he said that he regarded himself as an experimental writer but that all the experiments were hidden. So I think of myself as still experimenting, but, on the whole, the experiments are hidden, for good or ill, from my readers.

It surprised me that you got a degree in philosophy and literature because the stories at the center of your work are so compelling. I would think someone with a degree in philosophy would write illustrated concepts rather than stories. And I was even more surprised to discover that you often have a conceptual pattern in mind when you write, like the range of ideas about memory that you embody in The Missing World.

Well, I certainly had the idea of writing a novel that revolved around the issues and questions about memory. It took reading and research and writing the novel to get me to the point where I began to fully distinguish different kinds of memory and to evolve my own theories about the relationship between the individual and his or her memories. But it's true that when I start my novels I usually have a destination that I'm heading for that is something that you might describe as theoretical, but, like my experiments, I make considerable efforts to disguise that. (Laughter)

When I cast around for the idea for a novel, what I look for is an intersection between my private interests and public interests. For instance, in the case of *Criminals,* there was a lot of public interest at that time, the early nineties, about choices between adoptive and biological and surrogate and natural parents: ethical issues that hadn't arisen before in our Western society. Similarly, when I wrote *The Missing World,* there were lots of questions about buried memories and recovered memories and Alzheimer's and was it a good idea to try to invent drugs that would repress traumatic memories. I have a private interest in memory for a number of fairly blatant reasons: as a person living in a foreign country, I'm very dependent on my memory to make my life whole.

You've said that it's more challenging to write about the present than the past.

I have a number of dear friends who write wonderful historical novels and I admire what they do immensely. For me, the present still remains a big challenge: how to make sense of the seemingly endless chaos around us. I think that's the project of fiction. Fiction writers and fiction readers are deeply committed to this and even if you try to stop your readers making sense of something, they'll do it anyway, if they possibly can. So, for instance, if you have an adult character and he or she has some childhood memories, the reader thinks of the childhood memories as being causally significant in the life of the adult. Readers are very committed to motivation and motivation is a very comforting aspect of fiction. Whereas in the real world we often, rather disturbingly, can't figure out what motivates things.

■ *How do you begin to write? Do you write short pieces*
that eventually fall into patterns or do you have a plot?
If I have the right kind of opening chapter, then, hopefully, that will drive the novel forward. My novels are quite purposefully organized and, particularly in the case of *Criminals* and *The Missing World,* have an opening chapter that hopefully says to the reader, "Dear Reader, Come in!" (Laughter) "Come and spend some time with me, please." Sometimes, I spend a lot of time trying to find that opening or sometimes I get lucky and I find it right away.

■ *You said that you begin writing your works with an optimistic view*
that darkens as the novel proceeds. How do you explain that?
I don't know how that happens exactly. I was talking to an eight-year-old friend of mine about her stories and she said that the hardest part was writing the ending. I said, "Why is that so hard?" She said, "Well, at the end of the story you have to decide if the good guys or the bad guys are going to win." That's the dilemma of the adult fiction writer also: we're always divided, I think, between wanting that happy ending, that "Reader, I married him" sort of ending, in which marriage feels like the end of the story, and that other, lonelier, more existential, gloomier part of us that just doesn't believe in happy endings. I think it's quite a struggle for writers in this time and this century to figure out a satisfying ending.

■ *Settings are important to you in your work. And I notice you*
go back to England regularly and maybe even to Scotland . . .
Yes, Yes. I go back to both places. It's helpful for me to be confronted by the sensual detail of whatever I'm writing about. Britain is very different in lots of ways than America, so I'm glad that I get to go back frequently.

■ *You've said that doing research for your work gives you detail that*
sets off your imagination. Could you please explain that?

Well, I think we imagine the world in clichés. For instance, for *The Missing World*, I interviewed a woman who at a fairly young age had suddenly started having epileptic seizures and, as a result, lost her memory, and she talked about how disconcerting it was to have a friend come and visit her in hospital and the friend's hair was extremely different than she remembered and it was the first time she really had this visceral sense, "Oh, I have lost my memory." Little things like that make it real to me. That's why talking to individuals or looking at letters or diaries or interviews is just so helpful to getting a sense of the individual experiences.

▓ *Does teaching help your writing?*

Teaching has been very helpful to me in a number of ways. It gives me intimate access to the experience of many young Americans. I've learned a great deal about American life from talking to my students and reading their work. As you get older, you do lose touch with what it's like to be different ages, and your own imaginings and memories are subject to terrific revisionism, and so reading work in the presence of my students is also a very illuminating experience. To take an obvious example, it's very interesting to hear what they say about *Catcher in the Rye* compared to what I say about it. And we talk about the basic questions of making stories: What engages a reader's interest? What makes readers want to keep reading? What makes readers feel that they know characters? It's a luxury to be paid to explore those questions with other people. So I've felt very fortunate in that respect.

▓ *Some men I've interviewed have said that they found it exhilarating to write in a woman's voice because they loved getting caught in this other perspective.*

The challenge is always to imagine the other and writing as a man fascinates me in lots of ways. For instance, when a female character is hard pressed, we so often have her cry. If you're writing about a male character, you tend to use tears very sparingly, so you find other ways of expressing emotion; writing about men has helped me get better at thinking how to express emotion in a more interesting way for my female characters.

One of the hard things about writing about women is that women's lives are often very caught up in the particulars of daily life and the particulars of the body: what's in the fridge, how they look, how their child is managing. I think that's one of the great pleasures of reading things like *To the Lighthouse*, the way that Woolf captures so many of these small moments of being. For me one of the challenges of writing about women is to do justice to some of the minutiae around women's lives.

■ *You've said that all the books you wrote before* Eva Moves the Furniture *prepared you to write that novel. Could you please explain that?*

I began *Eva Moves the Furniture* in 1987 with the thought that I would write either a novella or a short novel very loosely on the life of my mother. And, almost immediately, I hit a wall and turned to other material: I wrote a novel called *Homework*. After I'd written *Homework*, I then went back to *Eva Moves the Furniture* and I worked on it fairly stubbornly for four or five years while also writing short stories. I simply couldn't make it work and I was driving myself and everyone I knew crazy by inflicting the manuscript on them and inflicting it on myself. So I decided to stop and I wrote a draft of my novel *Criminals* in three weeks with the help of my friend Andrea Barrett. We were at MacDowell Artists' Colony together. After this *long* struggle with *Eva Moves the Furniture*, I wanted to write something and know it would work. I didn't want to be sinking into another morass.

I revised *Criminals* for a year. When I finished, I went back to *Eva Moves the Furniture* and after four or five months had the same feeling of sinking into this quagmire of pages I couldn't fix. I turned away again to write *The Missing World*. After I wrote *The Missing World*, I once again had the feeling (that I had begun to regard as totally illusory), that I could finish *Eva Moves the Furniture*, that now I knew enough technically to finish the novel and I knew what the problems were. And, surprisingly, it actually turned out to be true. (Laughter) But I'd had the feeling so often by this point that I was not the first one to recognize that.

■ *You've said you had to learn to write* Eva Moves the Furniture *in first person. Why that was so difficult?*

A very few things came from the beginning of the novel in 1987; and one of those was that the main character was going to die as my mother had died at an early age, an early age for her and a still earlier age for me. So to use the first person voice for a character who is dead did not seem like a natural choice. Also, it was one thing to attempt to bring my mother to life on the page; it was another to say, "I will be inside your brain and your body." Initially, it felt like trespassing and I had to get over that.

Other women I've interviewed about their writing careers have said that their mothers played important roles. Does that make any sense to you?

For people who have mothers, yes. For many years I thought of myself as motherless. Writing *Eva Moves the Furniture* did finally give me the sense that I have a mother. Insofar as being an influence on my work, I'd have to say though that no project I've attempted has made me so miserable and proved so tiresome in so many ways, privately and professionally. I think, of course, the reason for my stubbornness in persisting with the project was because of the personal nature of the material, but that was also the trap. I was very aware that everybody has a mother: why should you be interested in mine? The personal nature of the material often seemed like more of a liability than an asset, so I don't know what I'd say about my mother being an influence on my work. (Laughter) One of the few things I know about her is that she did love reading and books, but other than that, I don't know.

The amount of time it takes you to write each novel differs, doesn't it? You said you wrote Criminals *quite quickly and . . .*

It seems to vary a lot for all kinds of reasons that I wish I understood better. Sometimes I'll write things quite quickly and then I'll spend a lot of time revising and adjusting them. Sometimes I write much more slowly and revise more as I go along . . . There doesn't seem to be one process or the other. But I do think that with each book, in a sense I'm learning how to write that book, so I don't think of novel writing as a very efficient process. There's always a kind of education going on.

Some authors consciously set out to challenge themselves by writing different kinds of things. Given the variety of ways you've found to test and complicate your perspective, I would guess you're one of those writers.

One of the dangers of getting older as a writer is that most writers use up their natural material; if they keep going as writers they have to start looking in a more intellectual way for material, to keep bringing in new stuff. So, of course, I'm concerned to try new things. I've also become increasingly aware that it's surprisingly easy to find yourself drawn into certain kinds of repetition. We all have blueprints that we come back to unless we make a very conscious effort to avoid them.

I do think as I get older writing, in some ways, gets harder because I would like to believe that whatever I'm working on next is going to be richer, fuller. But you have your own work at your back and then you also have the work of your many glorious contemporaries and predecessors . . . it gets complicated.

One's ambitions for one's work change as one gets older as well. In some ways, I'm a very typical writer in having begun by writing an intensely domestic novel, *Homework*, where almost everything takes place within the house. In later books my characters increasingly go out into the world and are less bound by the family. I hope that trajectory will continue.

▪ *Your work has gotten richer, I think.* Eva Moves the Furniture *is an incredible novel. How can you set creating fuller work as a goal and how do you achieve it?*

It seems an impossible goal to have because you worry if you look at the goal too directly, that it will sabotage you. In the case of *Eva*, finally being able to finish the book resulted from a sort of hopelessness about it ever being in the larger world. I thought, "I will finish the book to my own satisfaction and I will photocopy it for the dozen friends who've read it for me at various times and it will be *done*." It was very personally distressing to me that it was not *done*; all these drafts in my study weighed on me terribly. There was something liberating about not worrying about how agents and editors and reviewers would regard my efforts. I was very much writing for myself and the few readers I cherished. How one can capture that on other occasions is less clear to me, Nancy.

One of the reasons writing remains so interesting is that there is something ineffable about almost every stage of writing. Why as readers we look at black marks on the page and then picture Jane Eyre and Mr. Rochester, I have no idea. That ineffable quality stretches all the way from the mysterious origins of our work to the vexed commercial question of what makes a best seller. My hunch is that we come to reading and writing so early in our lives that it's harder to figure out what's going on, on either side of the page. Words are simultaneously our allies and our adversaries and it takes a special kind of energy to keep looking for the best words and putting them in the best possible order to tell our stories.

April 15, 2004

Bobbie Ann Mason

IT'S THIS IMPULSE TOWARD ORDER, THE PLEASURE
OF DISCOVERING DESIGN

Bobbie Ann Mason reports that the time she spent in the Northeast getting a PhD in English diverted her from the writing she had always wanted to do and even caused her to doubt that she could use her own experiences and perspectives to make literature. Eventually, she found her way back to both Kentucky and fiction writing. This interview reveals that the aesthetic sense she first developed making quilts with her grandmother shaped both her brief career as an academic and her long, extremely successful one producing fiction.

In addition to novels and short story collections, Bobbie Ann Mason has published literary analyses, a memoir, and a biography of Elvis. Her novel In Country *was made into a film. She won a National Book Critics Circle Award nomination, an American Book Award nomination, a PEN/Faulkner Award for fiction nomination, the Ernest Hemingway Foundation Award for* Shiloh and Other Stories, *a National Book Critics Circle Award nomination, and the Southern Book Award for* Feather Crowns.

▨ *You've suggested that going north to get a PhD in English interfered with your finding the confidence to write about the material that was natural to you.*

I came from a culture that insisted on your inferiority. Not only were you inferior in your own world, but you were more inferior when you went north because it was an image we had of Yankees (laughter): they were the winners; they looked down on us. I doubt if the Yankees actually had us on their minds, but when I moved north, I felt very keenly how I had been held back intellectually and had not been taught to use my imagination.

The intellectual part of it was the hardest because I was in graduate school and I wasn't prepared to be there. I loved to read and write, but

I had been taught to study in a very traditional way: memorize the material, consume it, and regurgitate it. I didn't come up with ideas the way other people did in graduate classes. It took me a while to realize that I didn't need to feel inferior for not being prepared. But still, that experience was shattering. It stopped up my mind so that I felt I couldn't get through this big mental block, created by fear. I've never really gotten over it.

I look at a book like Annie Dillard's *An American Childhood*, her memoir of growing up and her sensibility as a writer, and *Speak Memory* by Nabokov, and I see what talented people could do if they had the resources and the exposure as they were growing up. Nabokov knew all these languages and poetry and Annie Dillard had gone to the big library in Pittsburgh and was probably reading Jane Austen and Freud by the time she was ten, or eight. (Laughter) I didn't have any of that. When I went to graduate school, I had a lot of catching up to do, and because I was so frightened, I feel I didn't get to use as much of my imagination and mental ability that I might have. On the other hand, I had a unique background that gave me the material and the impetus to write. And I did write, so I'm very thankful for that.

> *You've said that reading Lee Smith's work*
> *gave you permission to do your own.*

In the mid-seventies, I read Lee Smith's first novel. I was probably about thirty-six at the time. And I thought, "Oh, I recognize this; I recognize the language." It helped me a great deal, as did Lisa Alther's *Kinflicks*. Those were the first inklings that there was a subject matter out there that I could do something with. I had been working on a short novel about a twelve-year-old based on my background.

> *When I read your book on Nabokov [Nabokov's Garden: A Guide to*
> *Ada (1974)] and then read The Girl Sleuth (1975), it was as though*
> *two different people had written them. The Nabokov book was an*
> *objective analysis, but The Girl Sleuth had a personal voice. You not*
> *only use "I," you talk about sitting around eating hard candy and*
> *devouring Nancy Drew books.*

Nabokov was a doctoral dissertation. I wrote *The Girl Sleuth* right after grad school as an antidote. It was like a vacation (laughter) and a full circle back to my childhood. It shouldn't be surprising that I wrote both, though, if you look at the kind of sensibility I have. Nabokov appealed to me more than any author because he was interested in the detail, the design, the shiver of recognition, the pleasures of life and the patterns we find, and, in retrospect, *The Girl Sleuth* seems an account of the sensibility of the writer, how I learned to look at things. There was a lot about my personal way of reading things, about coming from an isolated rural background with the desire to go on a vacation, to go to a big city. It was about dreams and aspirations; it was about textures—I was working all that through.

■ *You published two academic books quite quickly,*
so it seems odd to me that you felt like a failure.
Well, I felt a failure as an academic. I didn't really have that kind of mind. What I always wanted to do was write fiction, so I slowly, slowly made my way into that. I did have a great feeling of—I wouldn't say "ambition," exactly, but determination and perseverance.

■ *That seems brave.*
Oh, I didn't think it was brave. When I got out of college, I moved straight to New York. I didn't know a soul and people told me, "Oh, that was so brave." I didn't think of it as brave at all. I just thought, "I'm gettin' outta here." (Laughter) "I'm going; I'm going to New York." (Laughter)

■ *How did you find the confidence to send*
your first stories to the New Yorker?
Well, confidence is also a kind of naiveté.

■ *Oh, I see, you write a story, "Where am I going to send it?"*
"Oh, I think I'll send it to the *New Yorker*. Why not?" (Laughter)

■ *In some interviews you talk about how you began particular pieces.*
For instance, seeing people selling flowers got you started on In
Country. *Then you describe moving in an associative way from one*
thing to another.
Well, you write a book called *In Country* and it's about a Vietnam vet and his niece and so people think, "Well, this novel must have been inspired by some experience having to do with the Vietnam War." But it wasn't. It grew into that. That's generally the way I write.
If you're interested, I could describe the process.

■ *Great!*

I'm working on a novel now; this novel started with a sound. I heard a lab technician who was drawing blood from my mother's arm when I took her to the doctor, and I said, "You're not from around here, are you?" trying to place her accent. I guessed that she came from Wisconsin; she said, "No, Chicago." This sound of the way she talked with a Chicago accent wormed its way into my head, and that's one of the main things that got me going on the novel, which is not really about Chicago, although it plays a great part.

One thing led to another and I wrote a short story about a guy whose mother was in the hospital. I worked quite a while on that, and then I came across something else that was an even bigger subject for a novel, so I worked the short story into this subject and expanded it a whole lot more. Then I got going on this particular character, this guy. And, let's see, I made up more characters. I didn't know what the relationships were and I've spent a long time figuring that out. Meanwhile, I wrote a narrative that put the characters in various situations. I started off with a guy camping out in a wildlife refuge, so I got into his head a bit, but it's all mysterious. We don't know what he's up to or why he's so upset. So I spend the book trying to put this together. All of this is mystery and discovery. It's not like I have a huge thing on my mind that I'm carrying along that I have to express.

The pleasure of it is making discoveries, and that's usually done through specific words and images. If I come up with an interesting image here and find that it resonates another place, or if the two characters, the man and the woman, don't understand each other, then something they say might make it clearer. This is all very muddy, but, believe me, this is the way it works.

Somewhere along the line, about the sixth draft, say, I've got the narrative, but it doesn't hang together. What is this all about? Then, I make a notebook; I get the nicest notebook I can find that will be a pleasure to work in, and then I go through the narrative very carefully. I start making little categories of images and sounds and references and details and just bits of things. To my surprise, I discover a lot of images about dancing, like, "angels dancing on the head of a pin," or the character's parents used to dance to an old big band song—a whole page full of references, just images of dancing. I didn't realize that I had done all this, but it was telling me this had something to do with the way this character's mind was looking at things. And I noticed further that there's no actual dancing; it's all thinking about dancing or remembering or imagining. That intrigued me.

I tend to write a lot about nature, so I listed all the green things and all the flowers and insects and so forth. Then I found that there was a whole page full of dog references. So I realized that the dog is a bigger character than I thought and that this character has a special feeling about dogs. These discoveries I'm describing are elementary; it all gets very, very intricate. Then I'm able to feel my way and to understand the center of the book. I don't think in terms of themes or any of those reductive terms.

I know in classrooms generally they're talking about meaning, especially with undergraduates: what is the theme? And I think, "Well, all books are about love and death, so what's new?" (Laughter) There are no really new stories, so to say that a book is about love, or even a particular thing about it, is still reductive. Instead, I think of image patterns and sounds and when I'm looking at what I'm doing, I think of it as textures. I work on images, details, patterns, motifs, echoes, the way a sound or an image will echo on the last page that links back to something on the first page. Charles Baxter, in one of his marvelous essays, says that the reader may not notice that, but if it weren't there, it wouldn't be right. Those invisible things help build the whole story. The most important thing is tone; that's what you work toward: to make it consistent, to put it in the voice of the character. So I will try to analyze what I've done after I've basically done it: spewed out the main story and gotten the characters to come to life. Then the work begins—to shift it into place, to enhance it and then to see where it can jump out a little bit more.

■ *What do you mean, "jump out a little bit more"?*

There's an analytical or critical mode and a creative mode. If I'm thinking, "These characters aren't alive," it's hard to tell myself, "Well, I should do this, this, and this." That's when I have to shut my eyes and dream again. And see what happens. So in the latter stages I'm alternating between looking at it critically and looking at it imaginatively. I make up all kinds of terms to judge what I'm doing, like "balance," "emotional center," "continuity," and the "sound and tone."

I don't understand or know much about the new theories like deconstruction. I guess people have to find something to do (laughter), but I think of writing as an intricate construction project and it *is* the text, thank you. My story "Shiloh" was originally titled "Constructions" because each of the characters was constructing a fantasy: Leroy with his Lincoln Logs and his monologue memories and Norma Jean with her compositions and cooking experiments. I don't favor deconstruction. The *text* is the thing. Well, text, the textures, and the technicalities—the three "texes!" (Laughter)

■ *I don't quite understand what you mean by "texture."*
Could you please explain that a bit more?
The individual textures are the things that give you pleasure: the way something is described. The images. The senses. The sensations. The sounds. Particulars. I think literature is about textures and emotions. I think the aesthetic of reading is to experience the texture as particulars. I was indoctrinated by James Joyce's *Portrait of the Artist* and the aesthetic that Stephen discovers. And I'm grounded in Nabokov and Joyce. That defines the literature I enjoy and I can't seem to get off in any other direction, to think about literature as historical or feminist. I'm interested in literature as an aesthetic experience, not in expressing some idea.

Maybe I'm saying this against the way I think I've been read. Usually, I don't read what people write about my work; once in a while I'll see something. But they don't talk about tone. They don't talk about the words. They talk about popular culture and talk about people in a certain region. And I'm feeling a bit fitful right now, wanting to get beyond some of those things.

■ *What does "technicalities" mean?*
Oh, I'm talking about the artistry of it, the artist as the craftsperson, how it's put together.

■ *How long does it take you to write six drafts?*
Well, I'm on draft eight right now. I don't know. Two years.

■ *So you're working for two years without really knowing*
how it holds together. What keeps you going all that time?
Well, fairly quickly, the plot emerged. The plot, the direction, the form, so I had something to work with and then, it was a matter of trial and error to figure out what really was going on. Superficially, I can see where I'm going, but it's not written very well yet. So I just keep

rewriting it, trying to get deeper. The novel *Feather Crowns* I spent much longer writing; it's a longer book, probably took four and a half years. It's sixty-nine chapters and if I went through a chapter a day—they were short chapters—I could get through it in about three months. It seemed like I would never see the end of it because it was many drafts, maybe twelve—I wasn't keeping count.

■ *You must love the process.*

I do when it gets past those initial uncertainties where it's so scary; it depends so much on mood and confidence to get it to a certain place where I have enough to work with and can start to get excited about it.

■ *Somewhere you said that you make notes*
when people say striking things. Is that true?

I used to keep notebooks where I would write down things that would end up in my stories. Well, I'll tell you the remark that inspired the story "Shiloh." I overheard this. Somebody says, "It's *amazing* that I have strong feet considering that I come from two parents who don't have strong feet at all." (Laughter) And I thought, "I wonder what I could do with this?" So it is truly dumbfounding to me the things that they get out of "Shiloh" in colleges, since I remember writing it and thinking, "Well, would Norma Jean say this about her feet or her parents' feet?" I wasn't looking at the story as a finished product. Critics find all kinds of things in that story about popular culture, about marriage, even gender (because Leroy was doing needlework, I guess). When I'm writing a story, I'm piecing together many small bits, and I'm not usually thinking about the abstract. Well, it must hold up if people are finding so much to say about it.

■ *So those students who complain that literary analysis*
ruins perfectly good stories may have a point.

Well, in a way that's what I'm saying; I think criticism ought to be appreciation and not deconstruction—that's a destruction con. (Laughter)

■ *You've said that your writing gets harder and it sounds*
as though that's because you have more to say.

It just gets more complicated because the more complicated your vision . . .

■ *The more difficult to include everything.*
Yeah.

■ *Do you find yourself doing more research recently?*
I don't know; it depends. I'm doing a lot of research for this book I'm writing now. I tend to do my research after I've written. (Laughter)

■ *Yes, that was curious because you were already writing* In Country *when you went to see the war memorial. Do you visit settings like that systematically, or does that depend on . . . ?*
I never went to Shiloh. The book I've been doing now, I've been doing a lot of research on science. It surprised me that I needed to know all this and I got so fascinated by it.

■ *It sounds as though that's what really motivates you: you love to learn.*
Oh, absolutely. I've had a lot of time to think about why I write or need to write or wanted to write, and it goes back to the formative years when I helped my grandmother make quilts. One of my first toys was a jigsaw puzzle. I've done those all my life. And then I found Nabokov. His work is all about making designs and that's what I like to do: I like to make designs. It's this impulse towards order, the pleasure of discovering design. The pictures from the Hubble telescope are so *astounding*, so pleasing, so beautiful: they're like patchwork quilts.

March 22, 2004

I GET CURIOUS ABOUT A GROUP OF CHARACTERS
AND I START INVESTIGATING THEM

Larry McMurtry writes in order to find out what happens to characters who fascinate him. Although those characters who share his age and gender attract him the least, his comments suggest that the generous, optimistic females whom he especially likes share their creator's disposition.

McMurtry has published over twenty-five books and written over thirty screenplays. His screenplay of his novel The Last Picture Show *won an Oscar; his novel* Lonesome Dove *won the Pulitzer Prize. Recently, he has published* Sin Killer, The Wandering Hill, *and* By Sorrow's River, *all three part of a series called* The Berrybender Narratives; Paradise; Loop Group; Folly and Glory; *and* Sacagawea's Nickname: Essays on the West.

▓ *I think academics tend to assume writers write novels the way freshmen write term papers. You have a thesis . . .*

That's right. And you explain your thesis. But that isn't what happens. What happens is a process of discovery in which a writer is compelled as much by curiosity as to how things will turn out and how people are as anything else. I get curious about a group of characters and I start investigating them. Many, many writers have said this and it's true and not true: you feel after a time that the characters have complete autonomy. Faulkner said in his *Paris Review* interview that you feel like you're looking and listening and writing down what they say and describing what they do. Conrad also said in one of his prefaces that his attempt was to visualize as strongly as possible what's happening with the characters. I feel that way very much. I'm a visual writer. I feel like I'm watching them and listening to them; I don't feel that I'm making it happen. There's an element of trickery there, but psychologically, from the writer's point of view, that's how it feels: the character is doing it and you're recording it, not that you're in any way making them do it.

One place where your readership will make this issue clear is when a very appealing character dies, such as Emma [in *Terms of Endearment*] or such as Gus [in *Lonesome Dove*]. A number of people have asked me why I killed Emma or why I killed Gus and I have no sense of having done that. People die. They die at all ages. They die under all sorts of circumstances. So I don't feel like I killed Emma or I killed Gus. But they did die.

Coming to a book as a reader is very, very different from having done it as a writer. It's very different. It's got to be different because the writer writes in a burst and then forgets it. Very few of them will think about their own work much after they've finished it. I am intensely involved with my books when I write them. I start forgetting them as soon as I finish them. And I think this is entirely healthy because if I didn't forget them and they were stuck there in my mind, how would I go on and write other books? I never read them at all except in the odd way you read something while you're writing it. So I'm always talking from very distant memories of things that happened a long time ago.

John Barth said that writers talking about their work are like athletes talking about a game after they've played it: they can create ingenious explanations for why they did what they did, but while they're playing, they're essentially just hitting the ball. And they're hitting the ball well or badly because of highly trained intuitions, skills, disciplines, actions, etc. And I feel that way about trying to talk about my work. I don't think I should ever be taken as the definitive commentator on it.

Henry James did a great job of thinking about his own work when he came back to prepare the New York edition and wrote those prefaces. He read it all again and thought about why he must have done this and why he must have done that; but that's a lonely example in literature. Anything writers say about their own work should be taken with a grain of salt because mostly they're just sort of schmoozing.

Well, when Hawthorne wrote all kinds of notebooks, he didn't write good fiction.
I've never written any notebooks. I never keep any notes at all.

I was talking to a friend about doing this interview and he said, "McMurtry is such a wonderful storyteller. The academy doesn't value writers like that as much as it should."

Narrative art has been in disfavor for about fifty years. I think it's coming back into favor. There's been a reaction against the reaction and the unfashionability of narrative fiction, which started in the twenties or at least the thirties, is dying out. I just looked at a book by Robert Alter called *The Pleasure of Reading*. It's a kind of examination of the rise and fall of abstruse and esoteric critical theories: structuralism, deconstruction, etc., etc., and how people find their ways through this back to simply the pleasure of a narrative, so I think the tide is turning a little bit.

I'm conscious of being old-fashioned, always have been conscious of it. I'm sort of a nineteenth-century writer writing stylistically about a hundred years late, but I don't feel that to be a real problem. Literary fashions come and go. I'm not unaware of the benefits of the two or three experimentalist generations and I can use [them]; I write some fairly absurdist and even minimalist kinds of scenes occasionally, but it's not my basic mode. My basic mode is just old-fashioned nineteenth-century realism.

■ *I read all your books looking for a pattern in your*
characterization of women and it irritated me that
I couldn't find one. Then I realized that's good.
Yeah, that it's a little complicated. I don't think there's a pattern at all. I think it's just catch as catch can.

■ *I wonder if your women characters are so different because*
you're telling the story; you're not worrying about . . .
No, I have no theory of character at all. I just don't. I try to perceive and apprehend my characters truthfully and realistically. They do the things it seems to me it would be natural for them to do. I feel like they're doing them and not me. The order is within the life of the character. It's not within my conception of the character.

■ *I think that if I tried to pattern the male characters*
in your books I'd have an easier time.
Well, I think it would be less rewarding, though, because I don't think I have very many interesting male characters. It's always been a weakness, until fairly recently. In most of my books, the men are pallid compared to the women. I've always had the ability to write about old men or boys, but men my own age or in the middle generations don't inter-

est me. *Lonesome Dove* is deceptive in that regard because in my initial conception those men are much older than they finally appear. That was a book that started as a commissioned script for John Wayne, James Stewart, and Henry Fonda, and as I conceived it, they were old men; they were in their seventies, they were having a very late adventure and looking back on their lives. I was influenced by the fact that it's very hard to get major actors to play men that old because they feel they can never play younger again if they do. So I pulled the characters when ten or twelve years passed and I did write the book. I didn't really own the story because I'd been paid for it, [so] I made them about ten to fifteen years younger than they had been in my original conception. *Lonesome Dove* probably contains my most successful male characters, I would think . . . I don't know. I don't remember it that well.

■ *It seems to me that you're easier on women than you are on men. Take Harmony, for instance. If you had a male character with that kind of romanticism . . .*
Uh-huh, her optimism . . .

■ *It's seen as optimism.*
Her generosity . . .

■ *She's always walking into messes.*
I genuinely think women are nicer than men. There's no doubt of that: I just think that. In my experience, it's been true. My own life experience indicates to me that women are apt to be both braver and more generous than men and certainly more generous emotionally than men.

■ *It seems as though you're playing with that generosity all the time in your women characters.*
I'm struck with it all the time. I don't know that I'm playing with it. It's there and it's something that emerges in character after character, but to me that only seems realistic; it doesn't seem calculated.

■ *By "playing with it" I meant that generosity shows up in various characters in different contexts with different consequences. For instance, Jill Peel winds up being punished for it; she looks foolish compared to, say, Molly in* Leaving Cheyenne, *who is also generous. But Jill's generosity is clearly a mistake.*

Of course it's a mistake, but it's an extremely common mistake. It's the kind of mistake women make all the time. In fact, in this new book, Jill makes it fatally. She is already dead before this book begins, but there's a kind of recap of the last year or two or her life. But women do that all the time. It's not that I'm playing with it; I'm just observing it. It's something that I've observed and I observe it so commonly that it filters in there without my giving it the slightest thought.

It's just me looking for a pattern, again.

Well, there may be patterns. I don't ever deny that there can be patterns and if there are patterns in fiction such as mine it's because I have certain experiences that have either dominated or repeated themselves so many times that they filter naturally into my fiction without my being particularly aware of them. And I'm not particularly unaware of them. I am aware that my women are pretty generous people, but that's been my experience with women, that they are pretty generous people.

Are there any women characters you're particularly proud of?

Well, I'm proud of them as people because I think of them as people. Emma would be one and Harmony would certainly be one and I suppose Clara would be one. Those are probably the three women in my fiction I like best . . . and the girl in this new novel, T. R. T. R. is a wonderful character. Those are the ones I remember the best.

It seems to me that you're relatively hard on your male characters and that you're especially hard on writers, like Danny Deck and the narrator of Anything for Billy.

Wait till you read the new one, which is a sequel to the Danny Deck book in which he's in his fifties. It's even harder on him. It's an examination of the difficulties of being a writer. It's not that I don't particularly like Danny; I do like Danny, but insofar as . . . He's probably the most autobiographical character, not in terms of incident, but in terms of mood, in terms of ambivalence about writing itself. Consequently, I examine my own feelings about it, which are pretty harsh.

You've mentioned that putting aside Lonesome Dove *to write* The Desert Rose *was very important for you. Could you elaborate on that?*

I had been writing for about a decade without really liking my writing at all. I think this is a kind of boredom you fall into after you've written for a number of years. You have the unnatural situation of having to read one person, yourself, every day for a long, long time and it pales on you at some point. Everything seems stale and familiar; it seems like you're just repeating yourself.

The shallowest and weakest part of my writing is between, say, *Terms of Endearment* and *The Desert Rose*. In several years there I only produced *Somebody's Darling* and *Cadillac Jack*—neither very satisfactory books—and it's plainly because I was really tired of my writing, didn't have any sense of delight in doing it. It was a chore. I'd written a lot of *Lonesome Dove* in that period and found it uninteresting and boring and had dropped it twice. Partly that may have been because I was in a dubious legal situation [because I had started it as a commissioned script], partly it's the problem of the long book: the danger that you'll exhaust your interest in the subject long before you get to the end of the narrative. You can write a thousand pages about something; that's a good many pages. You may use up your interest in a given set of characters and get stopped and it's very hard to ever get up enough momentum to carry the story on. That had happened to me with *Lonesome Dove*. I wasn't very interested in it and I had laid it aside to write *Cadillac Jack* and then I laid it aside again to write *The Desert Rose*.

The Desert Rose was written in a month, so it didn't impede me very much. But it was very important for me because I loved writing it. It restored my interest in my own writing without which I don't think I would have finished *Lonesome Dove*; I think I would have just let it lie there.

■ *Do you have any specific sense of what the difference was?*

Well, it was Harmony. Harmony's voice. In the first place, I was writing about a character that I really liked and I was writing in the first person, which is very easy for me. And sometimes if you catch a voice and it just writes, it's a lot of fun to write. I never felt comfortable with the two books that preceded it and felt they weren't very good. And so it was a delight. It gave me a big kick to do it. And it restored my interest in the whole business and process of writing and I went back and wrote *Lonesome Dove*. The burst I got out of that has carried me pretty much up until now. I've written *Desert Rose, Lonesome Dove, Texasville, Anything for Billy*, and this new book all pretty rapidly.

■ *Just because of that shift?*

Well, it certainly made a big difference because ten years is a long time to do something that you're not really enjoying. So that I came back with some enjoyment was a very big deal, very big deal. Those things will happen. All writers that have long careers . . . it's not going to be consistent. You're going to have times when you just don't like doing it, when it doesn't have any meaning for you.

■ *It's interesting that writing in a woman's voice got you going. It's been argued that women have trouble writing because our culture doesn't take their perspective seriously.*

Well, I don't know. I just think the world of fiction is now dominated by women and has been for about the last fifteen or twenty years. It certainly is true that culturally all the things Virginia Woolf said in *A Room of One's Own* were true and that there were clear socioeconomic reasons why women didn't write, but those mostly faded out in the forties. I think most of the interesting fiction being written now is being written by women. I don't see much happening with the males right now. There are fifty or sixty young women loose in America writing very good fiction. So I think it's shifting. This is a cultural shift that's occurred within our time.

The other was true, to some extent, although there are numbers of gifted women writers back to the turn of the century. George Eliot was about as good as anybody. It hasn't been as slanted toward the male as some literary history makes it out to be. Probably a lot were squelched that could have been very good writers, but an awful lot of good women writers in the nineteenth century and an awful lot in the twentieth century, speaking just for fiction writers. I actually think better as fiction writers than poets, for the most part. Except in Russia, perhaps. Russian women poets have been very good. It seems to me that the women who have been great writers in the West have mainly been novelists, not poets. I can't think of a female poet that's as good as George Eliot, unless you go to the Russians.

It's my experience that the whole history of the novel is tied to female emotion to a large extent. Little Samuel Richardson who got it all started made his pocket money when he was a kid by writing love letters for illiterate girls in his village and then he went on to write *Pamela* etc., etc. And so novelists have always pretty much understood that if you want to find out much about the operation of emotion do it from women, not from men, because men don't tell you anything about it if they know anything. They're far less open about emotional matters and far less sophisticated about it, far less self-aware, it always seems to me, than women.

■ *I think that's all I wanted to ask you.*

That's fine. Thank you; that turned out to be interesting. I hope it's helpful.

April 16, 1989

SUE MILLER

I INHABIT EACH CHARACTER

It may seem odd that a writer of so many best-selling domestic novels spent her formative years collecting master's degrees from Harvard, Wesleyan, and Boston University, but Sue Miller's curiosity propels her writing; she is simply unlimited by stereotypes about education. She says little about how all those degrees fed her work but has remarked that she learned a great deal from working in day care. Similarly, the exploration that takes place as she writes is psychologically and intellectually sophisticated, but has a firm grounding in practicality, for she asks herself what would facilitate a character's transformation and what techniques would best convey it. As she answers these questions, Sue Miller not only learns about her self and the world, she enlarges her intuitive and stylistic capabilities, so that she can write an even better book next time.

Sue Miller has published six novels and a memoir. She received a National Book Critics Circle Award nomination for Family Pictures; *three of her novels have been made into films.*

You dedicated Family Pictures *to your father because, as you said, he helped you believe in your dreams. Could you please explain what he did?*

My father was intellectually and artistically curious and read deeply when something crossed his path which intrigued him. And he was very supportive of any interest of his children's he could share. When I tried to begin to write, he was *very* delighted for me—even well before I was publishing anything. I showed him rejection letters and he just said, "This is a very good letter." (Laughter) He was widely read in literature, so he was pleased, I think, to have a child who was interested in that too. But he was just as supportive of my siblings. My younger brother is a veterinarian; he and my father shared a fascination with animals and animal behavior and my father encouraged that: my brother always had snakes and rabbits and all kinds of pets when we were growing up. My sister was interested for a while in acting and he went to all of her plays. That's just the kind of person he was.

■ *You talk about first being conscious that there were better and worse ways to present things when your family would dissect sermons after church.*

Yes, listening to my parents gave me that notion that there were degrees of beauty in something. When I first heard sermons, of course, I could make no distinction: they were all boring and I had to sit through them. But then slowly I began to listen for the *way* somebody did it, began to notice when things were being done well, began to have a sense of the possible shapeliness of the sermon. That made me aware of the formal qualities of other written works. It attached itself to the way I read.

■ *You've said that your two early, unpublished novels were too conceptual. Is that how you see them now?*

Mostly the problem was that they were thin. Until I finished the second one, I hadn't really thought, "Well, you need to have a plot." (Laughter) "You need to have an action going on that engages the reader, that tells a story. You need to think about what the story is as well as what it is you're trying to get at."

Having been a mother helped me enormously. *The Good Mother*, the first published novel, relied on the feelings and emotions that a mother has for a child. That grounded me [and] allowed me a moral arena in which to move around in, in a way that the other topics I had taken up . . . which were so much more solipsistic, did not. I suddenly felt that I could construct a story that for me worked on many levels: it *was* a good story, it would be compelling scene by scene, and also would, I hope, affect the reader.

■ *Is that how you normally work, figure out a concept and a plot at the beginning?*

My process when I write tends to be very different book to book; whether I polish and buff up one chapter completely before moving on to the next—that kind of thing can change with practically every book I write.

But the way I begin hasn't changed at all. I make *a lot* of notes and I ask myself to understand why I'm drawn to the material I'm working on, what I'd like the reader to be feeling and thinking about it, what the most important aspects of it are. I ask myself to have a sense of what will happen, what I want going on at the end of the book. I don't always know the exact events that it ends with, but I know what resolution I want. That hasn't changed from book to book—except for the memoir about my father, which I kept coming at from a different angle every time I picked it up.

■ *How long were you writing the memoir?*
I started in 1991, 1992, I guess; about eight or nine years.

■ *I understood you to say that writing the memoir was harder than writing your novels because you couldn't begin with a shape.*
Yes, and that was at least partially because my reasons for doing it jumped around over the years. I didn't really know what I wanted a reader to get out of the memoir, particularly, or what I wanted to get out of it. I started off writing a chronological story of my life with my father, or of our family's life, which was not very interesting. (Laughter) I truly didn't know why I was working on it except that I knew that I wanted to write about Alzheimer's disease. Also, my control over that material—the research material—and my understanding of it varied over time. But generally the problem was just a sense of not knowing where I was going.

And, in fact, it's a book that's hard to explain to people who haven't read it—because it does include some material about our family's history, it includes material about my relationship with my father, it includes the story of his deterioration and his death, it includes material about the nature of Alzheimer's disease and what goes on in the brain when someone has it, it includes commentary about what it's like to be a caretaker. So it's not a memoir in some ways. But it's called a memoir. Even in the reviews, I noticed, it's hard for them to say what the book is about.

■ *That may be good, don't you think?*
I think it's perfectly fine, but the universe of publishing and reviewing likes to put a book neatly in a little slot on the shelf. There were people whose reviews complained, "This is supposed to be a memoir and we don't know enough about the people; we don't know anything about them at the end." So people do think that way a little bit and

more than a little bit in the publishing community. But *my* publisher was great; my editor was wonderful about it, she didn't care about how one might categorize it.

■ *When you teach, you talk to your students about "the dragon," but I didn't quite understand that theory. Could you please explain it?*
It's an analogy for the writing of fiction lifted from Flannery O'Connor—the notion that every character in a story must struggle with something: his dragon.

■ *You know, Jung talks about it, too.*
No, I don't.

■ *For him, the first stage in becoming a hero is facing the dragon, which is really the shadow or the part of yourself you've disowned.*
When [O'Connor] speaks of it, she's speaking of it theologically. But it's useful more generally too. Because one problem for students is that they don't know how to tell a story. They invent characters and then nothing happens and then more of nothing happens and then they kind of end it. So my argument has been that if you really look at any given character, there is, as Jung says—(laughter) as *I* can now say—a dragon for that character: something born of him that is the thing he ought to be confronting fictionally that you could make him confront. If you have someone, let's say, who's terribly prideful, you might bring him low. If you have someone who has trouble being attached to people, you might give him a desperate attachment or a need for a desperate attachment. It would vary, of course, from character to character, but if you look at each character, there is *something* that's the pickle he needs to be in (laughter) in order to make a story happen. When you create a character, if you ask yourself, "Why am I making this character?" "What is it about *this* character that interests me?" in a way you're asking, "What can I do to this character that will make a story happen?" and "What can I do that will be *just right* for *this* character to have to struggle with to make a story happen?" So that's what I conceive of as the dragon the students need to look at: what *is* the issue that this character needs to come to terms with or to struggle with? This doesn't suggest any necessary structure for a story. You can just have it be that at the end of the story, the character doesn't realize that there's a dragon he's about to meet. You don't need to work

it out in any given way. At different times fiction has fashionably done different things with regard to this idea, but I think it's fair to say that a dragon usually *happens* in a story: the character richly drawn struggles with something which emerges from himself that he ought to struggle with; or at least he learns that he's going to have to struggle. In a way, what fiction does is watch people struggle.

When I was writing the book about my father, I was in the book, too, and what I (laughter) hadn't understood was my own fate in the book. My own dragon. That's why I struggled with the book for such a long time. In the end, I came to several different conclusions about what my dragon was. My father, while being a wonderful father in many ways, was also always a bit abstract, gave himself almost equally to everyone else. Alzheimer's disease reminded me of that sense of [his] not being someone I could ever be close to, even though he was so supportive. Finally, some of my struggle was seeing him clearly, which I think I did over the course of writing the book; seeing how much he was a person of faith. Initially, I had wanted to redeem a life I thought had been destroyed. I was so angry towards the end of his life and afterwards. But I finally saw that Alzheimer's disease and death itself weren't a defeat for him. I came to understand him in that way and that was part of the book for me, too. Part of the struggle for me was that I hadn't *felt* him in the way that I came to when I had to struggle with what I was doing in the book.

■ *I was surprised when, in an interview, you talked about a character as though he was a person. Michelle Huneven said she thought Daniel in* While I Was Gone *was a workaholic and you replied, "I thought so too."*
(Laughter) Yeah. Each character needs to be real to me, as himself. I inhabit each of them. I try to give them my sympathy, even the ones I don't like very well: to understand why they are as they are, what they do to make what they do defensible to them. They do seem very real to me.

■ *Do you begin with a kind of notion about your characters and then they take shape as you write?*
I think of what kind of person they're going to be, but it isn't until I start writing that I fully imagine what they're like and begin to

understand who they are. A lot is giving them a voice in dialogue; as soon as [I] begin to imagine the way people talk and quirks of language and then the quirks of the way they're thinking, they begin to come to me, though I might have some notes before I started to write. But if I'm writing well, there's a kind of expansiveness in my imagination about someone.

■ *You said very early that you thought all your characters came from yourself and that included the male characters. That comment suggests to me that gender differences aren't that important.*
No, I don't think so. Obviously, they make a difference in what the character is like; I do think there are gender differences and they are important in life. But people of the opposite gender are not impossible to understand or to imagine. It's the job of a writer to cross imaginative lines, not always to be only himself—although there are some writers who have done fine with that. But I feel very comfortable with the male characters I've created: they're full and believable and sympathetic—some of them. So I don't see that as a barrier to moving imaginatively into a character.

■ *A couple of male writers have found it particularly valuable to write in a woman's voice.*
In the nineteenth-century men wrote a lot from the perspective of women, if not in the voice of. Think of the really great novels of Flaubert and Tolstoy. Maybe in the nineteenth century, the writer's life, Tolstoy's and Flaubert's in particular, was very domestic, very like a female life in some ways. They would have been comfortable writing women's lives because writers used to lead what the world would have thought of as women's lives.

I think American fiction in particular has fallen into the male-female division traditionally. It may be exciting now for American men to cross that line. They had gotten trapped for so long in what Leslie Fiedler proposes as a peculiarly *American* turning away from the domestic in fiction—the novel of the road or the sailing voyage or the trip down the river: leaving home was important in American fiction. The work of someone like Hemingway embodied this. It's been important for male writers in the past *not* to write domestic novels. Now they more and more are writing them.

■ *You said years ago that you thought domestic novels should be taken more seriously. Do you think that's changed, that they are?*

Well, to the degree that men begin to write them, they may begin to be. (Laughter) That's the way it works. Still, it's very hard for me to think of a writer of what we'd call domestic fiction, even a female writer of domestic fiction, who's been richly rewarded in terms of prizes and so on. When women win prizes, they tend to be for other kinds of work. Jane Smiley won for *A Thousand Acres*, which was fundamentally domestic; but I wonder if the frame hadn't been *King Lear*, whether that would have been seen as [being] good as it was . . . It's interesting to speculate.

But there are a lot of contemporary male writers who are doing more writing about the home and family. Some of it may be that they realize the people who buy books in this country are women. If you're going to have any success at all, you'd better be able to write about female interests. The male writer better come home from that voyage. (Laughter)

I would really be interested to have someone do a study of who used to read and who reads now and why; because when I was in my twenties and reading a lot, it was all men writers. It was Mailer and Roth and Updike and Bellow and Malamud, Cheever. Cheever and Updike were writing about the family, but not the others. In any case, there were just these *guys* and I can't believe that it was all women buying them. There must have been a wider readership of educated, literate men who made those books successful. Where are they now? Reading John Grisham or watching television, I suppose. I think women are really the audience for literature now; I don't know that anyone *knows* this is true because I don't know that anyone has a way of tracking whether men or women are buying and have bought and used to buy serious fiction, but I'd be *so* interested to have a study.

■ *You've said that when you wrote* The Good Mother, *you realized that you had to have a plot. And then in* Family Pictures, *you were focusing on point of view. In* While I Was Gone, *you said that you wanted to use an unreliable narrator. Do you generally set a technical problem for yourself with each book?*

Yeah, yeah. I enjoy constructing a book differently, figuring out how one makes a book that works in a particular way. When I read other books, I notice how they're put together technically. I often notice something that might be a pleasure to try and that would offer new opportunities to do certain things fictionally. I am always aware of trying to do something different and learn something.

■ *You said that you stopped working on the memoir to write* While I Was Gone *because you wanted to do something you could feel in control of and that you wrote it in first person because it would go quickly. Apparently, writing in first person feels especially comfortable to you.*

It certainly made it more instantly engaging to me, as the first person does. For the reader it works that way too, if it's working well. You think, "Oh, good. Someone is going to stop me and tell me her story." There's less work getting into it than there is with something that begins, "It was a rainy day and . . ." (Laughter) I was turning from the book about my father and wanted to feel (laughter) that I was working on something I was competent at; each time I would struggle with the book about my father, I would feel defeated as a writer in some ways.

■ *You've thanked people for helping you with research. How much research do you do?*

I do as much as I can, as much as I need to and probably then some. It's nice to have a way of stepping into the world and finding out about things. In some books I've had to do more than in other books. But it's always been pleasurable, that part of it, for me. In *While I Was Gone*, my younger brother helped me a lot with the veterinary part of it and I enjoyed that very much. For that book too I talked to some detectives about murders and how they worked on them in that period of time— the murder in that book occurs in the sixties. I read a lot about autism for *Family Pictures* and I read a lot about psychiatry and how it saw autism at that point in time. The book I've just finished and turned in is set in California and one of the characters is a vineyard manager. So I did a lot of talking to people who run vineyards. I read about how to grow grapes (laughter) and things like that. It was just great fun.

■ *A couple of times you've made an analogy between writing and dreaming. Is that just a metaphor you happened to use, or do you have any larger theories about that?*

It's not my analogy. I was quoting Cheever, who said in an interview that the use of autobiography in writing fiction is similar to the use of reality in a dream. You're utterly dependent on what you know and what you see, but on the other hand, what you're doing with it is as constructed and as unlike what really happened as a dream is. I do think writers move in a fluid way that probably is as deeply in touch with their unconscious as dreaming life is. It's a different way of thinking, certainly, about life—constructing characters and imagining problems for them—from someone who writes sociology. It leaves you freer from having to draw conclusions for people or make an argument. You can just present and think about it and maybe all you're thinking is that this is very sad and it makes you feel bad; it can be as simple as that. I do think there's a kind of play, like the play of dreaming, a pleasurable putting together of unpredictable, odd things that somehow seem satisfying to you as a writer, seems *right*. That is a privilege—to have such play as your work. There's a consciousness to some of it, obviously—it's not like dreaming in that sense—but there's also this sense that these things simply come to you. You *will* some of it, but then some of it is just *there*. You probably have a responsibility to look at it and to be sure of what you're doing, but sometimes it's just there. I think the more you do it, the more available it is.

Do you mean the longer you write each
book or the longer you write altogether?
The more deeply you get into each book and then also the longer you write. For me, anyway, the experience of writing has become richer as I've gone along. I feel more comfortably intuitive.

You once said, "One service fiction performs
is to honor the ambiguity in life."
Oh, what a good *quote*. (Laughter) Yeah, I think that's right and it is the privilege of the fiction writer to be able to live in a world in which you can write a whole book and have it remain ambiguous. (Laughter) No one would take that from a philosopher unless he was discussing ambiguity. And it seems to me the less polemic, the more open to ambiguity fiction is, the more complex and rewarding it is for a reader.

Your books are so compelling; I can understand why people
assume you write about things you've experienced. Do you
have any understanding of how you're able to do that?
By living in the characters, by really trying to imagine them. If it

weren't fun, if it were not an alternate universe that I could inhabit really fully, I wouldn't want to be doing it as much as I want to be doing it. (Laughter) I do understand my characters in an intuitive, felt way and I'm interested in their full complexity and I think people believe in them. If I have a gift, it is that: people believe that they're reading about real people and so they too are taken into another world. That's my hope anyway.

■ *What do you get out of that?*
Escape from myself, I imagine. But I also think it's a fresh way of thinking about life and *about* myself. If I'm looking at a character who is like me in this way but completely unlike me in six other ways, it's an interesting way of thinking about how another might act in this . . . It's a way of pondering questions of feeling and emotional response. It's useful to me, interesting to me—and fun. It's constructive.

■ *Some people have said that as they've gotten older they've become more interested in writing about characters very different from themselves. I don't see any pattern with you like that, but maybe you do.*
No, I don't. But I don't see much of a pattern of any kind in my work. I've moved around. I think probably every third or fourth book is a person that could be construed as being kind of like me, but then I've tried to write about other people, too, in between them. The book I just finished is about a whole family again, but in a very different way from *Family Pictures*. In part it's the story of a father and a daughter— a very different kind of father and daughter from me and my father, but some of the issues came up, in part, as a result of having written the book about my father. There couldn't be a man more different from my father than the one I created, and the daughter's pretty odd too, but they're struggling through some of the things I began to think about in my own relationship with my father. It felt interesting to write about a dyslexic man who doesn't read very much who's a vineyard man and his daughter. I felt very far away from myself; on the other hand, I felt completely connected to myself.

May 28, 2004

THOSE MOMENTS OF CLARITY ARE LITTLE GEMS

Kyoko Mori left her native Japan to attend college in the United States and stayed. Although she claims not to be an adventurous person, her work seems constantly in motion. Her first book, Shizuko's Daughter, *began as a dissertation combining poetry and short fiction, then morphed into a young adult novel selected as a* New York Times Book Review *Notable Book, the Best Book for Young Adults by the American Library Association, and a* Publisher's Weekly *editor's choice. She constructed her next novel,* One Bird, *with a much more direct plot line, but it, too, won multiple prizes. She went on to write a memoir, an essay collection, and a novel. She often begins a book with a format in mind, which she willingly abandons because she has the courage to let her writing tell her where she needs to go. She especially enjoys it when improving her work forces her to grapple with deeper truths about herself or her characters. She attributes her faith that her writing will take her somewhere worthwhile to her experience in a rigorous but affirming PhD program and to the examples of her mother and grandfather recording everyday pleasures on postcards and in journals.*

▪ *Your writings suggest that honesty came naturally to you; but, at the same time, you had to work at it. You've said reading American women writers and Asian-American writers gave you permission to speak in your own voice. What else has helped you write as honestly as you do?*

Going to graduate school to become a writer. A lot of people think this is not necessary and maybe it's not necessary for them, but choosing to go to grad school was giving myself permission and also responsibility: "I am going to take this time to do this," instead of trying to find work or go into literature. "Now, I have to do it; I signed up for it." It was supposed to be foolish to go into English, especially creative writing, with no prospect of getting a job, but I decided not to worry because what else was I going to do? If I ended up getting some non-writing job afterwards, I [would be] no worse off.

■ *Was graduate school helpful to you?*

Completely. I loved going to graduate school. It was a great thing. It was a lot of fun. I didn't go to a high-powered place. I went to a very solid and nurturing place, the University of Wisconsin–Milwaukee. I suppose if you're career minded you would try to go to a place that had a huge reputation like Iowa or Irvine or Columbia. I didn't apply to those places because I was only twenty-two. I didn't want to feel like I wasn't as good as everyone. I also figured pretty intense people go to those places. And I thought, "Milwaukee, this looks like a laid-back program." But at the same time, what they were going to make you do to get a PhD was *quite* rigorous, so I knew I would get a good education. I did a creative writing dissertation, a program where you took all your course work and prelims as though you were getting a literature PhD; but in lieu of a dissertation, you wrote a manuscript. This is one of the reasons that I did go to UW–Milwaukee rather than getting an MFA. I knew a PhD program would better prepare me for teaching and I always liked reading and writing about literature. I wasn't strong on all the theory; I also hate researching things and writing those endnotes. There was no way I could be a scholar because I felt defeated by all that, but I liked taking lit classes and writing papers.

UW–M turned out to be the kind of place where they had faculty–graduate student readings every month. So if you were a graduate student, you got to read with one of the faculty members; that was a way of bringing you up rather than putting you down and I did get to know the faculty. The few fellow students I really got to know were important to me and I learned a lot from them; I'm still in touch with many of them. But more than anything else, what mattered was giving myself time to do this and nothing else.

■ *Put it at the center of your life . . .*

Yeah, and live in a beautiful place. I lived a few blocks away from Lake Michigan in Milwaukee on the east side. Only after I moved away, I realized what a beautiful place it was because I took that lakefront for granted. To see that every day and walk to school, and sit around and talk about what you were writing . . . That was a good thing. I was a teaching assistant, [so] I learned to teach composition, which I hadn't taken because I had placed out of those classes; I also taught creative writing. All of that was enormously helpful.

And it was a good time. All these crazy things we did; I remember them fondly. I took [an] end of the nineteenth-century class, aesthetes and decadents, and we read a lot of Oscar Wilde. Instead of doing my graduate seminar paper, I threw a decadence party. People drank Pernod because we couldn't get absinthe. We put yellow drapes everywhere because yellow was the color of decadence. This fellow graduate student who was also a poet, Ken Pobo, and I wrote a skit instead of a graduate seminar paper (laughter); I gave the prologue pretending to be a French poet, Gerard de Nerval, who went mad and at the end of his life was seen walking along with a lobster on a pink leash; so I delivered this prologue and dressed my cat like a lobster. I had him on a pink leash and made paper lobster legs, which I tied around him. It was hilarious. It was a crazy and creative time.

▓ *Why do you see honesty as crucial to writing well?*

My first triumph as a writer was in second grade when we were all asked to write essays about the school lunch. All my friends wrote about how great the school lunches were even though nobody really thought this; the school lunches were *terrible*. So I talked about my experiences with school lunches and how they were not that great. And I won the essay contest. This made an impression on me (laughter) that you should just tell the truth. I didn't go on in a complaining way, but I tried to be humorous but honest about my experience of school lunch, which was not that positive. I loved getting that award.

I can't say that I always tell the truth in real-time situations. I try not to tell lies to manipulate people because I think that's bad. But to lie to be polite is different . . . You don't even think, "I am now making this up" because the urge to save the other person or your own self embarrassment comes so naturally. When you write you often even lie to yourself initially, especially when you write nonfiction: "So, this is what I learned from this experience." Half the time that turns out not to be the thing you actually learned. It's that veneer you put over the experience to make yourself think, "I have had closure." Writing is like peeling an onion. Usually when you write, you realize that the thing you thought was the truth was the inedible outer layer you have to peel away and then you start to see the truth. This is no different in fiction.

I love those moments in short stories when you finally see the light or the character has an epiphany that you didn't expect her to have.

I don't know if those moments of clarity in your writing radiate out to the rest of your life. Oftentimes you meet writers and you think, "God, this person writes with such clarity about their own lives and, therefore, they must be so self-aware" and then sometimes you're disappointed. That's true about your own self, too. Those moments of clarity are little gems; that doesn't mean the light is going to go outside the gem and light up your life. They're important for their own sake.

If you're the kind of person who writes, you're always generating words in your head and sometimes those words get in the way of perception instead of helping you to see better. It's like drawing; you have to learn to draw what you see, not what you think you see. That's always a struggle to see or to draw or to say without distortion or without your words becoming embellishments instead of clarity. But sometimes there's need for embellishment, too; it's hard to say, "Is this now a good time for the blunt truth or a better time to set up the context or to set up the mood for what's to come?"

■ *But when you talk about voice, you're critical of people*
focusing too much on the meaning or on philosophy.

Sometimes people are so anxious to get that secret meaning. You're reading something beautifully written and you don't see what's in front of you because you're always looking for some hidden meaning. That's what I object to; what is the moral of the story? I don't know what the moral of the story is. Maybe it doesn't matter.

■ *You said in an interview that you write in a journal, then that*
material becomes poetry, then the poems collect in a way that
convince you there's material for a story there . . .

I don't always write poems, but I do write in my journal. Working on a novel takes so long, by the time you finish, you may not be the same person: you may not live in the same place, or with the same person, you may look different; whatever you experience during that time tends to go into the novel through your journal or whatever cogitation happens in your head, that little movie in your head. So [journal writing] is part of my process. I don't write in my journal if I'm revising my novel; I figure there are only so many words that I can write every day; I don't want to waste my words writing in my journal.

I get up in the morning and I go running and I come back and I sit down with my coffee and then it'll be time to write. I don't do this every day 'cause I have to go teach; I tend to write every day during the summer when I'm not teaching. Other than sabbaticals, every year of my adult life I had to work in some way other than my writing; so, on days I write, I'm ready to concentrate. Even though I sometimes resent all these other things I have to do, I don't know if I can write five hours every day anyway. It's good if you could do it three or four days a week for three to five to maybe seven hours, depending on what you're doing. Once you're revising, you can put in much longer days. For one thing, it takes so long to read the thing that you've already written. This is the difference between working in prose and working in verse. When you're a poet, you struggle with those four words for four hours, but at least it doesn't take you three hours to read the stuff you wrote yesterday or last week.

■ *Your first book was written in short stories*
and then you realized that you had a book . . .
Yeah, yeah, yeah.

■ *Is that generally how you work, start with something small . . .*
No, no. That book was an exception because I thought that I was writing a series of short stories about these people. I was intimidated to think about a novel. I must have been twenty-four when I wrote what became the last chapter of that book: the story about the grandmother having a birthday. That was actually the first story I wrote about those characters. I would no more have written a novel than gone to outer space—that seemed so gigantic. But after I finished that story, I felt that I didn't do this one character justice, the young girl who is sitting at this Buddhist ceremony completely refusing to cry or show any kind of emotion. Her mother's been dead for seven, eight years; she's not going to be like that. I thought, "You know, I should write about her." And that's how it came about. But that's rare. This novel that I just sent to my agent, I knew from the beginning that it would be a novel, I didn't know what I really wanted to have happen, but I knew where it would take place and that there would be two central characters, a mother and a daughter, and I had a rough idea where I wanted it to go. And I started at the beginning. But I do have to say in the process of that, I took out whole characters. There are two char-

acters I collapsed into one at about revision number three. And I completely changed the personality of one of the other characters. So, clearly, I don't know what I'm doing when I start. You can't have it all planned out, but you have to know enough so that you can actually sit down to it.

■ *And you keep revising and then it slowly gets a shape.*
Yeah. Also, I did keep showing my manuscript to my agent: she's a great reader. And she suggested all these things and asked all these questions and in trying to address her concerns and questions, I thought, "Oh, I need to do this."

■ *Did you intend to write your first two books as young adult books?*
Not the first one because about one-third of it was a part of my graduate dissertation. I did a combined manuscript of stories and poems. I didn't think of them as having any particular audience other than the general audience of magazines and a lot of those chapters were published in lit magazines. So my first book wasn't really meant to be a young adult book, but it turned out that one of the main characters was twelve when the novel starts and twenty when it ends, the young adult age. The book was a collection of stories I rewrote as a novel. When it was a collection of stories, years would pass and there wouldn't be anything in between, so I had to straighten out the chronology. The revisions forced me to develop the character from twelve to twenty instead of seeing her in flashes.

My tendency at the time, and I still do this, is to rely on my ability to write good sentences and to put words together rather than to really investigate the psychology of the character and all the ambiguities the character must face. It's a cop-out to just write well instead [of looking] at the character and asking questions like, "Last time I saw her she was twelve; why is she like this at fourteen?" That made me delve deeper and get to know, "What is this about?" So rewriting the book as a novel forced me to focus on character and development and also the shape of the whole thing rather than thinking always like a poet and just going for the language. The manuscript was acquired by somebody who was putting together a young adult series, but he didn't ask me to do anything different except to make it into a novel rather than a collection of stories. The second book, *One Bird*, I had a contract to write and it was going to be in this same series.

I was in my twenties when I became a writer and I couldn't quite imagine writing about somebody my own age, but something I experienced ten years ago gave me the right sense of distance, . . . In my twenties, I wrote about people who are teenagers and then by the time I was in my late thirties, I started to write about the mid-thirties transformation. I see the adolescent years and then mid-thirties to, say, fifty, sixty, as times of transition. Whether she's a fictional character or even a nonfictional narrator of my book, some version of myself, the person I'm writing about has to be at point A and by the time the book is over, she has to go through B, C, D, E, maybe F, G. There has to be transformation. I don't think of my twenties as a huge period of transformation. I learned a lot to put in my head, but all I did was live in one place and go to school. Then I went to the new place where I learned to be a particular kind of a teacher. It's true, I got married during that time, but that seemed like more of the same because the marriage didn't take place in a fast way: we lived together and we kind of got married by default, and pretty much got divorced by default, so that didn't seem like a big deal or a sudden transformation. Divorce seems more like transition than marriage. Marriage seems more like a gradual trap that tightens around you, but when you reject it, that's transformation. The modern novel is not like the romance where the marriage is the final outcome; maybe for the modern writer, it's divorce that precipitates the novel.

■ *A lot of the writers I've talked with enjoy challenging themselves; is that why you've done such different kinds of writing?*

For me, the challenge comes by default. Some people love change and they like to challenge themselves to try new things. This is not me. I like to do the same thing over and over, if that were possible. But there comes a point where I have to admit that this is *not* possible! I wrote a novel thinking it was going to be a series of short stories because I already knew how to write a short story, but, of course, Marc Aronson, the editor, has to tell me, "This has to be a novel." So it was a challenge I had to accept. And then, I thought, "Hey, I now know how to write a novel." When I wrote my memoir, I actually wanted to write a novel about Japan and going to see my relatives because I had already written a novel, so I thought, "Well, I know how to do one of these!" *The Dream of Water* is nonfiction because when I went there and I saw my relatives, I decided that the story of my trip had to be done in a more straightforward way. Anything I made up would have been embellishment rather than transformation. The book had to be about my relatives and about my brief return into their world. So I reluctantly had to do a memoir, which I had never done before.

And for then my book of essays, *Polite Lies*, I wanted to do another memoir. I even put together a draft and it completely sucked. My editor and I looked at it and I said, "Marc, I know this is really bad. I don't know where I went wrong! I want to show it to you because I have nothing else to show." He [said], "What if you did this as a series of essays because there are these recurring topics." In every stupid narrative I wrote, there were these recurring topics such as need for honesty and need for polite lies, and the way women's lives are in Japan, the concept of beauty or integrity. Once we agreed on a group of possible topics, I had to start over. I ended up with a book of essays because it seemed like the only way to write about those topics, not because I was eager to try something new.

The new thing I tried last year was an essay about a thing, rather than about myself. Christina Thompson at *Harvard Review* called me last year and asked me did I have anything to submit and I said, "Well, I'm working on a novel, so I don't really have anything." Actually, I did have all this information about yarn because, at one point, I thought I was going to do a book proposal about fabrics. A few years ago, I spent weeks going to the Tozzer library here where they have anthropological books to read about how knitting and weaving started, all these different paintings that Renaissance painters had of Madonna knitting ... I loved reading the information, but I didn't know what to do with it. Information overwhelms me: dates, figures, facts. So when Christina called, I said, "Well, Christina, I don't have anything to show you, but I've been thinking about yarn. I have to leave right now because I'm going to a yarn store." Christina said, "Why don't you just write an essay about yarn?" I said, "OK, I'll sit down and work on it." I would never have done this on my own without being nudged. "Let's write this essay about yarn!" Why would I do that? But it was so satisfying to be able to finally use all the information I had gathered.

Especially in grad school, I spent a long time with friends, just driving around trying to figure out where to go. "Oh, we want to do something this afternoon." We go to the café and there's no place to park! So we can't go there. And then we go to the next place, but that place is too deserted. "There's nobody who wants to go there!" And pretty soon we don't know what to do: do we want to go shopping, are we going to get coffee? Sometimes all the stuff in my head is like passengers in a car driving around, waiting for the right café or shop to go into. There is a pleasure in finally finding a place for it.

So these challenges come my way and I'm good at accepting them, but it's usually not my initiative.

The writing takes you someplace you didn't expect to go.

Yeah, and I'm willing to go, but that's about all I can say for myself. I am not willing to say before the writing starts, "I've never written this, so I am going to do this now." I think, "No, I'm not going to do that." I'm the kind of person that goes into a restaurant and orders the same things. I've already eaten this; this was good; so stick with this. I go to the store and I buy clothes all the time, but all the clothes I buy look just like the clothes I already have. I'm not an adventurous person. People always think that I would be an adventurous person because I grew up somewhere else and I came here. But I have these two Siamese cats, they're four years old, this is my third group of cats; they're all Siamese cats. I never think, "You know, I've never had this other kind of cat, so let's go get this other kind." Why would I do this? These cats have always worked out for me. I happened to name my first cat Dorian because he was gray and I was taking that nineteenth-century class. So there was Dorian; then there was Oscar for Oscar Wilde, and then my current cats are called Ernest and Algernon. I don't know what to do if I get another cat. I've run out of all the good Oscar Wilde names. I stick with what I know.

When asked who was the most important influence on his work, the poet William Stafford said his mother.

Yeah, yeah, I would say my mother and my grandfather. Yeah. Definitely.

He talked about learning humility from her.

Yeah, yeah—and also discipline. My mother kept a journal. She wrote in a fairly disciplined manner. She wrote home to her parents once a week. And it was always a postcard. I have these postcards; they're like little prose poems, about what was flowering in the garden, some funny thing that happened with us, what she's baking, the clothes she's making. They're prose poems finding beauty in everyday life. And sometimes she made me write a letter, too, so we could send them together. So she kind of disciplined me to this. And I always saw my grandfather writing in his journal. That was the first thing he did every morning, with his tea. And it really did make an impression on me that this was something adults did: they read and they wrote. I took it for granted that everybody wrote something.

■ *Also, they wrote about everyday things instead of, say, scholarship, and your mother wrote about beautiful things.*
Yeah, yeah. And my grandfather, too, he was a retired schoolteacher, he would read, but he too made observations about what was around him. He wasn't so much a scholar, as much as he was a writer. His journals are records of, again, the flowers or the things that his grandchildren said or what his neighbors had said; it was a record of what he was aware of every day.

And I was definitely the kind of kid that when the teacher said, "Today, we're going to write a composition," I was happy. I looked forward to that. Writing was always fun. It's a rigorous discipline, but I wouldn't do it if there wasn't so much pleasure in getting it right, finally.

April 7, 2004

THYLIAS MOSS

I THINK THAT ONE SHOULD EXIST TRYING TO BE AWARE OF AS MUCH AS POSSIBLE

Thylias Moss wants to explore the many facets of ideas, so she likes using different media. While she sits at her laptop composing poems, she takes in the rhythm and sound of her typing, the emerging shape of her poem on the screen, and randomly changing background pictures of anything from a microbe to her sons. Not surprisingly, she has written in multiple genres: poetry, memoir, and a children's book, and she enjoys presenting her work both on the page and through sound. But even Thylias Moss can't produce all the possible renditions of her ideas alone, so it delights her that a choreographer and a filmmaker intend to reveal new dimensions of her narrative in verse, Slave Moth.

She has won the Dewar's Performance Artist Award as well as the Witter Bynner Award and a Whiting Award for her poetry. She has also been a MacArthur Fellow.

■ *You often talk about ideas when you're explaining how you write, but it's not as though you have a concept that you illustrate; your poetry is much too rich and complex for that.*

When I say something is idea driven, that does not mean that I have a full understanding of an idea. I emphasize more the necessity of making connections. I think that one should exist *trying* to be as aware of as much as possible; the more that one is aware of, the richer the connections that can be made and so, "I see this, I see this, I see this. Oh, my! Now I can put them together. Now this understanding is possible." That's what happened in the writing of the poem "Sour Milk." I had an awareness, something in an essay I read, a newspaper article, and a report on the evening news converged: "Hey, wow, I can see how these things *might* fit together. Let me pursue this." When I write, I pursue something to find out, "What is the result of examining these things?" I do not know the outcome. So it's not fully formed finalized ideas with conclusions! I conclude *nothing* at the time when I'm writing. If the conclusion comes before I've written it, there's no reason for me to write it. I will gain nothing from it if I know the conclusion. So I'll write something else.

These connections, of course, are very tenuous; they don't hold. But they may endure long enough for me to produce some kind of writing. While I am looking, time continues. I'm examining something that itself is continuing to change and so anything I write will be inaccurate because it will refer to something that has left whatever state it was in when I was commenting on it. I love that; that's very interesting to me.

I think of the idea as being a kind of polyhedron: it has many, many sides; many, many faces; many lines. And so one would think, "All right, if I turn this idea, because the idea is many faceted, I see it differently, I see another part, I expose a face that may not have been visible." Of course, an idea cannot be captured in its entirety, nor does one try to. Just have awareness that it is *possible* to look at it in another way, perhaps within the same poem. What if the ideas were rotated? What would that mean? What might happen to the writing?

To believe that an idea might somehow be complete with any particular treatment is erroneous. The idea exists in many manners of existence, many levels, and on many scales: one can look at it up close, then one can gradually increase the distance, the angle; there are many, many ways to approach an idea. Some of them are visible; some cannot even be seen. So one would use other ways to gather insight about the unseeable aspects of an idea. Some would produce sound to try to capture more of the simultaneous, more of the multiple existences of an idea.

In trying to understand the idea more completely, I use whatever media become available. I compose right on the computer. I find that absolutely necessary. I love the sound of it. The rhythms of language are exposed in typing; as the idea is shaped, it's wonderful for me because I'm hearing it. I also like the way things look on the screen; I can see it coming to existence in the way that I imagine it. When an idea is forming in my mind, it is not in manuscript, it is not in cursive writing, it is not jumbled. All my ideas have structure; the structure forms itself. I know exactly how to break the lines as I go along. It just all happens. That's one reason that I compose everything right at the computer. If I'm not doing that, there's either a power failure, the battery has been drained, I'm in some remote place, [or] all I have on me is paper and pencil.

If another idea comes, I will keep it. I always have multiple projects because that is the nature of idea. So all these little icons [on my computer screen] are writing projects. I keep many ideas going, so I have all my computer sticky notes: these are all ideas I'll get to. (Loud laughter)

I always surround myself with objects and replicas of the greater existence; I want to remember that whatever I'm writing about is embedded in this much larger thing. By immersing myself in mementoes of it, I can't possibly forget that. "Oh yes, I remember that! I remember all of this!"

Even on the computer, I have a wide range of image patterns that inspire me. The images change on my desktop at home every five minutes, this [laptop] might be set for fifteen-minute intervals, in random order. Most of the images are science related, so I'm very much interested in how things interact, what causes interactions, and what influences interactions. I love microbes. I'm interested in the limits of perception because I'd like these explorations to occur all the way to their limits. At the limits, you have the boundary of one thing and the boundary of another; that's where the most interesting interactions occur. So I'm interested in even writing to my own limitations, whatever they are. This causes writing to seem less polished, but it's far more authentic because I have taken it as far as I can.

■ *What would be a limitation in your writing?*

Well, according to the criteria I've given you, I must make these connections; I'm limited to that at this time. I should do something else. Maybe I will, but not today. I hope that I don't do this permanently; I don't say, "Here is *the way* to write." That will get stale, so it will have to change at some point.

■ *Your memoir suggested that a lot of people contributed to your being a writer. I wondered if you could explain how they helped you; for instance, your parents, your grade school teachers . . .*

I don't think anything that happened [in] elementary school caused me to be a writer. That had already happened. But there were certain teachers, certain situations in elementary school that were more compatible with my existing sensibilities as a writer. The first indication that I recall of [an] expansive style to thinking, an expansive style to writing probably occurred in elementary school. Mrs. Matthew was the first teacher in my recollection that understood me: I did not feel stifled in her classroom and, consequently, when assignments were given, I interpreted them my way without penalty. My self-imposed ceiling was always much more generous than ceilings teachers imposed; the teachers that I recall as being the greatest said, "Well, let me remove the ceiling and see what happens."

When there was a ceiling, I did not thrive; I felt spiteful even and I tended to withdraw. It was a wonderful, wonderful public school program at the time in Cleveland; these programs have probably met their demise. I started French in first grade; when I was in graduate school in linguistics class, I remember reading a study about those enriched classes in Cleveland. And we were all given instruments; we were all in the orchestra program and some of us were given private lessons. It was absolutely extraordinary.

In second grade, the format of the classroom was exciting. It was the reading club: groups with about a dozen children. We had about two questions assigned to us and we would have to write answers with page references in these notebooks. Then, someone would be appointed the leader of the discussion; that person would ask these assigned questions and we would have to discuss. We would always have to use some bridging phrases or transitional phrases, so a person would say, "Well, I can see your point, but on the other hand, if you look at page . . ."

Then we'd have to maintain a page of comments. In our reading, we'd think, "Hmm, that seems mysterious" and so we'd write "mysterious" and then we'd put down key words and phrases to make us remember. After we answered the questions, we could exchange comments: "I noticed this very mysterious passage. Didn't you find it. . . ." This would allow us to be able to begin to discuss the literature everyone had read. That format for English language and literature instruction persisted throughout elementary school within the enrichment and major work program. It was absolutely wonderful.

What was so valuable about that instruction?

To be able to articulate your ideas. Also, to be able to read with purpose. We were expected to have some kind of relationship with what we were reading. While we had questions to answer, we were then free to [note] however we felt about this and to create a record of our reaction to the various developments in the story. That was very useful to me; it was a good way to read. It made reading enjoyable no matter what it was that we read. We were reading to find something; that idea of reading to *find* something is the way I still read.

We also had to do presentations that were called morning talks; there were at least two a day, any topic. Each child would select a topic and then do research on this topic. We could have note cards, but we couldn't simply read a prepared speech. We would have to discuss this area that we had researched. We were expected to have visual aides of some sort. I always did more. Always.

In second grade, one of my topics was Susan B. Anthony. I had this wonderful book . . . my father bought a book for me every Sunday. We went on these walks, ever since I could walk, and I would come back with whatever book I chose. I never chose a storybook, but I had some fifty books in the Golden Library of Knowledge; I picked up *Energy and Power, Mathematics, Machines . . .*

One book I acquired was called *When They Were Girls*; it was about independent-minded women and the kind of childhood that they had. Susan B. Anthony was in this book, so, in second grade, I chose her for my morning talk and I made protest signs. Janice Skipper lived across the street from the school and there were all these clothes in her attic; I went over there [with] three or four other girls in the class. We found clothing we thought was suitable, so they wore it for my presentation. I had the lights turned off in the classroom, we all had flashlights and they were marching around the room with protest signs as I gave my presentation on Susan B. Anthony. I don't think that would have occurred in a classroom where a teacher would present instructions from which one is not to deviate. But since the assignment was given to me in a more open way, I felt free to pursue it however I might. Later, when I did Joan of Arc, fourth or fifth grade, my father helped me carry to school this *plank*, to which I tied Carolyn Smith. She was lashed to that plank wearing a white choir robe. I had this kind of cellophane fire. To show the stages of Joan's emotions as she was burning, I had the color wheel from the Christmas tree rotating; when the yellow was on Carolyn, I would talk about what the yellow represented in this burning of Joan, the red and the green. It was wonderful, a lot of fun for me. (Laughter)

■ *It sounds like the presentation of your poem* Slave Moth *at the Michigan Theatre this spring with visuals and your singing poems*

with your son accompanying you on the piano. It's as though you can't get enough into whatever you do. It's like this office.
(Laughter) Yes, yes, yes. That all started then.

◼ *How does that experience influence the way you teach?*

It's very important for me to teach the students to think for themselves and to give assignments where interpreting the assignment is part of the assignment. I design it to help them engage with thinking about existence in ways they may have not thought about it. I'll provide context and I'll tell them that they are free to do whatever they like within context. Context is a lens. We're going to look at this in this way at this time [I tell them]. You can look at the same thing with a different lens and find something else. It's important to me that the student have the responsibility of finding [her or his] own idea within the limitations I have given.

My emphasis is less on having a polished poem at the end and more on attempts. A semester is too short. Rather, [I tell them] "let's keep trying things. If it's flawed, who cares? That is not a problem. The only way to fail is not to try." It's to encourage them to have a different kind of relationship with the idea. I don't ever have answers to what I ask the students. I want to know myself. So I often do the assignments I give them.

◼ *Many writer-teachers talk about getting students to trust themselves. Is that the same as helping students find their voices?*

That's not what I mean at all, no. It has nothing to do with finding your voice. Voice involves a little bit, perhaps, how something is stated, [but] I think it's premature to address how something is stated until there is more content. Ways of perceiving, ways of thinking, lead to innovations in expression. I like to challenge how thinking is done: assumptions that one might have. It is [not] finding voice [but] arriving at understandings about existence that you may not have if you just continue to look in a particular way. So I'm more interested in providing other ways of understanding things, other ways of accessing information.

◼ *Do you love writing as much as you did when you were young, or more?*

Perhaps more because I understand now how I approach this. When I was younger, I would not have been able to articulate what I thought I was doing. I encourage my students to do that. For their final projects, I always have them put together a book, and write introductions or prologues so that they can really think through what happened in their projects. I think that's important: "What happened to your writing?"

■ *How did you happen to begin performing with your son?*

Initially, I had to start keeping up with him. In many, many ways, he's an unusual child. As he was turning six, he saw children having violin lessons after school; he said, "I'd like to do that." He tried the violin and it was the Suzuki method; he hated it. And he said, "This instrument just has four strings; this isn't enough notes." It was going to be some time before he would learn that all the notes were available to him. But *then* my husband had this old Yamaha keyboard; Ansted saw it, dusted it off, and turned it on. All the notes were there; there were no hidden notes. So the first thing he did was play his own song. When he was seven, he played his own composition.

Then I had to hurry. He's composing away; he also had drums. Now he's eight years old; he's playing and I can't help him. So I go to the Ann Arbor School of the Performing Arts and it's past the enrollment deadline, but I find an instructor who happened to teach piano and drums; I thought, "This is great" because those were Ansted's interests. So I was talking about him and saying, "Just listen to him play even though it's past the deadline. I'd prefer if you would meet with him" because I never like to speak for him. So we went, and [Ansted] starts playing the piano and then the instructor joins in and they're just playing and playing together. That's how Ansted became his student.

From second grade, he played in the middle school band; from sixth grade, he's played with the high school band. He played with the Wynton Marsalis septet in Brighton a couple of years ago. He had dinner with Wynton; he and Wynton keep in contact, and he became acquainted with Victor Goines, who's the director of jazz studies at Julliard and who was [a saxophonist] in the septet. Victor Goines said to Ansted, "When you're through with high school, if you're twelve when you're finished, that's fine. You just call me." So he's an unusual musician. He did not match expectations I had for a child that age despite my own experience with being a child, because he was far different even than I was. If I had imposed upon him the expectations of his age, there is much that he has done that he would not have done.

When the September 11th tragedy happened, he said, "I have to do something. What can I do? I can make music. I'm going to record a CD." "*Yes*," I said. I had no idea what to do. I mentioned it in class one day, "My child . . ." One of my students said, "Well, I've got a recording studio in my basement." Ansted went there; he recorded a CD; I took it to a sound studio to have it mastered; I learned to make the CDs; I made them, including the artwork, the label; they were sold locally at Nicola's Book Store; he raised $1,000 for the Red Cross.

He has a recording studio in the basement now; it became necessary. He has all professional equipment, this little boy, and he continues to record music. Occasionally, he would ask me, "I want some vocals on this one." So I would record vocals for him. That's how I became involved in his music, an *active* part, not just a sound engineer in a back room. We plan to try our hand at film. I don't know what's going to happen.

It doesn't sound as though you're just doing your motherly duty. It sounds as though you enjoy it.

(Laughter) Well, of course, of course, of course. He's just lucky that I'm so easily persuaded by ideas. "Great. OK. You want to make CDs, fine. No problem. Let's do it." Whatever it is.

I have a neurological disorder and I lost the use of my legs for six months, the use of my hands for about nine months. I couldn't write. I lost fine motor skills. I could pick up a sandwich, but toothbrushes, hairbrushes, combs, forks, pencils. I couldn't type . . . My son said to me, so wonderfully kind, that he could play and I could sing my poems. I don't like just reading at a poetry reading. No matter how much I love the poetry, it can seem tedious after a couple of hours. If I am performing, even if it is an intellectual performance in a classroom, I feel a little obligation to entertain. And so he's been accompanying me as much as possible. At the University of Chicago, there was a request for the poem "Glory." Ansted was playing the piano, an interlude, and for some reason, I sang it. I don't know why. It was unplanned. But once it happened, it was an extraordinary moment for the audience, for me, and that started the collaboration. So now I've reached the point where I always include music; there's a combination of reading the poems, singing them: these combinations become other dimensions of meaning.

■ *When you perform with your son, do you work spontaneously?*

We don't rehearse. We're engaged in a dialogue with the music and the words. What I say influences the playing and the playing influences the decisions I make as the person who will interpret these words and the music. Instead of shaping the language on the page where I'm creating a visual object, it is now purely a sonic object and I make decisions about the musical line that I can sing, what will repeat, how that might be. It is not planned because that would ruin the purpose of the dialogue: we're to not have the conversation we've had before; we want to keep talking.

■ *To what extent do you think about audience?*

When I was a child and writing, it was for myself; many people didn't know I was writing, many teachers didn't know. In fact, it wasn't discovered until fifth grade that I was writing because I left a poem on my desk and the teacher saw it. Prior to that, I had been careful about putting things away. My parents knew that I wrote, but they didn't demand to see it or anything; that was perfectly fine. But when I write now, even though I'm writing it in a way that is fulfilling for me, I know that when I'm done it may go to an editor; so I am aware that I am not the destination audience. The pleasure of the writing is all mine, but I have the illusion some discovery might occur that encourages the dangerous, *dangerous* arrogant notion that, "Hmm, I've discovered something. Somebody else might need to read this." It's not true that someone *needs* to read something I've written. I doubt that need. But it makes it false to then claim that I am the sole audience. I don't say, "Hmm, what might this particular audience want to happen here?" But I am aware that, if at all possible, I'd like to create an opportunity for someone else to retrace the journey I took in making the poem. I will write and I will be true to my idea, but the trueness of the idea is a little tainted by my awareness that it might be shared.

■ *Why is your book-length poem,* Slave
Moth, *easier than your other poems?*

Because I did have an agenda when I wrote that. When Ansted was in sixth grade, I went to a meeting of a parent focus group and some ninth grade parents were concerned about an ancestry project their children were assigned, some kind of genealogy project. Some parents argued that their children could not do the assignment because of slavery: "He couldn't get past slavery," one mother said. She was outraged by how embarrassed her son had to be by this assignment. I tried to be quiet, but eventually I couldn't, so I mentioned that my son had to write an ancestry poem in sixth grade; he had no problem with it. I said, "You put him in a box, he'll explore the box and he'll say, 'Nice box.' When he's done, he'll get out. Look at it from another way. Maybe he'll say, 'It needs a little door right here; it needs some windows.' He is not embarrassed by any part of his heritage or by anything else that is part of him." I said, "In the ancestry poem, Ansted went *all* the way back. He traced his ancestry to the big bang." He really did; he wrote about how we were all stardust.

We can have a relationship with information. There's a way of perceiving and looking that doesn't mean "Here is the only possible way to respond." I wrote this book to address that issue. I have a literate slave girl as the narrator, and despite her circumstance, she is going to find a way to have her self, to be a person, no matter the box of slavery, and by doing that, she has to push down the walls, she has to knock out the ceiling. It bothered me that someone could be so embarrassed that he couldn't look into the experience of slavery to see the complexity and the richness. We tend to talk about it as this singular experience; I wanted to create another model of a slave, one who did think, who had ideas, and who, despite circumstances, forged a sense of identity as best she could within the context she was in. So that's how *Slave Moth* came about.

I have this girl Varl sewing her poems in the book, and I wanted to know what that would be like. So I made a dress by hand on which I stitched lines from two poems, and then I bought this doll to wear it. This is my Varl doll. I told the publisher about it and the publisher was oh so excited when I sent them a digital image of the dress, that the image is on the cover of the book. A film version called *My Master Is a Collector* was in the Ann Arbor Film Festival. Now a dance version called *Slave Moth* will debut in the fall. I'm sort of peripheral to these projects. That's the point, isn't it? The idea exists and now a choreographer reinterprets it; visual artists reinterpret it, allowing it to become something beyond my limits. It's just wonderful.

July 30, 2004

I JUST THINK I'M REALLY LUCKY

*At the opening and close of this interview, W. S. Penn falls into
the perspective he sees as characteristic of the oral tradition:
everything relates. Penn's Nez Perce relatives introduced him
to this point of view and he has spent much of his career striv-
ing to render it on the page since it plays a central role in his
consciousness. This project has taken him through many genres: an essay collection, a short story collection, and two novels; in addition, he has edited two books about Native
American culture.* All My Sins Are Relatives, *the book where
Penn thinks he began writing what he wanted, was a Critic's
Choice selection and won the North American Indian Prose
Award. His most recent novel,* Killing Time with Strangers,
won the American Book Award.

    People start saying MSU is involved in this, that, or the other thing.
You can't divest yourself; you can't not be involved. You and I are
involved; we may not like it, but we're involved. Anyway. So where do
we begin?

    ■ *It sounds as though you were writing in
    a journal from the time you were small.*
    Very small, yeah.

    ■ *Then someone gave you another journal when
    you were twenty-one and you wrote stories.*
    Yup.

    ■ *But then you spent ten years in college trying
    to be a success. What was your field?*
    I went to graduate school twice in English literature. The first
time I was at the University of California at Davis and I got pretty
much ABD, I hadn't taken my exams yet . . . what bumped me out of

it is there was nobody except one person, Jack Hicks, who was qualified to give me the exam; they hadn't read as much as I'd read. I don't want to sound arrogant, but it wasn't going to work and I wasn't happy being a critic. I quit and went up to Port Townsend and helped run that writers' school up there. Then I ended up working as a maintenance man at Hearst's castle and decided to go back to school. I went to Syracuse, which was pretty much the only place that would take me because when I left Davis I didn't know you had to file forms to quit school. I thought if you just didn't enroll and didn't pay your tuition that you were not enrolled. No one wanted to take me because Davis . . . I'd vanished, so . . . And other places worried about it, too. They saw this caesura in my transcript and they said, "What happened? There's nothing in your file that says you withdrew."

George Elliott at Syracuse took me and then because I wanted to go on for the doctorate, George and I sat down and designed the Doctor of Arts together and I did it. They had thirteen people go through that program; twelve of those thirteen people are tenured professors somewhere in this country. Then they cut it back to the MFA again; so it opened, and three years later, it closed.

▧ *You've written that you tried to write realistic stories when you were in graduate school.*

Yeah. The book *This Is the World*, all but the last novella were done for my doctorate. The title story was, I think, the first story I ever got paid for. *Quarterly West* paid me somewhere between $150 and $250 for it. I remember the letdown I felt when I got the acceptance letter. (Laughter) I walked in George Elliott's office at Syracuse and handed it to him. He looked at it and said, "Well, that's nice." He knew exactly what I was feeling. At that moment, just as with the PhD in literature, I had this disjuncture that made me realize that what I was doing wasn't about getting paid or getting published. I don't believe in private writing. You meet poets who say, "I write for myself." Yeah, that's just—you're bad. But I still remember that day. At that time in the English Department they were refurbishing the Hall of Languages at Syracuse and we were housed in the old gym with these burlap dividers between offices, so that whenever one of the professors had a fight with his mistress, you could hear it. And I walked down to George's little cubicle from the mailbox . . .

■ *Do you think you remember it so well because
it was a moment when you discovered publication
wasn't exactly what it was all about?*

Yeah, I think that. I really loved George; he once called me his true son. I always thought of him as my true father, and so it was the entire atmosphere of the occasion, to go to my mailbox in the gym, which was the English Department, get this letter which . . . immediately, I said, "Oh, great!" *Quarterly West* is a good magazine; I love it; I love what they did. But it just seemed so after the fact. It seemed like "Yeah, I've been working for years to get to this point and it finally happened and now there was just another point to get to." That's true of all my books, everything I do. I try to do something new and different, I don't know if it is, I can't be the judge of it, but I can't write the same thing over and over again.

■ *In* All My Sins Are Relatives, *you wrote that you listened
too much to editors and agents while working on your
first book,* The Absence of Angels.

Yes, yes, yes. I was very young. Now, when I talk to students, I say you have to be very careful, but you should always work with editors because they mean well and agents mean well, but the purpose of being a writer, as far as I'm concerned, is to grow sufficiently so that you know when enough is enough. If you think editors are stupid and you just dismiss it, then I think you're foolish. I always look at it; I always think about it. I like my agent right now a lot because when she says . . . In fact, the novel she's shopping around, she called up, said, "You've got to cut this; you've got to cut that, you've got to . . ." She's very direct. I look at it and she's picked passages I knew I was going to have to cut that I was hoping I could sneak by. (Laughter) But she also says, because she's knows I'm particular, "You can fight me on this one; you can fight me on that one . . ."

But the first novel, I changed everything way too many times from the person it was told in, to its structure. My agent said, "Oh, you can't write a novel in second person." So I changed it to first person. I liked it in second person. Of course, I no longer have that copy; it was somehow lost. And a year after I did that, Jay McIerney came out with *Bright Lights, Big City*, which was told in the second person. So you learn something that way. Now I have a great luxury: I can write whatever I darn well want to write. And I can write it any way I want. If somebody doesn't want to publish it, "Oh well, that's too bad." I don't care. Eventually somebody will, if it's any good or maybe it doesn't deserve to be published; that can still happen.

■ *That moment when you stopped trying to please editors and agents, focused on pleasing yourself, and produced* All My Sins Are Relatives *fascinates me. How did you do that?*

I got tenure. I'm still proud of *All My Sins Are Relatives*; I read it and I think, "Gee, who wrote this? It couldn't have been me!" When *All My Sins Are Relatives* came out, everything happened quickly. I had three books come out in a year and a half.

■ *I remember you saying that you wished you were as smart in life as you were when you wrote that book.*

Yeah, I still do. I still do. When I talk to my creative writing students, I keep saying, the person the writer creates to be the writer of the book has to be better than the person the writer is. You have to be smarter because [what] comes out of uncomplicated anger or love is not necessarily a good book. So there's this person sitting on your shoulder, or wherever, who writes the book. You have to keep feeding that person. (Laughter)

■ *How do you feed that person?*

I can write anything I want to now. And so I don't worry about, "Are people going to like this?" I worry about, "Do I like the sentence? Do I like the character?" It's terribly self-indulgent. I'll sit down in my study and, as my wife told my department chair, she's not allowed to interrupt. Nobody can come down in my study when I'm working. I don't even go upstairs to use the bathroom when I'm working. And sometimes, I'll write a page or two and I'll be so enjoying the process of writing that . . . (Laughter) I have an idea what I want to get done that day and I'll get halfway through it; I'll sit back and I'll read it and . . . "This is funny" or "This is fun to do." I'll do that so long that I'll lose the momentum. It no longer bothers me that I do that; doesn't matter because the scene finally shapes itself. I just think I'm really lucky.

■ *What do you get from writing?*

I've said in the past and I still believe it: that if I don't write, I become a really bad person. If I write, I think I'm a better husband, a better father, and, in general, a better teacher, a better friend, a better person.

■ *Why?*

I don't know. I don't know. I think writing satisfies something in me that's very, very deep and I *have* to do it. If I don't write, I get bitchy, things irritate me too quickly. It's like going to the gym. You don't want to go, but you go to the gym for an hour and then afterwards, you feel good. I feel better. I'm tired, but . . . I get done with it and I think, "OK! Now I can go out to lunch with my wife or my daughter, or I can go to baseball practice with my son or . . ." I can do these things and it's all fine; it's all part of who I am and what I am. But if I don't write, it's like taking a chunk out of me. I can go two or three days, but I can't go . . . The time in England, my agreement is I don't take a computer with me because I spend mainly family time; if it weren't for all the books I haven't read that I can read over there, I'd probably go a little nuts. Even though I can't take a computer, I already have two blank spiral notebooks and I'm gonna, of course, take a couple hundred pages of the new novel I'll probably have done by then and I'll be exercising that part of the mind if not actually writing pages and pages. Because I can't not do it. I tell my students: "You're looking at one of the luckiest people you'll see in your entire life."

■ *Why do you think it gets easier for you to write?*

It's like any other activity you want to be good at. If you want to be good at the piano, you have to practice, practice, practice, practice, practice, until . . . you can call it "muscle memory," I don't care what. I watch my son, who happens to be very good at piano, and my daughter is very good at the flute so—I don't want to leave her out. For him, the piano is the same thing: when he's troubled at school, those kids all say that his vocabulary is too big . . . In the mornings, he'll go to his piano and play for about fifteen, twenty minutes practice and play things and I watch him and I see the same kind of meditative process going on. He involves himself in this thing he loves and he really does get completely involved and it's very similar to writing. You can see that in almost anything. Sports would be an easy analogy. They tested pro golfers by putting sensors on their heads and they noticed that the best putters were the people who had almost no brain activity while they were putting, which means it's completely muscle memory. Writing, if you just do it over and over again, you don't worry about sentences any more, you don't worry about, "Gee, am I going to run out of characters?" No. All of a sudden, I understand Dickens, although he's not my favorite writer. Virginia Woolf said whenever Dickens ran out of steam, he just threw another handful of characters on the fire. And she's probably right. That's probably exactly what he did.

Everybody kept saying, "Nobody wants collections of short stories; you've got to write a novel; you've gotta write a novel." So I thought, "Well, I'd better make myself into a novelist." So I worked really hard and things got longer and longer and I can't write a short story anymore. A short story should focus on one or two characters, usually, maybe three important characters. Now my imagination thinks up people all the time and I'm not interested in stopping at twenty pages.

■ *How do you begin your books?*
It depends on what kind of writing I'm doing. *Killing Time with Strangers* began two ways. It began with the first sentence, which is "Life may be a record of failure." I wanted to bring it full circle so that it came all the way back to that sentence. Then the other thing I wanted to do, in *that* case . . . When *All My Sins Are Relatives* came out, I'd had a research grant from MSU to do that book, so I had to give a presentation for our department. I was talking about the Nez Perce idea of Dreaming, which it gets called, a philosophical way of looking at the world and understanding what probably is going to happen. It's not prophetic, but it can sometimes be very close. Jim McClintock raised his hand and said, "In your last book you talked about Dreaming and then in this book you talk about Dreaming. Are you done with that now?" I said, "Yeah, probably I am," but the moment I said that I realized that if he had to ask, then I still had a book to write that conveyed this. *Killing Time with Strangers* was a complete novelistic attempt to clarify what it is I mean, so that the reader is going through the same process that I would have to go through in order to reach some of the same conclusions.

Part of the process is you have to keep revisiting territory and imagine with philosophy and as much wisdom as you can, if you have any, situations until you see essentially not only what could be, but what you might want to be. And then if that seems to be the best thing, you've envisioned it in such a way that you then put all the blocks in place that allow that to occur, and then many times that's exactly what occurs.

■ *I thought it was about how if you imagine and imagine and imagine that shapes you and what happens.*

But it does. When my children were born, people would say, "Just you wait until this age. Just you wait until that . . ." I call them the just-you-wait crowd. I finally took up smiling at them and [saying], "Well, fine, if it happens, I'll be prepared for it." But I knew in my heart it was never going to happen. The things that other people have encountered with their children, if they happen in my household, happen in such a small degree that most people wouldn't notice. The rebellious teenager . . . I have to pretend my teenager is being rebellious so she doesn't go any farther than she wants to go.

■ *This passage from* Killing Time with Strangers *seems to be about imagining; could you please explain it? "There is a big step that comes before words, precedes the making, a step that is difficult precisely because it is done without words. Indeed, you have to empty yourself of words and make yourself into a round and open receptor—sort of a human sweat lodge or hogan—that awaits what it does not know by naming but only knows by an active and involved waiting, a continuous reshaping of the potential to be."*

The closest I can get, the active way would be waiting, keeping yourself very, very still, kind of a Buddhist, or even Shintoist fashion, but being very alert so that when what is going to come to pass shows itself in the distance, you recognize it and you're not off chasing other things in your head. It's an actively pure form of meditation in a way, but it's not quite that and, again, I don't want to say it's prophetic, but it allows you to see that out of a hundred million things out there, only ten matter and only three of those connect in a way that keeps the process intact and keeps the self whole. It's not like nighttime dreaming; it's a daytime Dreaming. It's almost like your eyes are slightly out of focus and they're not aimed at the interior, but they're looking for relationships that are there but normally aren't seen. And by actively waiting you're alert to those connections when they happen or the possibility that they may happen.

You have to be active about it because otherwise you goof. I goof all the time because I forget—I get caught up in departmental politics or the emotions of the moment and in order to actively wait, you have to let them go. But it's almost impossible to explain, which is why that sentence is so convoluted. To me, that sentence does make sense; it's as close as I can get in words.

■ *Do you consciously try to write things that are part of the oral tradition or does that just happen?*
No, it's not conscious, but I understand how to get the oral tradition onto the page from the books I've done, but also the way I grew up. There's always a sentence where I'm writing along and it gets stagnant. Then I go back and reshape it or change the narrative or something for it to sound more like it's told. I've got to compromise because most people don't . . . There are certain ways that things can get told which are not the normal ways things get told; [for example,] it's become apparent to me that my sense of humor is not everybody's. I laugh my head off and my daughter will laugh; she thinks it's pretty funny, my son thinks it's funny, but I put it in a book and people aren't laughing as hard as I think they ought to be—although they do laugh. And it can also be sentence structure, it can also be that kind of summary; a lot of native stories end "and that's the way it was."

■ *Well,* Killing Time with Strangers . . .
Lack of chronology, yeah.

■ *Lack of chronology and also there's not much character description. It says, "If you want to know what Amanda looks like, she walks like a duck."*
He says too, "My Amanda will go undescribed so that she has the freedom to be who and what she needs her to be." The essence is Amanda; it's not what she looks like. So he has to wait and see. Just you like said you're superstitious about . . . I honor superstition. It's traditional, for example, for women of all cultures at least in Western cultures not to tell people they're pregnant until they're really dead certain they're pregnant, three months, four months in. They may tell their husbands or their boyfriends or whatever, but I understand that. And it's the same kind of thing: why do you want to jinx Amanda by saying, "Well, this is what she looks like"?
You've got the old showing and telling distinction, which is complete nonsense. There are times when you need to tell. Most of the

time my students tell at the wrong times and that's where we get into the show and tell. "You need to show this. You've got to have characters talk and let people see what they look like. People want to see them move. Do they walk like a duck? Do they walk . . . Let them be and let them breathe a little bit. Let your character have something you didn't expect your character to say," which they find very difficult. Letting your character do or say what you didn't plan on having them do or say . . . They go, "How do I do that?" They're wrenching everything towards an end. But that's part of the telling . . .

Then there are other parts where economy . . . Henry James knew about economy. James and Melville, both understood, I think, oral storytelling. You go back to *Beowulf*, you go back to any culture, you go back to oral traditions. My Mexican or southwestern Mexican Indian friends, I hear the orality when they speak. When I taught in the South Bronx I had a Puerto Rican colleague; she was fabulous because she would sit down in this teacher's area with coffee and try to tell you something; it would take half an hour for her to tell you something that most people could get across in five minutes, but it was wonderful to listen to—what people call digression—she'd get off here and off there, and it all connected at the end. To me, that's orality. Some people are what I call very written. Hemingway is very written most of the time. Hemingway, forgive me, bores me. Faulkner understands the oral tradition; Faulkner understood.

It does come from understanding things aren't linear and they aren't chronological. You and I don't live in a chronological time. We have watches and we're going to meet here at 12:30, but because I was talking to my contractor because we're remodeling and then the phone rang as I was walking out the door and I answered the phone, and I had to talk to this person for at least a few minutes . . . We live in a constant mixture of all different kinds of times. You probably still remember something you think happened to you when you were five. My sisters used to tease me because I used to always say, "When I was three, this happened. When I was three . . ." Somehow, all these memories like spider filaments, like web filaments have attached to this one age and it's not important whether you were three or four or two or whatever. What's important is the process, the context, the meaning. Everything happened and that forms the person you are now and it never leaves you. You can't ever get rid of it. Again, I'm still not making any sense about the oral tradition, but for me it's that everything connects. I write out of those connections. It's both a pleasure and a little bit frightening.

■ *Why is it frightening?*
Because it does so connect. You mentioned Vietnam. I could make an argument that we won the Vietnam War. Most of my colleagues would stop talking to me if I did, but the Vietnam War spent, I'm sorry to use that word, but spent [60,000] American boys' lives to open up Red China. When you see how Vietnam is not an isolated war, Vietnam is the extension of the war in the Pacific. Korea was an extension of the war in the Pacific. It was never completely, totally won, not that it ever could be. That's the interesting thing about war. I don't know that anybody ever clearly wins them. You can drop two bombs on Japan and scare people to death and kill a lot of people and sign a peace treaty and then become one of [its] strongest allies, at least economically. Or you can firebomb Dresden, which killed more people and yet they never, ever end. The Cold War just keeps on going. And I see them [as] parts, not always pleasant parts, of a connection that politically and economically and socially is wrenching. Globalism is wrenching. It's hurting us a little bit; it's hurting other people probably more, but it's gonna happen. So what you have to do is sit down and say, "OK, can we see the ways in which it can happen well, or can we just complain about it?" That's what I mean by connection. And that's why you can't not be involved.

June 4, 2004

NOTHING IS MORE MOVING TO ME THAN WHAT HAPPENS IN THE AVERAGE LIFE

Scott Turow's massive achievements as both a lawyer and a writer astonish no one more than they do Scott Turow. This capacity for disinterested amazement may well help explain how he has done so much so well. Every day when he writes, he records whatever attracts him. Making a novel of these pieces consists of sewing them together like pieces of a quilt. When he finishes, the product seems as compellingly mysterious to Turow as it does to his many, many readers.

Turow has published two nonfiction books and six novels that have sold more than twenty-five million copies worldwide and won several literary prizes. He recently published Ultimate Punishment: A Lawyer's Reflections on Dealing with the Death Penalty.

■ *When I read the three books you've published, it seemed to me each subsequent one had more depth.* The Burden of Proof *has, I think, a wonderful richness. Do you have any sense of progression?*

Well, certainly I thought *The Burden of Proof* was a much more sophisticated book than *Presumed Innocent*. That's only the author. I don't know whose aesthetic is supposed to dominate here.

One of the difficulties now, for me, is that I have this vast audience. When I take my shoes in to be fixed, give my name, there is somebody behind the counter repairing shoes who says, "Oh, I love your books." That's the audience I always wanted, but *The Burden of Proof* was a pretty hard book for a portion of that audience. Now, for the people who are doing PhDs, it's not. You try not to be defined by your own success and it's a *great problem* in some ways because you feel, "Oh, gosh, I'm going to disappoint those people. I'm gonna disappoint those people." And, on the other hand, somebody else will be pissed off at you, people who are sitting around saying, "Well, I wanted you to go even deeper this time." So it's complicated.

■ *You talked about learning at Stanford to*
try to write novels bus drivers would read.

The writing program was divided. The great ideological struggle between the writers of new fiction and the realist tradition of [Wallace] Stegner gripped that department and the Writing Center. Wally used to extol the view that it was important to reach every reader. Someone just said to me there was a technical mistake in one of his novels written fifty years ago. I said, "Write to Wally. He'll care about it." He'd always argue if you're going to write a book about farming, the farm equipment has to be just right, that the imitation of reality has to take place on that level.

But, to say the least, there were contrary views in that department and they were the more fashionable views at that time. The *smart* view was that novels were Andre Gide and James Joyce.

■ *Did you try to write like Joyce?*

Yeah, I did. I did. That was a great burden to me. Tillie Olson was a teacher and dear friend and [I] even tried to imitate Tillie's work. That didn't work for me either.

■ *Do you think the novel you wrote while at Stanford,*
"The Way Things Are," should be published?

I don't think it should be published now. It's written in self-contained scenes, which is how my writing tends to progress. And a lot of the prose is very good. Its biggest problem was it was finished at the wrong time: it was about sixties politics at a time that people weren't interested in reading about sixties politics. I've been working for a number of years on a book that in some ways picks up with "The Way Things Are." That was going to be the next book. About a year or a year and a quarter ago I was blocked with that book and started—pardon my French—fucking around with something else much simpler, much easier. I've finished a draft of that manuscript and I'm planning to publish that book next spring. I don't think anybody will accuse me of having gone deeper. I like this book. It is literally for me comic relief, but in some ways, it has a very mature vision to it, I think. We'll see what people think of it.

■ *How did you get the notion of proposing* One L?

I didn't propose it. I wrote to my agent and by way of apology for the fact that I was going to law school, suggested to her that somebody ought to write a nonfiction book about law school because there wasn't anything out there. I had a great deal of difficulty communicating with this woman. And it is symptomatic of those difficulties that what came back to me was a contract to write *One L*. She didn't *get* that I was suggesting somebody else write this book.

It's an amazing story. It's utterly bizarre. I had no intention of doing this and was literally presented with the contract . . . literally presented with the contract. I was just stupefied. I had sort of abandoned the literary life. And there I was with a book contract. I can't . . . I wish I could remember the rest of that day. I can remember opening the letter. I knew something was odd about the letter. My wife was at work. I was standing on my stoop in San Francisco where we then lived. I *loved* the idea as soon as it was presented to me. Just loved it. I'll have to ask Annette at dinner tonight, see if she can possibly remember what my reaction was because I was staggered.

■ *Did you keep a journal a lot that first year at Harvard Law?*
Yeah. Yeah. There was a lot to say. And it was very helpful to me. I look back now understanding more about myself and see that period as critical in terms of my psychological development. Certain issues rang enormous bells for me. This powerful man standing in front of this herd of young 'uns, intimidating them, played out the wrong dream for me. The thought reform that takes place in law school also was dramatic to me. I didn't like the fashionable tropes of the English Department at Stanford. And there was something very appealing to me in the way lawyers viewed the world. Basically, the law says, "First, let's find out where all the dots are. And then let's try to draw a straight line down the middle." It's like a Euclidean geometric problem. Of course, there are all kinds of different ways to draw that line. In fact, [the law provides] only one line; but you learn a great deal that way. So I was in deep conflict because I hated the process, yet I related to the fundamental enterprise.

■ *Before* Presumed Innocent, *you wrote a novella?*
I started another book which I *still* play with. Usually the times go past me. This was a great idea when I started it. There's something terrific in it. It's about a young man who's in his first year in college and he gets drunk the first big weekend and participates in a gang bang. Maybe

I'll finish it sometime; it still resonates for me. But I started that and I worked on that for about a year. And then I began to get this idea, very much like the impulse that gripped me last May: "Oh, to hell with this. This is too hard. I'm going to do something simple. I'm going to lay aside all of the baggage and write this murder mystery. I'm not going to strain for a literary voice. I'm going to write in what seems purely to be my own voice." And I started writing *Presumed Innocent*.

I went on about two years that way and, then, I just couldn't figure out the end of the book. I didn't know who killed this person. I had subplots, I couldn't imagine what the hell they were about. So I took time off and I wrote this novella about people of my generation growing apart from each other and getting into their kids and different commitments. It wasn't too bad, called "Cut Up in Pieces." I sent it to New York and also to friends in California. I then went back to finish *Presumed Innocent*.

I sent ["Cut Up in Pieces"] to Gail Hochman, who represents me now, and she showed it to Jon Galassi who was then at Random House. He thought it might be worth publishing if I wanted to do more work on it. Gail calls me up and, you know, not very easy to get a first novel published, and she says, "I think I may have somebody interested in it." I said, "Forget it. I'm back at work on this other book; I'll finish it in a year or two. It will be much easier to sell this book." That's one of the problems of writing on the side. You get driven emotionally by everything else you're doing and by then the issues of *Presumed Innocent* seemed more important to me.

When I went back to *Presumed Innocent*, I just let it go. I took three weeks off from the U.S. Attorney's Office and I was going to work on a series of essays about the criminal justice system. I spent the first week writing that and somehow that transformed itself into the impulses of fiction and I wrote, in the next two weeks, the entire ending of *Presumed Innocent*. I still had to fill in the middle, which was the trial, but I went back to the beginning and began rewriting again. And by the time I had left the U.S. Attorney's Office, I had gotten back to where I had been when I had put the novel aside, had rewritten all of that, and was ready to go through to the end. And I did that. I did that.

■ *I read you plotted it while you were gardening.*

I did. [For] a couple of years while I was writing this novella, "Cut Up in Pieces," it would be my task every Saturday to think about the plot [of *Presumed Innocent*] while I was in the garden. But I didn't realize I had resolved any of this until this period in 1984 when I took three weeks off. And, all of a sudden, there I was writing the end of *Presumed Innocent*. I thought I was nuts, by the way. I thought it was just, just lunacy. Just lunacy. All of these twists and turns and counter-stories and very self-consciously written against form, convention, genre. Thought I knew exactly what I was doing, but . . .

■ *And I read you wrote every morning on your way into work.*

That is absolutely true. That is not only how *Presumed Innocent* was started but also how these two other novellas I'm describing, one about the man in college and "Cut Up in Pieces"—they were all written the same way.

I don't know if I'd ever have published any of these books if it were not for the computer because the time to write was so fractional. I would write whatever I wanted to write. And I couldn't put myself back in that place because I didn't have the time to get back there. I would just pick up in a free associative way and eventually with the computer I was able to sew all these little pieces together. But it was like a quilt: this patch and that patch.

■ *Oh really, I had the notion you started with this big plot . . .*

The beginning of *Presumed Innocent* was sort of written that way in the sense that as I go through those notebooks which I still have it seems like the story is developing up to a point, but beginning with 1984 when I got the computer, I wrote the ending and I wrote all over the book. I'd go back and this passage, that passage. The first passage I have on the computer is a file called "Barbara," which is descriptions of Rusty's wife.

■ *Could you give me a sense of your process*
when you wrote The Burden of Proof?

Initially, I'd come into the office on the 8:52, so I'd get up at 7 and write til 8:15, then I'd get dressed. So I was writing for about an hour and fifteen minutes and doing better than you would think that way. And that went on until, I think, October of 1988, I agreed with my partners that . . .The summer of 1988 was one of the hardest periods I've had practicing law. I represented brokerage houses in disputes they had with their customers in the wake of the stock market crash of 1987. A lot of those cases went to hearing. I had been hired as a special prosecutor by the village of Oak Park and was investigating its police department. Two of those cases went to trial—dismissal cases against two officers who were both ultimately discharged from the police force. And then I had one other civil case that I was trying for an aircraft manufacturer that went to trial. I tried six cases in a period of four or five months and it was just way too much, *way* too much. As one of my partners put it, I retired the Sonnenschein trial trophy. (Sigh) It takes these periods when things get out of control to say to yourself, "Gee, is this really what I want out of my life?" I have always enjoyed practicing law. My partners are wonderful people and have been very kind to me, but enough was enough.

I'm in my fifteenth year practicing law. And it's really weird to have done something fifteen years and think that people know you because you do something else. It's taken me a number of years to adjust to the fact that having wanted *desperately* when I was younger to be a writer and to be known as a writer, and having accepted that was not going to happen, having taken on another profession and having succeeded in it, that nevertheless, I'm back to square one, that what I wanted to start with is what I have. To enjoy that has taken a bit of adjustment. It really has.

It took me a while to unplug; but by the end of 1988, I had begun to spend more time at home and I was writing for increasing periods of time, usually three or four hours at a stretch. At that point, I had renewed this process I'd begun with *Presumed Innocent* of writing all over the book and I did that and . . . I then began in early '89 going straight through again to get a draft and then I guess it would be by July of '89, I had a good draft and sent that to [New York]. But the real collecting process . . .

You have to imagine a bunch of computer files: this one is called "Helen," this one is called "Clara." Usually they're character's names and there are various passages about the characters and sometimes it was Stern's reflections about his children. All those ruminative passages tended to be written in these hour and fifteen minute sessions in the mornings. Sometimes I'd get a little time at night.

■ *How did you decide what to write?*
Just what I wanted to write. I do very little rewriting in that phase. Sometimes I'd write the same passage three times over a period of a month, three different ways, if I was absorbed with a particular idea.

■ *So you'd write these intuitively.*
Right.

■ *And then eventually they'd begin . . .*
Once you find the voice of a particular book, at least I've found now, things come pretty automatically. I'm talking about the authorial voice of that book; this third person voice inflected heavily by this proper speech of immigrant Sandy Stern, and his occasional love of American idiom. That's the voice of that book, and there's a kind of pompousness to it. Once it's discovered, though, it all moves from there. And Stern's dialogue is a subset of that voice. He is very stilted and formal in his speech.

■ *The idea of people trying to stay in control recurs in your work. And you take that issue to another level of understanding each time. Carolyn in* Presumed Innocent *needs to control, but instead of seeing her as bad, in the same way Perini [from* One L*] is bad, she's sick.*
I didn't realize what *Presumed Innocent* is about thematically until long after I was done with it—which is one of the problems with writing books. But if you say to me, what do you think that novel is about, my answer is the uses and misuses of power in the private and the public sphere. In that one sentence you unite virtually all of the action of the novel. This theme is certainly one I continue to be drawn to profoundly.

■ *And Sandy Stern the courtroom performer in* Presumed Innocent *resurfaces as vulnerable, confused Sandy Stern in* The Burden of Proof. *You go straight to the underside. Do you have any idea how you were able to access that?*
No. I don't. The manuscript I'm finishing now doesn't seem mysterious to me. The voice it's written in is a voice I recognize and its conventions . . . , all of it are things that I know. When I look at Sandy Stern and I look at *The Burden of Proof,* I don't know how in the world I was able to write that book. Now if it were somebody else, it wouldn't surprise me. I'm not holding it up against Tolstoy. I'm just saying given me and what I know of myself, it's shocking I would write a book about an immigrant who was about fifteen years older than me and would know him so intimately. It's really beyond me. But it worked. At least it worked for me as the writer.

■ *It worked for me as a reader. I was sobbing at the end.*
I was sobbing at the end of it, too. I don't apologize for that novel. I know that it was in an absolute sense not as popular as *Presumed Innocent*.

■ *It seems to me your books suggest women can save men. For instance, at the end of* One L, *you say you hope more women go into law and change the law. In* Presumed Innocent, *Rusty is looking unsuccessfully for salvation from Carolyn and Barbara. In Sandy Stern's case [The Burden of Proof], it's more complicated, but the theme is there. And you've talked about your wife being supportive. Do you talk to her about your writing?*
Well, I talk to her about it when it's done. She's an artist. This is her work on both walls. We talk a little to each other about process; we talk to each other a lot about the finished stuff. We don't talk much about what's going on in between. Our principal interest is our life together: our kids, the stuff we share. The artwork for each of us is pretty much an individual enterprise.

Annette always paid me the homage of considering me a writer, even when that seemed sort of absurd, and it was very helpful. She was always on my side when I said I wanted time to do this. She wouldn't say, "What the hell are you doing?" when it was eleven o'clock at night and I was down in the corner of the living room, tapping away. I bought this computer for $2,500. I'm staggered by that because at the time I did it, I was making about $40,000 a year. That's an enormous investment. That's just an enormous investment. And she never even thought twice about it. She has always taken for granted that this was something I was going to continue to try to do.

I am one of these people who believes that, and having raised three children now, gender identity comes relatively late in the game. I think we start out pretty much imagining both alternatives as kids. And I think to the extent [novelists lose] track of [both], they lose track of a very positive aspect of our imagination.

■ *In something I read you were asked why the women are so terrible in* Presumed Innocent.
Yeah, right. I always had . . . *always* had enormous sympathy for Carolyn, whom I *thought* I was presenting pretty clearly as the victim of an abused childhood. I've felt a certain fear, just because of some of

the feminist hostility to *Presumed Innocent*, of writing from a female point of view; but in the next book, I'm gonna do it. It will be half and half. There will be two first person narrators and there is also a section that will be written third person and sometimes from the point of view of a woman. Actually, Sonny Klonsky from *Burden of Proof*.

■ *You talk about crying when you finished* Presumed Innocent . . .
It wasn't *now* that was moving me. It was the past. What I kept saying to myself was, "I had wanted it so badly in the past . . ." That was gone. I had found other ways . . . I felt amazed; the way things work out is utterly bizarre. Nothing is more moving to me than what happens in the average life. And I looked back at the desperation I had felt, the wild ambition . . . I had wanted so badly to achieve something in a literary life and had given it up. [I] felt in some way that the ambition was unrecoverable and realized, I guess, that I had suffered a lot, suffered my own ambitions terribly. So that was what was so moving to me.

■ *Does it make you feel good to write every morning?*
I sure like to write. I sure like to write. And it's never as frustrating as practicing law can be. The law at its best can be . . . , trying a case, waiting for a verdict, you can't do anything more suspenseful. The thing that always used to blow my mind away when I was waiting for a jury, especially in a prominent case, is you watch them come back in and whatever it was going to be, guilty or not guilty, you knew in some small way history was happening. The society was reaching a fork in the road and it was going to go that way or another way for this individual and if it was a prominent individual, for the community and the people who depend on him. You don't get that kind of high writing. It's not that dramatic and exciting, but in terms of fulfillment, it's terrific, terrific.

■ *You've talked a bit about law helping your writing because
it deals with moral issues. Do you stand by that?*
Yeah, I think that.

■ *Do you have anything else to say about it?*
Well, I puzzle on it all the time. I learned a lot about narration trying cases. You take a bunch of people off the street and you have to explain things to them. And all of the sophistication that gets pounded

into you in graduate school about enjoying and admiring the elusive, the subtle, the elegant, suddenly gets kicked the other way. Mere gestures are not going to do it. It was very helpful to me to see the mesmerizing effect that stories have—no matter how many you hear, you haven't heard enough. The star witness, when telling a story well, will capture the courtroom. And I learned a lot about how those stories are organized to make them accessible to this listening audience.

I learned a lot, writing briefs with fifteen-page limits, about the preciousness of my own language. Somehow, the world didn't collapse when I cut that sentence, that paragraph, that page. And I've also learned that writing is work and that to a great extent, conjuring with rules and conjuring with the situations in my own constricted plots are not that different from one another. This division between work and creativity strikes me as utterly puzzling. There's an enormous amount of creativity that goes into writing the average brief or scholarly article. What distinguishes the novel is that the materials are entirely imagined. But once they're there, it's not a lot different as a process. You're still working on a confined playing field.

■ *It seems as though most of the writers I've talked to like to try different kinds of books.*
Well, they're under the illusion they're doing that. It's always easy to stand back and see that they haven't succeeded very well. There really is one book every author is writing.

I *think* I'd like to do different things. You want to try out the variety of your personality. But you are only one person. I look at John Updike, who has written a lot of different stuff and is a great writer; but whenever he tries to be funny, to me, he doesn't succeed very well. He keeps coming back to these Rabbit books, and I'm one of those people who mourn Rabbit's death. He's done it four times and I thought the last book was a magnificent novel, Tolstoyan in its depths. And here's a guy who's tried a lot of different things, does many things well, but there's something about that particular character and voice that allows him to tap into a certain greatness.

As a writer, I don't feel I've done my best work yet; I suppose everybody feels that way. There is a yawning Faulknerian voice in here somewhere and I don't know if I'll ever tap into that or not. But I may get my arms around it eventually. Who knows?

October 30, 1992

ACQUIESCENCE TO THE UNKNOWN ALLOWS
WRITERS TO STAY VITAL

Katherine Vaz wants to create work with a voice that speaks to her readers of intimate matters too subtle and important for direct explanation. Vaz identifies patience as the most important quality she brings to this quest because she writes until she has an intuitive sense that her work has taken off. Because her aesthetic instincts require constant nourishment, she reads widely, sometimes copying literary works by hand so she can savor the words.

Her two novels, Saudade *and* Mariana, *were best sellers in Portugal and in 2002, Katherine Vaz was named the Portuguese-American Women's Association Woman of the Year. The Library of Congress selected* Mariana, *which has been published in six languages, as one of the top thirty international books of 1998. As a result of winning the Drue Heinz Literature Prize, her short story collection,* Fado & Other Stories, *was published by the University of Pittsburgh Press. She has also published nonfiction and children's stories. She is currently a Briggs-Copeland Lecturer in Fiction at Harvard University.*

> *You said when you were twelve you wrote something and you didn't know where it came from . . .*

It was in the days when we had vocabulary books; the book was called *Word Wealth* and Sister Delfina put a couple words on the board. I can't remember what they were, but I remember writing a paragraph with them that I thought came from some place outside myself, almost as if it wrote itself; I found that very thrilling. I don't believe there's anything magical about that: something in me just got unlocked and came out. I remember feeling very exhilarated by writing this clean, wonderful paragraph . . . I played piano for nine years; I remember a couple of times playing a scale where I thought the scale took over for me. That exhilaration made me want to be a writer. It was that simple.

We have two voices in the world. One is the practical one that we use to get through the day and the other is a voice inside us that we can't use and don't use because it almost is destroyed when it's let out in the air. It can be too romantic or too philosophical when we try and translate it. But books of fiction put that voice into stories in a way that makes letters important, makes writing important and reading important. It's not that we speak of these profound things; we describe the world with that force below them, so we feel that voice radiating out. That's important for writers and for readers. Certainly for me, when I read a book that makes me feel like I'm speaking on that level with someone . . . it's not solemn, but it feels profound and, to me, almost musical. Music hits us the way that level of language does, which is why people universally are attracted to music and absorb it without needing to criticize it or to make comments; they simply receive it. That level of voice is why we read and ultimately why we write. We write to speak that way to other people whom we may never meet. That's what keeps me going.

I sometimes think that's why I like to swim so much. It's a very bad week when I don't go swimming because there's that floating or lightness that is the way music works and the way writing works when it *catches* you, when it tells a good story. People hunger for stories, the way human beings always have, because it's such a random, busy world. When writers pick things out of the chaos and make a shape out of it, there's something beautiful about that, the way we see a painting or the way that we listen to a piece of music. Someone has created something highly selective for us so we can fall into a sense of the mystery of the world put in front of us, but in a way that contains all the things that we know and recognize.

There's an odd rule that the more specific we make a world, the more universal it becomes.

▪ *That does in some way work, yes.*

It *does* work because we feel like someone has invited us into something that's true, something that's whole, something that is fully and keenly realized and with a certain sense of authority. Even if we've never used a samovar, to feel it in a story, we feel connected to yet another part of the world, but through objects, through what people specifically do. I think that's why we love stories so much.

■ *Well, your books make me cry.*
I hate to say it, but that's really good to hear. (Laughter) That makes me glad. They were difficult to write. *Mariana* in particular was a wrenching book to write.

■ *I read it took years because at first it didn't work.*
I spent a long time writing stuff that even I couldn't get through; it was boring. I had Mariana as a character appearing in a contemporary story. It was just dreadful. I had her visiting a contemporary woman and I wrote hundreds of pages . . . One evening, I went swimming and I remember later lying on my bed, saying, "My head is splitting in two; my head is splitting in two." Then suddenly out of nowhere I said, "I think she wants her own book." The contemporary thing all fell away and I thought, "Why don't I just write the story of her life?" I wrote the book in almost to the day nine months. I finished on the fourth of July; I was really in the seventeenth and eighteenth centuries. I went into the living room, looked at my husband, and said, "I think I just finished." He said, "Well, then they're setting off fireworks for you to celebrate," which was appropriate because in the last scene of the book, something happens in the sky. The question is, did it take me nine months to write or four years? It really took four years because that included going to the convent in Portugal and doing the research. It's important to get things right, calmly fully realizing every scene, not for accuracy's sake so much as for authenticity. Walker Percy has a line about you need the feel of a place on your skin, to paraphrase. So I wanted to feel the place on my skin rather than just in my head.

Writing is always a process of getting beyond that, "Gee, I think this is working." "OK, that's all right; that will work . . ." and just knowing that something works. More and more I think writing has to do with patience. I'm disciplined but that's not enough. I had this training of going to a school run by Spanish nuns and they were big on a couple hours of homework every night; I had no trouble being disciplined; I still don't. More than just discipline, though, it's quietness and patience and waiting for whatever it is to click. I grew up near San Francisco, so the analogy I always think of is the trolley drivers: the cable would fall off and they'd have to step out and throw it back on the line that was over the street. Sometimes it would take a few tries before the cable hooked back on. Writers know when it clicks, when the cable is hooked; they know when it's just good or OK or passable or competent, and they know when the rhythm seems to be upon them. Sometimes that's a long process of patience and attention to get there.

You've said that your father set a good example for you by painting every day.

Yes, it was a quiet settling into doing work that he enjoyed. I have a sister-in-law who took some of his paintings finally and sold them at a fair. He would give the paintings away. He painted for the pleasure of it. He was quite good, but it was settling in with pleasure and surprise; he wasn't sure where something would be going; he would try all sorts of styles and it was something that he enjoyed. So that must have seeped into my consciousness that a person can settle into that kind of quiet, focused attention to something artistic and that's a good thing. I'm sure that I absorbed a lot of that.

You've said that when you were young, you copied stories so that you could learn how to write.

Oh, I actually still do that because it slows me down, because we get too rushed when we write, we get impatient, and to feel the formation of each letter in each word settles me down into the lines of other stories. I find it a good exercise to center myself. It's a matter of feeling that it's a handmade thing and I drop into the calmness of someone else's sentences. We read awfully fast, too.

Here at Harvard, we were talking about setting and students brought in examples of what they thought were good settings authors had done. I finally stopped them because they were reading *so fast* that they were stumbling over the words and missing . . . And these are very, very smart, good students. They all laughed and said that they're used to reading that way. It was an interesting and funny exercise. I actually was stopping them after reading a paragraph and they couldn't recall all the details of the lines and they should have; they were missing things even then and they knew it. We're taught to do everything fast and not to do things deeply or carefully, so I have to catch myself and sometimes even now I'll copy things out to see how stories are built: how did an author smooth the transitions in? I like to pick writers who are very different from who I am and how I write just to see how other people work. Then, of course, the main point is to put those all aside, forget about them and not to imitate, to wait for something that comes with its own form, its own content to me and is my own because all those other things work *because* they're unique. It's a process of being patient for something coming out of who I am.

■ *Do you write every day?*

Flannery O'Connor has a wonderful line about believing more and more in inspiration the older she got, but that she'd sit at her desk from nine to twelve every day so it would know where to find her if it came looking. I believe you do have to sit there and see if it comes. You don't get this clarion call. If you're in touch with that process every day, that doesn't mean every day is going to be good. After a while you get patient with that. I try and be consistently in touch with the process, at least thinking about or sitting at my desk first thing every morning. I think everyone is born with a different nervous system and that dictates times and habits and that those aren't as much of a consequence as how well a writer can be quiet and attentive and focused and patient for that story to arrive. Since I am such an early morning person, I find it easy to sit and go over things and see if there's something there pretty much every morning and almost write at random if nothing is. Then the day sometimes comes and takes things away from me; I have other obligations, but I try and have lots of time when I don't have my day too fractured because I do my best thinking when I'm uninterrupted. When I know I've got something, I focus on that. When I feel that it's catching, then I work very intensely; I can write twelve hours a day.

Sometimes, though, I'll go for weeks or months when writing feels stale, lacking in fresh air, with the whiff of the lamp. Then I have to get up from my desk and go out in the world.

Not all of my ideas pan out. I tell students that ideas can only go so far because putting words on paper can help us figure out what we think and feel. Alice Munro has a line I very much like because people are always saying, "Should we write about what we know? Should we write about what we don't know?" and she remarked once that she liked to write what she didn't know about what she knew. I'm always trying to go to that. That means pushing into the unknown part of the known world, so it's an informed view, but trying to get to the mystery of it. Again, that's Flannery O'Connor's idea about stories being a frame around mystery, and the mysteries we might be after vary at different times in our lives.

▨ *You're frequently identified as a Portuguese-American writer; how important is your background?*
Well, the three books I've done thus far have had that as the inspiration of the subject matter because my father's family came from the Azores and I grew up in California . . . My father wrote a book called *The History of the Portuguese in California.* He was very involved in the Luso community in the Bay Area; he gave a lot of speeches, he wrote this book. A lot of people would come to our house or send us letters or tell us stories. And we grew up around my Portuguese relatives. Carlos Fuentes has a nice quote about writers giving voice to those who have none. It seemed to me there were lots of amazing stories that people weren't turning into fiction. For example, I was sent one day to the house of my godmother because her housekeeper, Mrs. Correia, had locked herself out. She didn't speak English, just Portuguese, and she couldn't read or write, and my father blurted one day that he thought she thought in color. She couldn't use the telephone because she couldn't identify numbers either, so he colored the numerals on her phone with paint and made a placard with different necklaces of dots of paint; that's how she dialed, in color. Even then this seemed a metaphor for being in a different world. But I had to go and let her in the house; I remember being very moved by how patient she was because she had been locked out for hours and didn't think to do anything but sit there til someone rescued her. I had some cousins in Hayward, California, and the man of the house was having an affair with the woman next door and his wife closed all the curtains on that side of her house so she didn't have to look at his mistress's house any more. The children grew up thinking that all houses had a dark and a light side, like the moon. When I was a young writer, I tried to write what my mentor Oakley Hall referred to as "brittle-people-saying-brittle-things-to-each-other" stories and then one day I sat down—I can even see the room in Los Angeles—and thought I should look to who I was. In one day I wrote a story from my family's history about a priest persuading my great aunt to give her land to the church when she died; the story still sometimes gets included in different California anthologies. I finally had written about something close to me.

But having Portuguese-American characters in a story isn't about sociology; telling a good story with specific details is what matters. I wanted to tell stories about people who didn't have what I saw as a voice, at least in American letters, but I want to write for everyone, just as I don't pick or choose what to read based solely on the nationality of the characters. Being in a certain hyphenated category isn't the point so much as saying, "People of any nationality, any combination, are mainstream. All that matters is good writing and good stories."

I'm proud to have written about the Portuguese-American community, though. They've been wonderful; the Portuguese community has been terrific. When I go to Lisbon, they call me the American cousin and they're very pleased that I've written these stories, but no one wants to be on a separate, special shelf. It gets into defining a little too much who we are by blood or nationality.

▪ *Your father painted . . . what struck me about*
your books is that they're so rich sensually.
I've had eye surgery twice, and so colors and what they mean and the science of the eye is fascinating to me. I did a lot of research about that for my first book. Books document who we are at a certain time and I wanted a drenching of the senses in that way—a lot about color and the eye and . . .

▪ *You're talking about your first book, right?*
My first book, *Saudade.* I was trying to get across how women and their physicality and mentality describe the world. Right after I sold my book, I went to see a movie as a treat and it happened to be *The Piano,* which is of course about a deaf woman also who is trying to achieve her own language. It's really about how a woman learns to speak when she doesn't seem to have a voice in the world. I thought, "Oh, heavens, heavens, on completely different continents, we seem intrigued by the same thing." So we're trying to document who we are at a certain time.

▪ *You said that some of your collected*
short stories were parts of Saudade.
Actually, it was the other way around: I wrote some stories where I found my voice, however haltingly, and I wanted to see if I could expand that, and that's what made my first book be about the Por-

tuguese in California. It seemed to me that I had so many stories from my past about that. I'm now a decade and a half beyond that. I'm in the beginning stages of trying to do something that corresponds more with who I am now. I don't want to do the same thing again.

■ *Have you done that consciously as you've gone along, pursue different projects . . .*

I wish I could say I've been completely conscious at every move, but I haven't; I've been stumbling around and trying to see what clicks. The story of Mariana got handed to me by a friend who'd read the translations of her love letters by Rilke, and she said, "Oh, you know a lot about Portuguese things, maybe this is a book you'll want to do." I ended up writing that one in that four-year process and I thought I was going to just sell it here, but my agent sent it to London, to a fellow named Patrick Walsh who was then at the Christopher Little Agency, and he sold it in six languages; it's only this year that it sold here. It's had a strange route: that's why I got sent on a book tour in Italy. There were benefits that I hadn't predicted. It's dangerous to try and predict too absolutely what's going to happen, but there was something in the story of Mariana that captivated me. Again, it's about a woman trying to find her voice in the world; it's a woman who's in a cloister for decades and has this love affair with a soldier—a very different story from my first book about a deaf girl who comes from the Azores to America, but I'm fascinated by how women express themselves in the world.

■ *You were drawn to the story about the nun and started . . .*

And just started. And then had a lot of miscues and then it took a strange route in the world. Doing very well overseas: it did very well in Germany, and certainly in Italy and in Portugal it was a best seller . . .

■ *That must have been fun.*

Yeah, I did a lot of interviews there. I was on television, so people would send drinks over to me in restaurants when I was in Lisbon, which was kind of fun . . . and strange, because I'm an American from California. Maybe it was my lesson that it's a big world and that there are readers in all sorts of guises and facets and places that we don't always know about. I'm a believer in writing for readers, that we write because it means a lot to us to read a book and fall into a world and feel that a voice is speaking to us. I also believe that writers have to go out in the world and [see] what befalls a person. I'm a believer in putting something out in the world and seeing what comes back. There's a rigidity with the way we live now. We always want to know what we're going to be doing a year from now or five years from now. Acquiescence to the unknown allows writers to stay vital; otherwise, they're in danger of closing down or having too many limits.

We can be open to surprise and what the world gives us. At the age of forty-six, I moved to the East Coast because I didn't want to live my whole life in California, so there's that leap into the unknown. Then I happened to get hired at Harvard because I thought, "Gee, well, I'd better do something now" and sent out applications. That wouldn't have happened if I had stuck with the known. Now, this is going to lead somewhere else. I'm curious as to what that will be.

■ *In your essay "Baptism," you talked about all these sad things happening, your friend dying, for instance; you said you were learning to have compassion for everyone's story. What did you mean by that?*

Even though I was in a lot of pain when my friend died—we were both twenty-six—it enabled me to realize that the rest of the world was walking around with that kind of pain, too. There's a Chekhov story I love called "The Lady with a Lap Dog." The main character Gurov suddenly realizes he's really in love for the first time in his life and he's getting older now. Because he's got this great secret love within him—he's married and so is his lover—he looks around Moscow and he's full of contempt for everyone's frivolous habits and empty ways and gambling and so forth. He's walking his daughter to school before he's going to meet his mistress, Anna, feeling that no one on earth knows what he's thinking or feeling or where he's going or where his heart lies at that moment. He suddenly realizes, "Wait a minute, wait a minute, everyone must be walking around this way, too." He goes from looking at the world with this impatient, jaundiced eye to great compassion; it's a beautiful story for that reason. So it's not just understanding our individual pain; it's suddenly realizing, "Oh, wait a minute, if I'm walking around or going to the grocery story or the stationer's and aching with pain at having lost my friend, then who knows what has happened to the clerk or this person or that person?" In the Chekhov story, there's a feeling that the best part of all of us is hidden, and that taps into what I was saying before about the voice of writers and where they try and connect. When I lost my friend and felt bereft, I realized that one must have great compassion also for what it would have been like for the mother to have lost her daughter and for anyone to have suffered . . . a kind of quietness in realizing we never know what's going on with someone else, entirely, even people who are close to us.

■ *Jim Harrison said that one of the things he liked about getting older was that it was easier for him to lose himself in characters unlike himself.*

I absolutely agree and that's where I am now: not thinking so much about the immediate people I grew up around, or who was I then, but looking at the big world out there. We become fascinated by the distances we all feel from each other, which is why marriage is one of the timeless subjects to write about, because two people who are supposed to be intimate have such enormous chasms between them. That's painful and endlessly fascinating for that reason. So, yeah, that is one nice thing about getting older.

April 26, 2004

Every interview in this collection was re-edited after January 1, 2004 and then reviewed and approved by the interviewees or their literary executors. My first interview collection, *Finding the Words: Conversations with Writers Who Teach* (Swallow/Ohio, 1985) included earlier versions of talks with Allen Ginsberg, Clarence Major, James Alan McPherson, N. Scott Momaday, William Stafford, Wallace Stegner, Diane Wakoski, Anne Waldman, Richard Wilbur, and Helen Yglesias. Other published versions include: Marvin Bell, *Black Warrior Review* (2000); Allen Ginsberg, the *Washington Post* (1984), *Spontaneous Mind: Selected Interviews 1958–1996*, ed. David Carter (New York: Harper Collins, 2001); Etheridge Knight, *Flying Island* (1993); Clarence Major, *San Francisco Review of Books* (1982); *The Point Where Teaching and Writing Intersect*, ed. Nancy Larson Shapiro and Ron Padgett (New York: Teachers & Writers Collaborative, 1983), *Network* (1996), and *Conversations with Clarence Major*, ed. Nancy Bunge (Jackson: University Press of Mississippi, 2002); Larry McMurtry, *San Francisco Review of Books* (1992); William Stafford, *The American Poetry Review* (1981), *You Must Revise Your Life*, ed. William Stafford (Ann Arbor: University of Michigan Press, 1986); Ruth Stone, *Kalliope* (2003); Richard Wilbur, *Conversations with Richard Wilbur*, ed. William Butts (Jackson: University Press of Mississippi, 1990); and Helen Yglesias, *Fiction Writers Market*, ed. Laurie Henry (1988).

independence, 45, 94, 124, 127, 130, 141–142, 148–149, 160, 172, 208–209, 210–211

integrity, 94, 95–96, 122, 126, 131, 139, 141, 144, 148–149, 160, 163–164, 172, 210–211, 212, 221, 232

isolation, 4–5, 33, 48, 63, 111, 129–130

journals, 86, 90, 132–135, 145–146, 165, 168, 171, 191, 196–197, 208, 220

language, 30, 32–33, 85, 117–118, 141, 160–161, 191, 193; and fiction, 183; and poetry, 29–30, 72–73, 85, 89, 125

law, 45, 220, 221, 222–223, 226–227

life experience, 56, 62–63, 80, 116–117, 173–174, 179, 232, 236

literature as model, 8, 9–10, 13, 24–25

memoir, 180

MFA programs, 25, 29, 107, 130, 209

morality, 142

music, 146, 204–206, 229

narrative voice, 150, 157–159, 175–176, 185, 210, 211, 224, 226

notebooks. See journals

objectivity, 37, 86, 97–99, 102–103

obsession, 9, 53–54, 58

occupations, 44, 56–57, 68, 82, 147–148, 173. See also law

openness, 69, 86, 236

oral tradition, 29–31, 51–52, 215–217

physical exercise, 125, 192, 229, 230

plot, 146, 165, 167, 171–172, 181–182, 221–222

poetry: nature of, 85–86; process, 10, 105, 121–122, 123–129. See also language; writing process

publication, 25–26, 61, 83–84, 112–113, 124, 180–181, 209–211, 221

reading: aloud, 19, 23, 41–42, 58–59, 75, 77; fiction, 154; poetry, 29–31, 86, 99, 106; as source of inspiration, 62, 75, 92–93, 97, 104, 113, 151, 154, 163, 231–232

rejection, 5–6

research, 62–63, 136–140, 151, 155–157, 169, 185, 195, 230

reviews, 115, 117, 180; of women's work, 7

self-absorption, 102, 151, 179

self-realization: and writing, 34–36, 42, 60–61, 70–71, 73, 93–94, 127, 128–129, 159, 182, 187, 190–191, 211–212

self-trust: and teaching, 14, 18; and writing, 14–18, 36, 49, 58, 61–62, 70–71, 72, 74, 76, 86, 93–94, 112–113, 124, 154, 158, 160, 162–164, 189, 194, 203, 207, 210–211, 221, 232, 233

settings, 137, 156

social class, 40–41, 44–45

social concerns, 81, 141–142, 206–207

spontaneity, 35–36, 64–65, 69, 97, 125–126, 127, 206, 223, 236

students: criticism of, 60–61, 65, 74–75, 87, 88–89, 90–91, 115; praise of, 65, 86, 90–91, 96

subject matter, 59, 62, 105, 116–118, 179

teachers as models, 28, 31

teaching: fiction writing, 53–54, 110, 115–116, 181–182, 231; impact on instructor, 7, 24, 44, 49–50, 54–55, 56–57, 67–68, 80–81, 87, 109, 114–115, 157; literature, 22–24, 50, 77–78, 105–106, 166, 168; of oneself, 153–154; poetry writing, 7–10, 13–18, 31, 64–67, 86–87, 88–93, 102–105, 123–125; writing, 13–18, 37–39, 43–44,

51–52, 58–60, 74–75, 96–99,
117–118, 203–204
translation, 9, 104
travel writing, 81

unconscious, 10–12, 144–146, 186

variety: importance of, 78, 97,
159–160, 175, 184–185, 210, 227;
resistance to, 194–196
violence, 31–32
visual influences, 85, 147, 170
voice, 42, 63, 203, 221, 229. *See also*
narrative voice

women writers, 62, 176–177; as
models, 6–7; issue of taking
themselves seriously, 3–6, 82–85,
112 176; poets, 101, 176; subject
matter of, 59, 157. *See also*
domestic novel; gender

writers: in academia, 16, 18, 19–20,
25, 29, 57, 80, 95–96, 109–110, 117,
130, 188–190, 208–211; as models,
13–14, 46, 95–96, 110, 116, 130, 142
writer's block, 27
writing: classes, 73; as educative, 155,
169, 182, 187, 193, 194–196,
198–200, 232; exercises, 7–8, 31;
for money, 39–40, 76–77, 80; as a
practice, 60, 75–76, 97, 100,
212–213; value of, 39, 42, 45–46,
56, 62, 76–77, 106–108, 116, 130,
153–154, 188–190, 208–210. *See also*
self-realization
writing process, 10, 79–80, 85–86,
143–151, 191–196, 198–200, 211–217,
219–225, 228–229; compared to
painting, 47–48, 231; enjoyment
of, 48–49, 87, 110–111, 115, 124–125,
139–140, 175–176, 184–185, 197, 211,
226; poetry versus prose, 26–28,
147. *See also* poetry, fiction